Just a Liverpudlian

Thirty - Eight Short Stories

by

Allan Francis Scott

Order this book online at www.trafford.com
or email orders@trafford.com

Most Trafford titles are also available at major online book retailers.

Note for Librarians: A cataloguing record for this book is available from Library and Archives Canada at www.collectionscanada.ca/amicus/index-e.html

Printed in Victoria, BC, Canada.

ISBN: 978-1-4269-1861-2

Our mission is to efficiently provide the world's finest, most comprehensive book publishing service, enabling every author to experience success. To find out how to publish your book, your way, and have it available worldwide, visit us online at www.trafford.com

Trafford rev. 09/15/09

www.trafford.com

North America & international
oll-free: 1 888 232 4444 (USA & Canada)
phone: 250 383 6864 • fax: 812 355 4082

Liverpool 1938

DOUBLE TROUBLE

As my father and his friend Jack opened the front parlour door and carefully stepped over my toy soldiers and wooden fort, I sensed all was not well. No laughter, no busmans' banter, no pats on the head, only a gesture of the thumb from my father, for me to leave.

Curiosity sent me to my hiding place; the cupboard under the stairs. A great place to eavesdrop on all the gossip. Here, I learnt about the outstanding attributes of the new barmaid at the Crown and Anchor, my aunts indiscretions with a sailor at Blackpool, and my mother's perpetually tight rein on my father.

But on this June evening in 1938 the conversation between Bill (my father) and Jack lacked any indication of humour.

'Well, Bill, what do you think about this carry on?' and Jack continued, 'I told you bad things always happen in threes.'

'It's only two.' My father countered.

'No, we're changing from a single-decker bus to a double-decker and our company is being sold to Crossville. Lastly, it will mean time clocks, inspectors, managers and all that stuff.'

My father and Jack were a team. Dad, the conductor and Jack, the driver of a beautiful blue and cream bus, or charabanc, as my mother called it. For several years, Jack and dad worked six days-a-week around Liverpool, enjoying flexible hours, and extra cash, if the customers paid and neglected to ask for a ticket.

But, on Sundays, the bus belonged to Dad and Jack.

The owner had agreed that as long as they kept it clean and in good running order and it was back on the road at 7 a.m. on Monday mornings, they had a deal.

On Saturday evenings, Herman, as the bus was affectionately named would be parked outside our row house, cleaned inside by me, and outside by two bigger boys.

Lastly, be inspected by my father, who would then place a folding chalk board next to it that stated:

Sunday 2 p.m. Mystery Tour.
Return by 8 p.m.
3/6 for adults. 1/6 for children.
Two stops for refreshments.
Book now as seating is limited.

We always had a full bus and any overflow were seated on folding wooden stools placed in the aisle. The last tasks for these two entrepreneurs was to arrange the route and phone the two pubs that would benefit from the arrival of a bus load of thirsty

Mystery tourists. My mother kept a low profile, as she was the hat lady. Her job during the return trip was to make her way down the aisle between the singing patrons. Wave the inverted driver's hat and suggest a tip for the driver and his mate, who generously gave up their Sundays, so we could all have a good time.

Once back at home, it was clean out Herman and share the money. We all prospered, the kids who cleaned and polished Herman, my mum, Jack and the pubs we stopped at. Even I made two shillings a trip, plus a refund from any empty bottles I found rolling around in the well of the bus.

However, my eight-year-old mind realized, that the days of Sunday mystery tours and the extra cash tossed in my direction from happy trippers, would soon come to an end. No bus, no trips and no money.

'We can still sneak a bus out on Sundays,' I heard Jack whisper.

'No, it will be a double-decker and red at that,' my father countered.

'All we can do is wait and see how the new owner is, or maybe we can buy Herman,' Jack replied hopefully.

'Old Herman would cost more than our wages for years, then we would have to pay for gas and oil and a mechanic,' my dad explained.

There was a moments silence, then I heard my name called. I waited a second, pushed open the door of my hiding place and trotted into the front parlour.

'Go to the off license and get three bottles of brown ale. That's a good lad.' My dad ordered.

As I was about to leave mum was sitting in the kitchen talking to my aunt. I heard her say, 'I knew it was too good to last. No more holidays in Ostende for Bill and me.'

My aunt looked up, 'Maybe a war too,' she sighed and added, 'Allan, get us a couple of bottles as well,--to drown our sorrows.'

The sale did go through as Jack had predicted. Crossville buses were to dominate the streets of Liverpool. All was not doom and gloom however. My father and Jack were chosen to pick up the first double-decker bus from the factory in Sheffield and drive it back to the newly painted Bus Station on Edge Lane.

The Bus Station was the focal point for a gathering of VIPs to receive what was to be the first of six, new shiny red double-decker buses. The arrival time was to be 4 p.m. It would be spruced up, then christened by the wife of the new owner.

As mum and I arrived at the Bus Station, we saw two tow trucks leaving and a glum- looking man in a dark suit talking to the group of VIPs. We overheard, that sadly the arrival ceremony would have to be cancelled for today. Due to a mechanical problem en route.

However: the mechanic's lunch room was anything but glum. When we peered in the door, Charlie, the head mechanic waved my mum and me over. 'You'll never believe this, but the new bus, plus Jack and your old man are stuck under a bridge near Salford, about thirty miles from here. I told Jack he shouldn't try to drive a fifteen-foot high bus under a fourteen-foot bridge.' This observation was greeted with howls of laughter from the three grimey, oil stained mechanics, seated at their lunch table.

We were both very subdued as we walked home, and I hoped my mother wasn't going to cry. My aunt greeted us as we walked in, 'that was quick, how's the new bus look?'

'It hasn't arrived yet,' my mum softly replied. ' Bill and Jack have the new super-duper Crossville bus....stuck under a bridge near Salford.'

My aunt's eyes widened. 'You're pulling-my-leg!'

My mum shook her head. 'No it's true,' and I was afraid she would burst into tears.

'What a couple of clowns,' my aunt roared, 'they just wanted a single-decker again.'

It was rather a subdued pair that guided the bright red double-decker into the bus station the next afternoon. Jack at the wheel and my father standing at attention on the rear platform. I noticed he was holding on tightly to the handrail.

The VIPs applauded as Jack halted his new charge adjacent to the red carpet. A round of laughter was generated as my father rang the bell,–– 'ding-ding.'

The christening was performed with the traditional bottle of champagne. Then it was announced by the proud owner that for the maiden drive, all were welcome aboard.

The merry throng of VIPs followed by the workers climbed the stairs to the upper deck. Charlie, the mechanic shouted to my Dad, for all to hear. 'I hope Jack remembers that bridge round the corner!'

Allan F Scott

The End

Liverpool 1940

THE TALE OF TWO DIARIES

On October 29th 1940, Dr. Joseph Goebbels wrote in his diary: 'Massive Luftwaffe air attack on Liverpool.' Then he went on to write: 'Our new house in Berlin is ready.' He continued to describe how comfortable and modern it was and how Magda (his wife), really loved it.

He was forty-three years old and had been the Minister for Propaganda for seven years, had four beautiful young daughters and a son. His wife was in a nursing home having number six, another daughter.

I was ten years old, and in my diary I wrote: 'Bigger than usual raid, but they missed the rail yards, the bombs landed in the Edge Hill area, one in front of our house that cracked the front walls. This morning I picked up a lot of shrapnel.'

Had I the capability to travel through time and space, I would have stood by Dr. Goebbels' new writing desk, looked over his shoulder and said: 'We also had a nice home, until last night, when your Luftwaffe missed the railway yards and destroyed the front of our house.'

Bombs did strange things. This one landed in the street, and left a crater about five feet deep, but didn't break any windows or hurt anyone, just cracked our house from top to bottom. We had to move immediately.

Dr. Goebbels had a member of his staff by the name of William Joyce. His job was to broadcast propaganda in English, which he did very well. His nickname was Lord Haw-Haw, due to the posh and superior tone of voice he adopted.

His was probably the most listened to broadcast in England and at seven each evening, most homes would be tuned into the program, Germany Calling.

He knew which areas had been bombed and at what time the town hall clock had stopped. He told us what time to expect a raid and where, which ships had been sunk at sea, and whose families had lost a son, father or husband.

This used to frighten me. It was like being watched by an invisible bogey-man. However, the adults used to treat him as a joke, and as the war progressed, his predictions became more and more erratic. But I still felt that cold shiver when I heard his voice... 'Germany Calling.'

December 23rd, 1940. Dr. Goebbels wrote, 'The Royal Air Force made a moderate incursion into Germany: Berlin is untouched, but we attacked Liverpool with 250 bombers.'

My diary: 'Dad, who was in the Fire Service, arrived home about nine this morning. I had never seen him look so tired and worn. He was covered from head to feet in black grease, but his Liverpudlian sense of humour prevailed, and he broke into Al Jolson's Swanee. What a strange sight he was dancing round the kitchen in his wellington boots and helmet, black from head to toe. Swanee how I love you, my dear old Swanee. My Aunt laughing, rushed to hug him, then we had two smoke and grease stained people dancing round the kitchen.'

During his scrub down he told us of his saga of the night.

The docks and warehouse area had been bombed and were on fire. When the fire engines tried to climb the hill to the burning warehouse, they were met by a flood of melted butter, which made it impossible to drive up the hill, so all the hoses had to be carried up, and in turn became soaked in grease. As the fire increased, the butter started to burn on the streets, and the firemen had to hose each other down as their clothes started to smoulder. Add to this the continuing bombing of the already burning targets, the perpetual rain of shrapnel from the anti-aircraft guns, not an enviable position to be in, and not one that you would think would create... my most memorable version of Swanee.

Dr, Goebbels finished his entry for that day with, 'Enjoyed a pre-Christmas evening, but how tired and battle weary I am.'

I would have liked to say, 'Your're tired--you should see my Dad.'

A job that I enjoyed, but the adults complained about, was putting masking tape on all the windows. The theory was, in the event of an explosion, the tape would stop the glass from splintering. Artistic license was ripe in this project: crosses, squares, circles, stick figures in various poses, and many rude suggestions were spelt out to Adolph.

Lord Haw-Haw proclaimed, 'Last night Berlin was bombed and thirty people were killed. Now is the time of the full moon, and Liverpool will be our main target.'

This time he was not exaggerating, and Dr. Goebbels could write in his diary, 14th March 1941: 'We attack Liverpool with 400 aircraft in good visibility with devastating results.'

My entry for Friday 14th March displayed the tunnel vision of an eleven- year- old. Friday was the night I was taken to the movies, and Lord Haw-Haw and the Lufwaffe were not going to interfere with this weekly treat.

In spite of the full moon and threats from above, Mum gave into my nagging and off we went to the six o'clock show: Pinocchio.

An hour into the program, we heard the sirens; the manager came on stage to say that the movie would continue as long as possible, but if we wanted to leave, we would have our money refunded. Mum looked at me and could see how enthralled I was, and she whispered, 'Just get under the seat if anything happens.'

Pinocchio was to be locked in the caravan, and as the door was slammed on him, there was a tremendous explosion from the rear of the cinema. The screen went blank, the lights went out, and debris fell from the ceiling. I don't remember getting under the seat, but there I was with the rest of the patrons,with one hand trying to stop the seat tipping up as I sheltered under it.

Slowly the dust settled, and the staff shouted for us to leave by the side door, as the foyer was blocked. With the help of flashlights probing the dust-laden air, we scrambled over the debris and rubble to the street.

It was almost as light as day, with the searchlights, flashes of anti-aircraft guns and the flares that the bombers had released. The streets were deserted, except for the odd rescue truck and fire engine, but the noise was increasing as the next wave was approaching, the searchlights whisking across the sky, catching the silver glint of the barrage balloons in their fingers of light.

As the anti-aircraft guns began to open up closer and closer, we ran and dodged into doorways to avoid falling shrapnel after each volley. It was only a few blocks to home, but having to door hop all the way made it seem a much greater distance.

At home the family had already settled in the basement, which had been re-enforced with wooden pillars.

As this was our home most evenings, Uncle Frank had made it comfortable by setting up all our beds, so we avoided having to leap out of bed and dash downstairs for every air-raid warning.

Tea was made, and Mum and I recounted our adventure of the partly seen Pinocchio. The intensity of the raid increased and we tried to guess what the target for tonight would be, but it seemed the explosions came from all directions.

Sleep was impossible and for the first time we heard the battery of rocket guns fire from the park. From hanging around the park, I had been told what they sounded like by one of the gunners, and I enjoyed airing my knowledge to our very frightened group. They go, 'Whoosh-Whoosh.'

My attempts at sound effects were interrupted by what sounded like an express train descending on us. Then we felt a thump, the ground shook, we froze as we waited for the explosion.

There was only an eerie silence.

The door bell rang, we all jumped in fright.

Then a shout, 'Everyone out!...Unexploded bomb!'

We all had small cases packed, and gas masks over our shoulders in their issue cardboard box, except for Mum who had splurged on a patent leather case with a picture of Clark Gable on it. The theory on this, women would be less likely to forget their mask if it had a picture of Clark Gable on it. I had wanted one with a picture of Judy Garland, but was told, 'You're too young to be interested in that stuff.' Lastly the cat was put in his basket, the dog on his lead.

It was out to the street again, but this time we were five, plus the dog and cat. As we left the front door I dashed over to have a look at our near miss, it was just a hole in the road about four feet diameter and the pavement lifted several feet around it.

'Allan, get away from that; you'll ruin the whole evening if you get blown up,' my uncle yelled.

We did the door hopping for a few blocks to the big public shelter under the Technical School. This was my day school shelter, and considered super-safe, due to the basement being re-enforced with steel beams. Plus it was a four story brick building.

Here we were met by an officious air raid warden who said, 'Hurry in, but you'll have to leave the dog and cat outside.' To our pleas, he grumbled, 'Rules are rules ...no pets.' We huddled in the entrance and decided to try Aunty Dorothy's house, a few blocks away.

Considering it was 3 a.m. she gave us a warm welcome, and we settled in her basement . As the noise increased again, I started to get the shakes and was allowed a cup of strong sweet tea, which I found out later contained a sleeping pill.

Next morning I dashed out expecting to see not a house left standing, all looked well, but what I at first thought to be snow, was flakes of ash falling. This continued all day with the ash piling into little drifts in the corners and gutters.

I continued exploring the district and had my usual haul of shrapnel, when I saw a rescue truck. These unsung heroes, usually cheerful in the morning when their shift was over, looked worn and dejected. The driver was sitting with his hands over his face. 'What's wrong?' I asked beginning to feel their grief. The driver raised his head, his eyes devoid of expression and gestured with his thumb down the street. 'Don't bother looking for anyone there; they all died.' I looked and could see more rescue trucks. Turning the corner, a pile of rubble that had been a four story brick building, the Technical School and my day time shelter. Three hundred people in a fraction of a second, gone for ever, and it still took two days before the last survivor was dug out.

Aunty Dorothy was laughing and dishing out the porridge when I arrived back for breakfast. I tried to break into the conversation, but be seen and not heard was the order of the day and I was ignored, until I shouted.

'The Technical School has been destroyed!'

Everyone eyed me with disbelief, my uncle dashed out the door and was back a few minutes later. Downcast he said, 'It's true,' and began to name the neighbours who used that shelter because they considered their homes unsafe.

'God, that could have been us.' his voice faltered.

There was a second of silence, while realisation sank in. Grabbing the dog under one arm and the cat under the other he shouted. 'Here's two that are going to have the best meal they ever had.'

Out came the week's bacon and meat ration, the two pets hesitant at first, soon began to chomp away with that air of urgency pets have, when they feel this is too good to last.

Saturday 15th March 1941.

The Minister of Propaganda wrote in his diary. 'Yesterday was a high pressure, crazy day. Tonight, we attack Liverpool again, with 250 aircraft. It is 1a.m.and the British have still not come, so I am off to bed.

BUT THEY WILL, DR. GOEBBLES, THEY WILL.

Allan F Scott

The End

Quotations are from the 'Goebbels Diaries 1939-1941.' Translated and Edited by Fred Taylor. Copyright Fred Taylor and Hamish Hamilton Ltd.
Published by G.P.PUTNAM'S Sons. New York.

======================================

Blackpool 1940

FIRST LOVE

Here is a question I'm sure many of us ask, but the reply can only apply to the individual asking it. When did the emotion of love first appear? How old was I, with whom, how did it affect me, and lastly, did it always have a beginning, a gestation period and an end?

At first it crept up on me, then later in life I could detect the early symptoms and either avoid any further contact, or leave it to Qui Sera Sera. That is assuming one has enough emotional strength left after cupid's arrows have found the Achilles Heel, and the potion has started to invade the brain and body. Placing one into a condition of temporary insanity called--Love.

I've been called shallow, and I admit it. I can fall in love with a beautiful blond lady in a mini-skirt, very easily, even if she has little academic learning and little knowledge of anything. While a rotund T-shirted, blue-jeaned clad intellectual, would flicker on and off my male radar screen unnoticed.

Women don't like shallow men... so they tell me, unless, they are very good looking, wealthy or in positions of power. All of the above, being labelled aphrodisiacs.

So that's three counts out for me! What a mystery I found it all as a thirteen-year-old.

But, I'll go back to when I was about eleven-years old and evacuated to Blackpool. Barbara and her family had a bed and breakfast and they were also my parents' best friends. Never having any sisters, staying in a house with Barbara was exciting. Another plus, the other residents were Polish airmen from the nearby airfield.

Barbara and I had a common interest--roller skating. We were both quite good and enjoyed racing each down the straight, then grabbing a hand and swinging round the corners.

The hit song at the time was Scatterbrain, hard to explain to our Polish airmen.

When you smile it's so enchanting, when you sing it's so insane.

Isn't it a pity that you're such a scatterbrain.

We'd sing along fitting our stride to the tempo and laugh as we tumbled trying a few fancy crossovers in time with the music.

The airmen called us The Whiz Kids. Then later, as our attachment was noticed, Mr. & Mrs. Whiz. Barbara and I in our youthful innocence were amazed that someone who was.... maybe a pilot, couldn't skate, which non of them could. However, they treated us royally, and we were never short of candy-floss, pop, or someone to take us to the movies. But, as most good things do, it all came to an end, and for the time being, the predicted bombing never occurred and back I went to Liverpool.

It was not until I was eighteen that I met Barbara again. Her parents had bought the Glen Helen Hotel on the Isle of Man and my parents and myself went to stay for Christmas. She was now about sixteen, myself, eighteen and doing my military service.

I noticed in many ways she had outgrown me, she was very attractive in an aristocratic way and mixed with all ages and types in the bar with ease.

It was when we wandered off on our own that it became like old times, and we chatted about the fun we had had, and wondered how many of the airman, who had been so kind to us, survived the war? Had our favourite teddy bear, Rollerbear survived, after we hid him behind a large oak wardrobe the night before we had to go our separate ways. Our plan, was to wait until we were really grown up.... say twenty, return to Blackpool, rescue Rollerbear and the three of us would live happily ever after. I guess he was the son we never had the ability to create.

We were in the garden, it was moonlight, the sounds of a waterfall behind us had cupid put his arrow gun on rapid fire and I was captivated. I stroked her hair and tried to kiss her. 'Just one for the good times,' she laughed. I closed my eyes and time stood still, until she placed her hands on my chest and gently stepped back.

'I have a boyfriend,' she whispered.

'I don't want to know that,' I sighed.

'Well I am being honest with you,' she smiled up at me, 'and I bet you have a girlfriend.'

'That's different,' I complained, 'plus, I like you much better.'

'Typical man, just love the girl you're with, and see if you get lucky.'

'I'm not like that.' Even then, I thought my statement lacked conviction.

'Rubbish! all men are like that, that's what makes you all so exciting.'

This was my first experience with mixed messages women constantly leave you bewildered with.

'How would you like a drive round the island?' she looked up nodding her head.

'I can borrow dad's motor bike,' she whispered.

'The one he used on the TT Race?' I queried nervously.

'It's dark.' I stated the obvious, regressing from a hopeful seducer to a potential nervous passenger. She ran up the path, turned and shouted, 'I'll just check with Dad.' She trotted back a few minutes later. 'Dad wants us to use the MG, it looks like rain or snow, I'll get us leather coats and we can have the top down.' Slowly I walked to the garage and arrived as the MG growled into life, the lights flicked on, indicating all was ready to go. Behind the wheel, Barbara in leather coat, helmet and goggles looked like an eager Biggles heading for a dawn patrol.

She pointed at a similar coat on the passenger seat. It was far too large, and when I added the goggles I complained that I felt like, Toad of Toad Hall.

'Don't look so nervous, this will be fun,' she assured me. Then she let up the clutch which slumped me back in my seat. The lights reflected off the wet parking area then softened as we hit the gravel.

Barbara expertly used clutch and gears as she accelerated down the hill and into the corners. 'You sure know how to handle the gears,' I shouted above the noise of the engine and wind.

'The less I use the brakes, the better, there's quite the drop off coming up and a skid could be dangerous.' I held on tightly to the dashboard handle as we snorted round another corner.

'How far are we going?' and was about to add ,'my mother will worry if I'm too long,' but that hardly sounded like a statement from a 'man of the world.' So I bit my tongue and hung on.

'Once round the island is about thirty-eight miles, but if the rain keeps off we may try a hill climb after.' Barbara glanced at me, 'don't look so stiff, you make me nervous. Sit low, press your feet on the floor and relax.'

Barbara leant towards me, 'I know this road like the back of my hand.'

'I'm glad about that, because I can't see a thing.'

'Don't worry I've been driving it since I was fourteen. We used to do it Sunday mornings with Dad on his Norton bike, Mum sitting passenger with a watch and me learning the ropes. As dad said, 'it's either this or go to church.' Most times he was at least ten minutes ahead of us.'

To my right, in the distance I could see the sea and knew we must be near the coast road. 'You'll like this, six miles down hill, then Hillbury.' She whooped as we hit top gear and rocketed down the hill. I'm not sure if there where any turns because I'd closed my eyes.

Barbara changed down and I opened one eye and was relieved to see houses and a few street lights. 'You can change gear if you like,' she glanced at me taking her hand off the gear stick. I put my hand on the vibrating lever and gentle moved it, there was a horrible grinding noise. 'No--into third,' Barbara shouted. I must have looked as helpless as I felt. 'You don't know anything about driving do you, what do they teach you in the air force?'

'Well, I'm at the school of music,' it seemed rather a feeble excuse for my present lack of expertise.

'Hmmm,' she huffed, and jockeyed the shift onto third. Just as I was beginning to enjoy the coast road and admiring the crashing waves she tapped me on the shoulder. 'We'll head to the hill climb, I'll take it easy, it's hard to see the ruts in the dark.'

In a few minutes, the coast behind us, we started to climb, we slid side to side and the mud sprayed around us. I sat even lower in the seat. 'Sorry about this,' and Barbara folded the windscreen down. 'Can't see through a muddy windscreen.'

I wiped my goggles hoping to see something, but thought better of it and let the mud build up. I felt a tap on the knee, 'use this,' and she offered me what had been a white scarf. I feebly obeyed, but in two seconds I was blind again.

I felt the road surface change, and the fish tailing ceased. 'I'll just clean the windscreen.' Barbara stood leaning over the dash and wiped the mud encrusted glass. 'That's better, it's not usually this bad, must have been raining more than I thought. Now.... home for a hot toddy before Dad has to close the bar.'

My fear and muddy discomfort was replaced with--cold and discomfort--as we drove the half-hour back to the Glen Helen.

Barbara slowed the MG in front of the garage and hopped out. 'Sit here and keep your foot on the accelerator, pump it when I say.' She guided me into the driver's seat, 'don't touch the gears or the clutch.'

I watched as she crouched down aiming a jet of water under the car and over the wheels. 'Keep the revs up,' she shouted. She raised the bonnet and sprayed over the engine, 'more!' I pressed the pedal the engine roared and steam rose from both sides of the engine.

She produced two buckets, 'here, we'll just wash the seats then our coats, and that's it.'

The pub was in full glow as we edged and squinted into the bright lights. Barbara was soon surrounded by several males laughing at her mud caked legs and neck. Her father put his wrestler's arm round my shoulders. 'You've been rolling my daughter in the mud again?' He laughed over at my mother, 'never trust an air force chap, one quick roll in the mud and they fly off.'

'You should know, Jack,' my father shouted. Louise, Barbara's mother came to my rescue.

'Ignore them, here's a rum toddy.'

I liked her mum she seemed to understand me. I had been told that daughters usually take after their mum, but Barbara was definitely more like her father.

Barbara turned from her admirers waving her glass in my direction, 'Allan, if you're up early, we can take the horses out.'

'Do they have any gears?' I joked.

Her dad grinned, 'no, but they'll give you the gears if you don't show them who's boss.'

'Just like your daughter,' I grinned back.

Several years later our respective parents made a last attempt at uniting their offspring. I hadn't seen Barbara for about three years and was surprised when my mother told me Barbara was coming to London, and would I like to spend a week with her in a hotel.

The dates were arranged and I, though apprehensive, felt we would have a good time, even maybe several skating evenings in one of he big London rinks.

It was a small hotel, our rooms several doors apart but on the same floor, with a nice dining room three doors down. All should have been very romantic, but it was not to be. She was not the same Barbara anymore, serious, rather dour and given to moods of gloomy silence whenever we were alone. Of course, I assumed it was either: my appearance, my attempt at conversation or lack of funds to visit the nightlife.

When the week ended I'm sure we were both relieved. I know I was, but what puzzled me, was, how my little fun loving skating mate had changed.

I mentioned this to my father. His words of wisdom: 'Women are like that, if they're not enjoying themselves--they make sure you don't.

Allan F Scott

The End

Liverpool 1941

ADORATION, JEALOUSY, REJECTION.

Walking home from school with my sealed report clutched in my grubby hand and seething with curiosity as to its contents I met John, who also had his report clutched in an equally grubby hand.

'Wonder what it says?' I asked John, waving my report at him.

'My mum's out; let's boil a kettle and steam them open,' was his instant reply.

I was always amazed at John's man-of-the-world attitude. 'Will it work?' I asked nervously.

'Of cause it will, read it in a book on spies,' this eleven-year-old James Bond replied.

John was always top of the class, while I floundered about twenty-sixth.

He even had his own front door key, while I had to climb through the bathroom window, if no one was home.

John put the kettle on and we laid our reports on the table. Soon a healthy head of steam rose from the kettle spout, over which he carefully held his envelope. After a few seconds, he winked at me, put a pencil under the flap and eased it open.

'Hold the envelope open until the glue dries,' he said, handing it to me.

I was delighted to be part of this espionage, and did as instructed, while John unfolded his report.

'Pretty good: first, first, first,' he boasted out loud. 'Oh . . . a twenty-fifth in gymnastics. I hate gym,' and he continued. 'Why are humans always trying to compete with horses? Show me a horse that can work out the coefficient linear expansion of its metal shoe and I'll practice jumping over fences.'

Now it was my turn, and he eased out my report from the curling envelope. I started to read it, and very depressing it was.

'Maybe, I'll settle for jumping fences,' I whined.

The final entry was the headmaster's notation, which thankfully ignored all my intellectual shortcomings, but did state--posture needs attention.

'What is posture?' I questioned out loud, hoping John would volunteer an explanation? But he was too engrossed with his own list of triumphs.

When I arrived home, I nonchalantly asked my aunt what posture was.

'Something to do with your bum, I think. Why, what's the problem?'

'Oh, nothing,' I murmured, but that was not good news, attention to the bum meant one of two things. It was going to be hit, or, if Father Bum Squeezer (as our priest was laughingly known) was within arms length--squeezed. Neither alternative a pleasant prospect.

Later in the day, I stood next to my father who was seated at his little desk, and awaited his judgement on my scholastic efforts.

'Not very good, and the headmaster says your posture needs attention.'

I faked surprise at this statement.

'Well... fancy that,' I said. Then hesitated, not wanting to hear any more bad news, but ventured. 'What's posture?'

My father looked up at me,'The way you stand and walk. You stand like an out-of-work docker and walk like a drunken sailor.' This was something I had never thought about. One just walked and stood without thinking. My father added that he would talk to my mother, but, if there was no improvement by my next report--something would have to be done.

April 1942, my next report was equally depressing. The entry headed Physical Exercises, I sensed, sealed my fate.

It stated: Only fair: he must stand erect.

At dinner that evening my mother interrupted my conversation with my aunts and whispered to me, 'I'm going to enrol you at Miss Bagley's School of Dancing and Deportment.'

Aunt Lil, noticing my startled expression asked, 'What's wrong?'

'Mum says I have to go to Bags Acad.' The terror I felt was evident in my rising voice, and all eyes turned in my direction.

'Why?' Aunt Lil asked, a look of sympathy showing in her eyes.

'I'm not erect enough,' I replied.

There was a second of silence, then I noticed my aunt's expression change from sympathy to delight, and a peal of laughter erupted around the table.

My mother wiping her eyes said, 'We'd better send your father with you,' this generated more laughter, and I noticed my father also got quite red in the face.

My aunt added, 'Maybe you'll get a discount; two erect men for the price of one.' More merriment, at my expense.

I was bewildered and upset. What was so funny in all this?

Aunt Lil--usually one I could rely on for sympathy--just burst into laughter every time she looked at me.

I was horrified. What would the kids at school say? This was worse than when my aunt told me because my name was Scott, I had a tartan, and should wear a kilt.

Many times on our way home from school, my chums and I had tried to peep into the window of Bagg's Acad (as we called it) intrigued by the perpetual rendition of the Teddy Bear's Picnic;

which was always audible through the partly open windows. However: they were too high, preventing us from seeing the intriguing happenings that we imagined must be taking place, just above our visual range. Sometimes, a tall intimidating lady would glare out, as we crouched out of sight behind the wall.

The teasing soon began at home. Aunt Lil telling me, I would have to march round and round a room with a book on my head, in time to the never ending dreaded Teddy Bear's Picnic. Then worse, I'd have to dance with some of the prim girls we had seen entering the academy. Girls we had teased, calling them Baggy's Bags, and worse.

This was a nightmare for a twelve-year-old Liverpudlian.

The first attendance was to be the following Wednesday. But, I planned to leave the house, hide in the park, and return home after two hours with what-ever story I could invent. However, my plan was thwarted, when my mother insisted on coming with me to register.

As we neared the academy I looked fearfully in all directions, hoping to evade any of my school chums. It was bad enough to be seen out with your mother, but to be seen entering Bagg's Acad. I would be the laughingstock of the playground.

Miss Bagley, was the intimidating figure who glared out the window at us, and I was afraid I'd be recognised. She smiled at my mother, the two of them glanced in my direction and shared a joke. I heard my mother say, that I didn't have a girl friend yet . . . and Miss Bagley whispered, 'I'm sure he will soon.'

This was worse than I imagined, and this was just the registration!

'Master Scott follow me,' Miss Bagley commanded. She led me to a large room, where three boys and four girls sat on upright chairs arranged against the walls.

I was introduced to 'Miss so and so,' and 'Master so and so,' all names I promptly forgot. None of them looked threatening; in fact, they all looked as uncomfortable as myself.

'Now!' Miss Bagley shouted, 'I want you all to stand with your backs to the wall.' This we obeyed with the enthusiasm of a group of dissidents awaiting the arrival of the firing squad.

'Shoes off!' was her next command.

Having new socks, I obeyed with alacrity. I had all new underwear as well. My mother insisted on this, whenever a trip of more than two blocks from home was planned.

'What if you got run over by a bus?' Was her logical explanation.

My worldly friend John extended this theory by adding. 'If you want to avoid being run over by a bus--wear dirty socks and underwear.'

However, one of our group had not anticipated this invasion of privacy, and on removing his shoes, sported two protruding toes. This started the girls giggling and the poor boy turned a strawberry pink.

'None of that ladies,' Miss Bagley shouted, enforcing the order with a swish of her two foot ruler.

I was the first in line and as Miss Bagley approached, ruler in hand. I prepared to duck. A ruler in an adults hand meant only one thing--a slap to come.

'Heads up, I want your bum, heels, and back of the head, against the wall.

Good, now stretch as tall as you can.' Miss Bagley snapped out her orders with the authority of a drill sergeant.

'Now, Master Scott walk in that position to the opposite wall, turn and walk back.' I wobbled wall to wall. Hearing the girls giggling behind me, it was my turn to change colour.

Soon we were all marching wall to wall. The girls seemed to move with grace and ease. The boys slouched, in my case, I slouched--and wobbled.

Miss Bagley exchanged her weapon for a plank of wood about four feet long. It had a handle on the back, this enabled her to press the plank against our backs as we marched.

'Straighten up, or I will tie this to your back!' and she darted between us plank in hand. 'Practice this at home,' she shouted as she guided us into the hallway.

The hallway had two white ropes stretched the length of it, shoulder width and height, I thought these were for decoration, but no––. These we had to march between, whilst avoiding touching the rope with either shoulder.

This I found impossible and received a tap on the offending shoulder each time I brushed the rope. 'Hold your head up, stomach in, and don't wobble.' So it went for the rest of the lesson.

Later at home, I demonstrated what I had to practice, much to the amusement of the household.

'Maybe she'll teach you to walk like a sober drunken sailor,' my aunt said as she tried to stifle her laughter.

'Yes, but an erect one,' my other aunt added, again to much laughter.

I was looking forward to the next lesson with the same enthusiasm as a dental appointment. But Saturday morning found me walking to Miss Bagley's, with clean socks and underwear, my hair cemented with Brylcream, and trying not to wobble.

As we waited for the arrival of our mentor. I stood, my back to the wall, stretching and pressing. She arrived, with another victim, who was introduced as Miss Sharp.

'Master Scott, I want you, to demonstrate to Miss Sharp last weeks lessons.'

I removed my shoes, pressed my rear against the wall, stretched and wobbled to the opposite wall.

'Miss Sharp, your turn.'

The class giggled and Miss Bagley frowned as she wobbled worse than I did.

'Don't wobble like Master Scott, that's what I'm trying to eradicate,' Miss Bagley commented.

Miss Sharp turned and said, 'It's not a wobble, it's a skater's stride.'

At last I had a compatriot. 'I skate too,' I said, quite excited at this explanation of my wobble.

'Rubbish ,' Miss Bagley replied, 'Do you think Sonja Henie wobbles?'

I felt I had found in Miss Sharp, a soul-mate, and as I looked at her I experienced emotions that until now, must have been dormant. This feeling of adoration was new to me. I had never really looked at a girl before, but her self-confidence, poise, and lack of embarrassment in this situation had me intrigued. I wish I was like her, I thought, as she silenced the other three giggling females with a menacing stare.

'Now class,' Miss Bagley continued, 'Follow my tempo and walk wall-to-wall.' She set the pace by tapping the ruler on the floor.

'Heads left, heads right. Stop!--Scott and Sharp, walk on the insides of your feet; like this.'

Years later, when I saw Jerry Lewis doing a comedy routine, I remembered where I had seen that walk before. However, it did stop the wobble but gave us rather a knock-kneed stride.

As the class ended I looked for Miss Sharp and saw her walk out hand-in-hand with her mother. No longer the self-possessed woman of the world, but a little girl with blue eyes and shining red hair.

The next four lessons we paraded up and down as Miss Bagley played the Teddy Bear's Picnic, with extreme gusto.

I started to look forward to the lessons and would try and insert myself next to Miss Sharp in our warm-up march.

We then advanced to our next challenge; which was sitting.

'Approach the chair directly, turn about, knees together and sit . . . try not to miss the chair,' she added softly. This was the first glimpse of humour I noticed in Miss Bagley's dialogue.

'Now, sitting at a table,' she continued. 'Approach the chair from the rear, pull it out and step round it, press the backs of your knees to the seat, and sit.

'And note--gentlemen, you always pull out the chair for a lady--.She steps around you, then you gently push the chair until it touches the backs of her legs; that is her cue to sit. Beware, gentlemen, if we have any antics, you will feel the weight of my ruler on your head.' This threat was enough to eliminate any urge we had to do the obvious.

By now, we were seated, and Miss Bagley placed a glass in front of each of us. 'How to accept a drink,' she announced.

'The waiter will always approach you from the left, so move the glass with your right hand so he can conveniently pour.' As the orange juice was poured, I couldn't resist a sip, and raised my glass. However, this movement was met with a slap on the back of the wrist with her ruler, which hurt. Miss Bagley frowned down at me, then left the room to refill the jug, or decanter, as she called it.

Miss Sharp leaned over to me and whispered, 'Did that hurt?'

'Yes,' I replied tearfully.

She took my hand, kissed it and said, 'Poor baby,' which provoked giggles all round. Her lips were like an electric shock on my hand. I was left mute and blushing, but a little excited.

I knew the next phase of suffering was about to commence, because Miss Bagley had said, 'Scott, if you dance like you walk, you'll make your partner seasick.'

I had seen my mother and father dance, and it looked very difficult.

What was the difference between dancing and embracing? I had seen my father and the lady from the sweet shop doing what I thought was embracing, but my father informed me he was just showing her a few moves.

Next lesson, I was to learn.

'Now, Master Scott,' Miss Bagley shouted in my ear. 'Right hand round my waist, left hand high. Move closer and grip me in a firm embrace. Now, left foot forward, one-two-three.' I was propelled round the room to my first waltz.

We changed partners every few minutes, and ecstasy for me, was to grip Miss Sharp very firmly, relish her smell of toothpaste and talcum powder--then forget to dance.

'Come on you two wobblers,' Miss Bagley would yell, 'keep moving.'

My first feelings of jealousy, were aroused when I saw Miss Sharp being held in the firm embrace of the other male members of the class, and obviously enjoying it.

After the class I noticed a green bow that Miss Sharp had been wearing. She had left it on a chair. I picked it up, ran outside hoping to catch her. She was just leaving with her mother. I dashed up to them extending the bow in my hand.

'You left this on a chair,' I said.

Miss Sharp took the bow, curtsied and said, 'Oh, thank you, kind sir.'

I bowed in return and her mother said, 'What a nice boy.'

It wasn't the word nice that hurt, but the shrug of indifference Miss Sharp directed at her mother.

'You, are becoming quite the little Madame,' her mother said, enforcing the statement with a light slap on the back of her head; then off they went leaving me to cope with the experience of another new emotion--Rejection.

Allan F Scott

The End

Liverpool 1941

THE TRIO

This was my second term at the Academy of Dancing and Deportment, run by the dictatorial Miss Bagley. Though her treatment of us was a little kinder, she was still yelling at us. 'Stand erect, don't wobble, walk with your shoulders back, dance smoothly, and lead firmly.'

The dancing, I used to practice in our front room to the radio.

With the diagrams of the various dance steps in hand I had to avoid the furniture, the dog in close pursuit and the cat always in the corner where you wanted to perform a half turn.

My Aunt Lil let me practice with her, but she liked to tease me by either going completely rigid, or cuddling me saying, 'Try to be more romantic.'

Sometimes my father would put his head around the door.

'How's he doing?'

'I think I've got rid of his wobble,' my aunt laughed.

'Works for me,' my father replied with a wink. More laughter at my innocent expense.

After our first class Miss Bagley announced, that for the next two months she would be holding Saturday night dances. Four to six p.m. and parents were invited.

I tried to keep this a secret, but to no avail. Mum announced that she and Dad would be attending our first dance.

So on Saturday afternoon the three of us set off, with me trying to walk as far as possible behind my parents. I was hoping to have an exclusive on Miss Sharp, but who had the first dance with her--my father. He even made her laugh and gave her a playful pat on the shoulder at the end of the dance.

Who was I dancing with--my mother. This was not going at all well, and I was debating sneaking out the side door when Miss Bagley approached. Oh no, I thought, she's going to ask me to dance.

But she smiled and said, 'Your father tells me, you would probably rather be playing your drums than dancing.' I nodded, not sure where the conversation was headed.

'Well, why don't you bring your drums round here tomorrow afternoon, and Mr.Bagley and I will see if you fit in with us, we could become a trio.'

I was quite excited at this prospect, and when I eventually danced with Miss Sharp I told her my news. She was not in the least impressed and kept smiling over my shoulder at the other boys. I knew this, because I felt her cheek twitch, and I would try to turn her, to see at whom her smile was directed. She would refuse to rotate, and give me one of her blue-eyed-icy-looks.

It's going to be more fun playing my drums. I thought.

On the walk home I warmed to my parents, in fact, I felt quite proud of them. I had never really seen them dance before, but they were good and won a prize for their Charleston. They even seemed to be enjoying each other's company, which gave me a warm secure feeling.

Sunday afternoon two friends and I lugged my drums to the academy and I started to set up in the ballroom next to the piano.

Miss Bagley arrived several pieces of music in hand, smiled at my friends and said, 'I'm Betty, my brother Fred, will be along in a minute with his fiddle, by the way, he's stone deaf, happened in the war, but he gets by.'

Fred arrived, and smiled broadly at me as he tuned his violin, by holding it above the open piano and pressing the body of the instrument to the side of his head.

'Let's try a fox-trot,' Betty said, and placed a copy of Blue Moon on Fred's music stand then tapped four beats with her long ruler on his shoulder.

Well, that's an new way to start, I thought.

But it worked and when she wanted to stop, she poked him in the back. We then played a quickstep, a rumba and a tango.

'Good,' she said. 'I'll just check with Fred,' and wrote a few words on a legal pad then handed it to him. He added a few words and passed it back.

She turned smiling at me. 'We think you'll fit in fine,' she lowered her voice, 'but I can only pay two and sixpence.'

'Great Miss Bagley,' I replied enthusiastically.

'Allan, please call us Fred and Betty.'

The next Saturday I sat behind my drums, watching my former dancing friends arrive and of course Miss Sharp. Whom, I thought, would be very impressed with my performance, especially when I spun the right stick in the air and kept the beat with my left, but she hardly gave me glance.

Betty referred to her piano playing as tickling the ivories, and her brother's violin performance as scratching the cat. As I got to know them they treated me like a fellow musician, and I found they both had a wonderful sense of humour.

Fred, had in his violin case a set of filing cards, one for every occasion. These little notes he waved at us at what he thought were appropriate times. Printed neatly on them were phrases such as:

How about a drink?

Is it intermission yet?

Not Blue Moon again, and my favourite, How do like that girl in the blue dress? but, where blue was indicated, he had listed every alternative colour and would point with his bow to the appropriate one.

I used to just nod my head, laugh, and keep playing away. Then one day at school during prep, I created a few suitable replies.

Next Saturday when he held up, How about a drink?

I held up my card which read, Did you know alcohol was bad for your hearing? He held up, Sorry can't hear you.

For his, multi-choice card. How do you like that girl in the blue dress?

My card read, You're too old to be looking at young girls.

His favourite reply was, There maybe snow on the roof, but there's still fire in the furnace. So it went on for several Saturdays, with Fred and I creating endless permutations.

Betty, we thought, was too busy playing and watching her dancers to be interested in our humorous card flashings. Until one day she turned from her piano, and held up a card that said.

If you two don't stop pissing about with those cards I'll get myself a blind drummer and violinist.

Fred wrote. She doesn't mean it.

She wrote. Oh, yes I do!

I wrote. If we were blind, you'd have to write in braille, and we'd have to stop playing to read it. Our laughter ended both the discussion and the music, to the bewilderment of the dancers.

Each Saturday by the time I packed up my drums, the object of my affections had left with another admirer. I began to feel that playing drums had it's drawbacks, but it took fifty years, three wives and many unsuccessful relationships for that to sink in.

Allan F Scott

The End

Liverpool 1941

THE ENGLISH LESSON

The following statement, will be greeted with howls of derision by persons who have ever put pen to paper, or finger to keyboard.

I hate Shakespeare.

Sixteen letters that mark me as an ignorant illiterate.

That's not how I wish to be classified, so I'll explain how I arrived at what to me, as a twelve -year- old, was but a logical conclusion.

Ever heard of Fats Waller? If not, I'll give a short biography. To my twelve-year-old mind, he was everything I'd like to be. A famous American pianist, singer and entertainer, enjoyed and imitated by many a Liverpudlian jazz lover of the thirties.

Why not a drummer that sang? That was the thought that sowed my seeds of interest.

I skipped three days lunch, hiding the 2/3d in my school bag. I put the money to good use, by buying a piano copy of Ain't Misbehavin. The photo on the front shows a huge black man, eyes wide, cheeks puffed, pounding the keyboard and obviously voicing this statement to a cute young lady, reclining enticingly on the top of his grand piano. This was a revelation, he was so big and black. This made it all the more exciting. Having previously never seen a photo of my mentor, I'd never thought of him being black.

My first challenge was to learn the words. It was four days to our next rehearsal and I wanted to surprise the other three members of our group with my impression of a 300 pound black man's version of Ain't Misbehavin.

My piano copy was under my 'Complete works of Shakespeare,' wedged under the lid of my Wrinch school desk. All I had to do was to open the desk top about two inches and I could read Fats Waller's words of wisdom, mouth them silently, thus committing them to memory.

Mr. Bont, like most of our teachers at the Liverpool Collegiate was intensely disliked, with justification I might add. Each week, we had to learn and recite a paragraph of Shakespeare. With no idea what most of the words meant, nor why they were used. It was my turn.

'The quality of mercy is not strain'd it drops er..er.'

A thump, on the back of my head from the Complete Works of Shakespeare, applied with a strong hand.

'Next,' our teacher of the indecipherable shouted. The victim at the next desk tried to remedy my failure, with the same lack of success.

'Useless nincompoops!' Mr.Bont yelled as he again lashed out at our ducking heads. During my evasive action, my desk top flew open and the vigilant eyes of Mr. Bont sighted my open copy of, Ain't Misbehavin.

'What is this?' he spluttered, lifting my precious musical gem and holding it between thumb and forefinger like a wet dish cloth.

'It's a piece of music, Sir.'

'It is a sheet of illiterate nonsense, you ignoramus.' I felt a firm grip on my left ear. 'We are going to the principal's office, we'll see what he has to say about this piece of rubbish'

It was a painful trip down the hallway to the principal's office as I tried to keep up with the angry Mr. Bont, my head tilted to ease the strain on my firmly grasped ear. Plus, I expected the culmination would be at least four painful strokes of a very slender, flexible cane on my outstretched hands.

'Come in,' the voice of our new principal echoed off the panelled walls.

Mr. Welesly, his feet propped on the desk looked very relaxed as I was pushed towards him.

'So, Mr. Bont, what has this young miscreant done to incur so much displeasure on your part?

'Sir, I caught Scott furtively reading this in his desk during my lesson. This, after he failed to recite the Shakespeare I assigned him.'

My now creased version of Ain't Misbehavin was plonked on his desk.

'So, young Scott what have you to say for yourself?'

'I was trying to memorise the song, Sir.'

'I'll deal with this Mr. Bont, your class is probably getting a little restless.'

Mr. Bont glared at me, as he moved to the door. I heard it close behind me.

'Do you know anything about Mr. Bont, Scott.?'

'No, Sir, just that he's our English teacher.'

'Right, did you know he's sixty-five, he could have retired five years ago, but when the war started, young men like me were called into the forces. He came back to teach, so youngsters like you, would still get an education. He's been teaching English and Shakespeare for forty-seven years. Now... do you wonder that he gets annoyed when young lads like you pay no attention, and never even think of a thank you, for his dedication?'

I nodded, looking at the floor, my hands clenched expecting the worst. He swung his feet off the desk and moved to the piano bench in the corner, sat down, and motioned me over.

'So, that is the dedicated Mr. Bont, to whom you are going to apologise when you return to class. Not only that, you will promise to learn your assignments and treat him with the respect you owe to him.

'Yes, Sir.'

He nodded and smiled, now.... 'what do you know about Fats Waller?' I looked up quickly at the mention of his name.

'He's plays the piano and sings, he's very big and a black man.'

'Right, he was 300 pounds when he died last year, at the age of 39. When I was your age I saw him in playing in London. Wonderful, he was a master of the'stride piano style.'

He saw my puzzled look, 'like this,' he swung round to the piano and moved his left hand over the keys at a walking pace. 'See, what I mean, now the right hand,'

Out flowed Ain't Misbehavin during which, he softly mouthed the words.

I was entranced--the school bell rang and broke the spell.

'Now Scott, head back to your class room, apologise and learn whatever Mr. Bont gives you. By the way, did you know Fats Waller was a great fan of Shakespeare?'

I looked up and shook my head.

'They were both troubadours, who used their beautiful language to tell a story. Sometimes sad, sometimes funny, but always entertaining. If you don't understand a word Shakespeare used, look in your dictionary. If Mr. Fats Waller gives you a problem word, ask me, because it may not be in a dictionary yet. He lifted my music off the piano, passed it to me and pointed to the door.

' Back to Mr. Bont young Scott and I want an improvement in your performance and attitude.' Yes, Sir and I practically bounced through the door.'

I hesitated at my class room door, the class was on break. I knocked.

'Come in! You again Scott.' He took the music from my hand, looked at me and I was sure he was about to rip it in half and toss it into the waste paper basket. Instead, he placed it on his desk, glanced at me and read out loud,

> No one to talk to, all by myself,
> No one to walk with,
> I'm just happy on the shelf.

'I think this Mr. Waller wrote it for me, Scott.' He almost smiled.

'Yes, Sir. Mr Welesly told me Fats Waller was a great fan of Shakespeare, they were both troubadours.' Here was a good time to segue into my apology, which I did with as much humility as I could muster. Ending with, 'I have to thank you for teaching us for forty-seven years.'

Again I saw a flicker of a smile, 'thank you Scott, words are easy, I'll expect proof next week, and it feels like a hundred and forty-seven years! Off to your next class you ignoramus.'

'One question, Sir.' He frowned.

'What is an ignoramus?'

'Look in the mirror, young Scott.
In the mirror!'

Allan F Scott

The End

Liverpool 1942

THE TRAM RIDE

Each afternoon, on leaving the Oulton High School my routine had been monotonous and boring. Run to the corner adjacent to the Adelphi Hotel, wait for the tram to slow down as it negotiated the curve, run along side, grab the post and swing myself aboard. Keeping the momentum I would run up the stairs to the top deck and flop on a rear seat. Most of the conductors were friendly as they punched my ticket, but would add something like: 'You'll break your neck one day lad,' or 'You get on at a proper stop next time.'

Then--in 1942 the Americans started to arrive. Their base was just beyond the terminus of my 6A tram. Instead of getting off at my usual stop, I would extend my ride and try to sit behind them, just to hear them talk. Especially the black soldiers, in fact, I would ride to the end of the line listening to every word, trying to understand the conversations, fascinated, intrigued and curious. The forty minutes it took just flew-by. In my twelve-year old mind, anyone black, must be either a jazzman, a tap dancer, or a comedian. The movies gave me, Louis Armstrong, Cab Calloway, Ella Fitzgerald, Fletcher Henderson and the love of my pre-teen life.... Lena Horne.

I had torn her picture from a Life Magazine in my barber's shop, carefully trimmed it, and gently pasted it on the wall at the head of my bed. Her head tilted back, laughing, I thought she was the most beautiful woman I had ever seen. Then one evening as I listened to the American Forces Network, I heard her voice. She had the most wonderful voice I had ever heard. Stormy Weather echoed through my mind for months.

Rationing, allowed me three 78 records a month and Lena Horne had to be one of them.

I was surprised when the grouchy man who owned the record store knew her name, and stated, that if I paid in advance, he would order it for me.

Then, I had the return trip to look forward to. Here, would be a fresh batch of soldiers intent on a wild night in downtown Liverpool. They seemed to be intrigued with Lime street, the Rialto and the Grafton Rooms. They would argue as to which was the best place to pick up babes, as they called the available young ladies of the city. Sometimes, noticing me, they would ask my advice. My knowledge of the nightlife was limited to the Roller Rink or the Ice Rink. 'Lots of girls there on Friday and Saturday nights,' I would proclaim, trying to sound worldly. 'Lots of sixteen-year-olds, and some ladies as old as twenty.' That statement would produce several wows and whistles from the lonely GI's.

If it was a Friday, sometimes I'd see some of them had taken my advice and were attempting to ice skate. It was disappointing to watch their feeble attempts. However, usually after a few minutes a young lady would skate up to them, and offer assistance, which is what they wanted in the first place. So.... maybe my advice was not wasted after all.

On one of my extended tram trips I noticed a black soldier with a trumpet case.

'Are you a trumpet player?' I naively asked.

'Sure kid, just going to sit in at the Stork Hotel.' I glanced up at him. 'How come all the best jazz players are black?' I asked.

'Well--they're not. Take Harry James, Bix Beiderbecke, Artie Shaw, Buddy Rich, they're the best, and pure white,' he was smiling at my bewilderment.

'How come you don't know that boy?' he grinned down at me.

'Well, I've only heard them on the wireless, I've never seen any pictures.'

'Here,' and he produced a few magazines from his case. I noticed the name Downbeat. 'If you can show me the way to the Stork Hotel, you can keep these.'

It didn't matter that I had to retrace my steps down town again, I was just intrigued with our conversation and continued asking questions.

'That's Lena Horne,' I exclaimed, pointing, as I thumbed through the pages.

'How come you know her?' He winked at me.

'She was in Life magazine and she is so beautiful. I just got a record of her singing, Stormy Weather.'

'What good taste you have boy, but I'll give you some advice. If you ever come to the States, make it New York. You maybe disillusioned if you go South. To know what the South is like, read Erskine Caldwell. Things may change after the war, but it'll take awhile I'm sure.'

We'd arrived at the Stork Hotel. I pointed at the sign. He put out his hand, 'Henry Powell Junior.'

'My name's Allan Scott, but why junior?'

'My father has the same name,' he explained.

'That's not very imaginative is it, couldn't your mum think of another name?'

He started to laugh, 'it's a great compliment to be called after your father, but around the house, I'm just.... junior.'

'That seems silly for a big man like you to be called junior,' was my puzzled reply. I swung my school bag from my shoulder and started to reorganise my books to make room for the magazines.

'What's all those books you have there?' Junior inquired as he looked over my shoulder. 'Well, this is En Route for French, and this is Music Theory by John Tobin, he teaches at my school.

'I bet you enjoy music kid,' Junior beamed down at me.

'I hate it, that teacher hits us on the head really hard with his book if we sing out of tune. Last week he made me write out the 23rd.Psalm twelve times. It took me to midnight, then when I gave it to him, he never even looked at it--just threw it in the waste paper basket. When I grow up I'm going back to my school and punch all the teachers that hit me.'

'Now boy, don't you go getting yourself into no trouble. He's probably just envious of your youth, maybe even a frustrated jazzman.' I laughed at the thought of the obnoxious Mr. Tobin playing jazz. I held up another book, Civis Romanus, 'that's my Latin book. The teacher's not a bad old guy, he just goes asleep when we read for him.'

Junior opened the book, 'sure looks difficult, read me that bit.' His large black finger pointed, 'Mens cuiusque is est quisque,' I read out loud.

'What does it mean kid?'

'The spirit is the true self. Cicero said that about 100 years BC.' He looked at the cover of the book. 'What's it called?'

'Civis Romanus sum, I am a Roman Citizen.' I was surprised he was even interested. 'You are one clever boy, sure you want to be a jazz musician? Say something else in Latin.'

'Well....you're from New York. You could say, Civis New Yorkus sum. I am a citizen of New York.'

'I like that.' He mounted the first step and grinned down at me. 'Yes, I like that, but I've got to go play.' He climbed the rest of the steps to the swing door, half pushed it open. Turned and waved. 'Civis New Yorkus sum. Yes indeed!––Everyday I learn something new,' were his partiing words.

Allan F Scott

The End

Liverpool 1944

MY FIRST FLIGHT

I had been looking forward to this day for two months, but Murphy's Law crept up on me. I had caught the flu. 'This is not going to prevent me taking my first flight.' I said to myself in the bathroom mirror, as I reached for another bottle of aspirin and a box of throat lozenges.

This prize had been awarded to myself and two other Air Cadets for winning the aircraft recognition test, and having the skill to reassemble the many pieces of a Browning machine gun in the dark. Though I must admit, I felt a little guilty, as I emptied the left over bits from my pockets to my bedside table later the same evening.

At fourteen I had the ability to override my conscience in such matters, especially if I was going to enjoy a benefit. The prize I lusted after were four flying lessons in a De Havilland Tiger Moth to be taken at an airfield just outside Liverpool.

The day came, the sun shone, and we, as the chosen three boarded a small blue airforce bus that arrived in front of our Air Cadet office. Our officer, who was also our maths teacher, stood in the front of the bus and reminded us to be respectful and to salute properly at all times. 'Remember, you are from the Liverpool Collegiate,' were the closing words to his pep talk.

We arrived, stopped outside the guardroom and a military policeman saluted our officer, then asked our destination.

'You lot are not very popular,' the policeman said. 'The Australian instructors were supposed to have a wild weekend in London. You'll find them in the crew room, hangar three.'

As we arrived at the hanger line I caught sight of several yellow Tiger Moths neatly lined up on the tarmac. I chewed on my aspirin and sucked the throat lozenges in eager anticipation.

'All out and fall in by the hangar door,' our officer commanded. Here he inspected us, making sure our collars were done up and our toes pointed out at 45 degrees. He then entered the hangar.

Even outside, the sound of the profanities from the crew room reached us.

It was then, I realised that Australians are bilingual. They speak Australian and profanity.

Our officer returned looking a little flushed and distressed, but ordered us to follow him to the parachute store. The three of us marched in single file, our leader striding alongside calling out the step. 'Left, right, left right,' echoed off the cold grey steel hangar doors.

With much pulling and tugging on the straps between shoulder and groin, the three of us were fitted with what seemed a too large and too heavier bag. The straps of which pulled between our legs ruining the carefully ironed creases in our trousers. The bag had the tendency to wedge between the knees, but, by keeping my legs together it rested behind me.

'Not really meant for little kipper runts,' the NCO complained as he tugged at my shoulder straps. 'Anyway, you can come back and get another one if it doesn't work.' His last words of consolation were interspersed with more indecipherable profanities that had his colleagues laughing and us fourteen-year-olds perplexed, but we laughed anyway.

Our march back to the flight line was slow and ponderous, as us, 'little kippers' tried to keep in step as the chutes flopped against the backs of our legs.

The three pilots were slumped on the grass, beer bottles in hand as we arrived back at the hangar.

'Halt!' Our officer shouted, then turned to the instructors and saluted.

This display of military protocol drew a round of applause. He then added, "three cadets reporting for training." This information was received with a string of profanation's and grunts of dissatisfaction from our instructors. They slowly rose to their feet, then waved for us to follow as they strolled towards the line of Tiger Moths

'Front seat,' the burly Australian growled down at me. I looked up at him.

'Well--what?' he said.

'I've never seen an Australian before,' I replied.

'What do you think then?' he almost smiled.

'You're very big, and you swear a lot,' I observed.

'What makes you say that you little bugger,' and two large hands lifted me in the direction of the front seat but left me suspended over the edge of the fuselage and the seat back. Another lift and I was plonked in the front seat.

'Don't touch anything and remember, if anything goes wrong, this thing will burn up in about fifty seconds. If we have to bail out I'll invert it, you just fall out, then don't forget to pull this handle or it could spoil your whole day,'

The last sentence was shouted through the speaking tube by my ear.

'Right, Sir.' I softly replied.

'Speak up kid, and here we go.'

We bounced and jiggled across the grass onto the runway and slowly picked up speed. The rattle and vibrations of the wheels on cement ceased, and for the first time in my life--I was flying. I tried to turn to grin at my instructor, but he was making a rude gesture to his colleagues in the aircraft behind, and slightly below us.

'We'll climb to 2,000 ft. then we'll let you have a go,' he growled through the tube.

It was a beautiful clear day and the Irish Sea glinted to our right and the smoke and grime of Liverpool smudged the horizon far into the distance.

'Right, listen up.' My burly intimidator mouthed in my speaking tube.

'Hold the joystick in your right hand and slowly pull back.' I did as instructed and slowly the nose of the aircraft moved above the horizon.

'Good, centre it again, then move it to the left.' We started to bank and I could see the fields far below us over the side of the cockpit.

'Now to the right.'

So it went for a few more minutes, as I was instructed to add pressure to the pedals in a turn, though I could hardly reach them. Then I heard a whoop of excitement from the rear seat and he practically stood up waving at his colleagues in the other two aircraft and pointing below and ahead.

In the distance I saw the silhouettes of sixTiger Moths. They were flying perfectly in line astern and below us, on what I knew to be the downwind leg of the landing circuit.

'Hang on kid,' the voice shouted through the tube and over we went in a steep dive. I looked behind and the other two Moths were behind us. We flew straight down towards the six approaching aircraft and pulled up directly in front of them. They didn't seem to notice us for a moment, then they suddenly banked and side slipped in all directions.

My Australian Biggles was whooping and waving with delight at the confusion around us. 'How do you like that ripper, kipper?' he shouted. 'Those Pommies never learn, they always try their parade square landings.'

'Now we'll try some aerobatics.' He slid away from his two companions and straight down we went, then straight up, and over. 'That's a loop,' he shouted. 'Hold tight.'

Those were the last words I heard, until I opened my eyes and found myself lying on the grass, the concerned face of my instructor looking down at me as he patted the side of my face.

'What's wrong kid, I thought you'd died on me.'

'I've got flu,' I moaned as I was helped to my feet and removed from my parachute. 'Lean on me kid and we'll get you to your bus.'

One of the other instructors walked towards us laughing.

'What'd yer do Joe, zoom him out?'

'Shut it Charlie, or I'll zoom you out. The kid's sick and he still came flying.'

He helped me to the back seat of the bus, placed a small open bottle of scotch in my hand, tousled my hair, slowly walked the aisle of the bus, turned, laughed and gave me the thumbs up sign. My first hero.

Allan F Scott

The End

Liverpool 1945

MY FIRST SYMPHONIC EXPERIENCE

It was 1945, and having reached the age of fifteen, for my birthday I was permitted to enjoy my first official date. What better way to celebrate this degree of sophistication than by taking a young lady of interest, to a symphony concert at the Liverpool Philharmonic Hall.

When I arrived at her house, her older brother opened the door and I knew, by his lack of surprise, that I was expected. As he led me into the front parlour he said, 'She's just tarting herself up; she'll be down in an hour or two.' He used the tone of voice that an older brother uses when talking of his sister. A tone that conveys, he cannot possibly believe anyone would want to be seen in public with her.

A few minutes later she appeared, and I had the usual palpitations males have when in a temporary condition of insanity, called love. Her brother seemed oblivious to this vision of loveliness and asked, 'Where're you two off then?'

'A symphony concert,' Doreen replied. A note of superiority in her voice.

Big brother rolled his eyes. 'That should be a barrel of laughs.'

Doreen glared at him as we edged past him and out the front door. Big brother laughed, and yelled for all the neighbours sitting on their front steps to hear, 'Keep your knickers on then.'

She smiled at me and yelled over her shoulder, 'You ignorant prick!' I could see Doreen was no shrinking violet.

I had hoped to take her for tea and dessert. Very adult, I thought, but as time was short we settled for an ice cream cone each, and headed into the theatre.

Not being able to afford the best seats, I had taken the on-stage special seats, which were behind the orchestra, but I was assured that we would be able to see and hear everything that was going on.

The usher took our tickets. 'Hurry, it's the back stage door and the concert is about to start.' We headed back stage, trying to follow the usher's directions, but backstage can be quite the labyrinth and took a few minutes of gently pushing doors open, before I pushed the right door, and below us was the orchestra and audience.

As we started down the stairs, applause erupted for the entrance of the conductor. It was the legendary Sir Malcolm Sargent.

Doreen, with a typical Liverpudlian sense of humour nodded in the direction of the applauding audience and smiled at me. 'Someone must have told them it was your birthday.'

At this point, I had an ice cream cone in each hand and the programs in my mouth, whilst Doreen held both our coats. This made it difficult to hurry; I had to keep saying, 'Excuse me,' and still retain the programs in my mouth, plus not brush the people with the ice cream cones, which, by this time had started to melt, leaving a trail of white spots on the carpet.

Our seats did have a good view--of the percussion section and we were behind the timpanist. Sir Malcolm acknowledged the applause, and turned to face the orchestra baton raised. He noticed us struggling to our seats and slowly lowered his baton.

Someone at the end of the row was one seat out, so for us to obtain two seats together, we had to ask them to all move up one. Doreen said, 'Either, you move up or I'll sit on my boyfriend's lap.'

So the great shuffle began, by now, not only the audience was watching us, but the orchestra members had also turned to see what was holding up the maestro's downbeat.

At last we were in our seats, coats on our laps and ice cream cones in hand. The baton fell but it was the National Anthem, so we all had to stand up again.

'Jesus Christ,' Doreen said in a stage whisper, loud enough to make the timpanist turn and utter, 'Shush,' in her direction. She countered this remark by sticking out her tongue in his direction.

On Doreen's left, was a gentleman with a musical score on his lap. To his left were several of his rather bored looking music students, to whom, during our settling in, he had been explaining the finer points of 'Finlandia', the first piece on the program. His voice was rampant with authority.

He leaned over to Doreen and said, 'Young Lady, it is not done to eat ice cream during a concert.'

'Well you're reading a book,' she replied, and gestured with her now nearly liquid ice cream cone. The top of the cone landed on his score. He was not amused, but the rest of the row erupted in laughter. I looked up to see the baleful eyes of Sir Malcolm fixed in our direction, his baton still hovering on the downbeat.

I had been playing drums in a dance band for two years, and it was a great thrill to sit so close to the timpanist and percussion section, in fact, it changed my life.

Finlandia has lots of timpani and percussion, it was exciting. I walked around for days singing the snare drum part. " De-dum-de-diga-diga-dum-dum. I was on a musical high.

After the concert I talked to the percussionists about lessons, as my academic knowledge was nil. They were very friendly, mainly due to Doreen flirting with them, as only a pretty 15 year old can do. I left with a day and time for my first lesson and the suave musician said, 'You can bring your girlfriend if you like.' I was very naive, and wondered why.

Twelve years later, in London, I was booked as extra percussion with the BBC Symphony Orchestra and yes--it was Sir Malcolm on the podium.

As he turned to cue me for my percussion entry, we made eye contact, and I wondered if he had a former vision of me holding an ice cream cone instead of a ambourine. If he did, he neglected to mention it.

Allan F Scott

The End

Liverpool 1946

THE EARLY DAYS

Liverpool, in 1946 was not the cultural centre of Europe; in fact, many miles of it looked like a disused parking lot. The rebuilding had not yet begun; all that had taken place was buildings partly destroyed by bombs, had been completely destroyed by the wrecker's ball.

In this grey and bleak city one pleasure left was dancing, which many people did, sometimes six nights a week.

Having hated school, I regularly pressed my mother to let me leave. Eventually I was told, 'You can leave but I will arrange a job at Littlewoods.' But really, what I wanted to do, was play in a band.

I was lucky and within a month had two jobs to contend with; I would leave home at seven in the morning, return for dinner, then out again at six- thirty for my drumming gig at the Gordon Institute on Scotland road. I'd arrive home at about eleven thirty p.m., a long day for a sixteen-year old.

I was a complete mystery to my aunts, who could not understand why I listened to all that American stuff, especially that skinny Italian chap, plus use my ration of three records a month, to buy more American 'jungle music.'

'What is wrong with Gracie Fields and George Formby?' my aunts used to ask.

Pictures of Count Basie, Duke Ellington, Lionel Hampton, Ella Fitzgerald, and the other 'greats' littered my room. 'What a rough looking bunch,' my aunt used to say. 'And they give themselves Royal titles like Duke and Count, what would the King say?'

'They have a King too,' I added, just to upset her a little more. 'King Oliver,' and I showed her a picture of the Creole Jazz Band with King Oliver holding his cornet and looking sombrely into the camera.

' Really!' My aunt eyed me with great indignation. "I've a good mind to write to the King about this, maybe he could send a gunboat or the Coldstream Guards to sort this out, only the British Empire is allowed Royal personages.'

Well, if she thought my collection of 'Jazz Greats' looked rough, she should have seen the clientele at the Gordon Institute, which was situated on Scotland Road, one of the poorest areas of Liverpool with a large Irish population.

Every night fights would break out on the dance floor; just a few tussling figures at first, then it would escalate until most of the dance floor became a battle ground, but the rest of the patrons just kept dancing.

When this happened we would immediately change to a waltz, hoping it would have a soothing effect--our fearless band leader, all 5ft 4" of him, would put down his sax, leap over the wire safety screen into the fray and drag the combatants apart. Climb back on stage, smooth his brylcreamed hair and continue playing.

The stage was raised about four feet and the wire screen was to stop bottles, glasses, etc.that some of the patrons tossed at the band in a moment of Celtic frivolity.

If the situation became too dangerous, our leader would open the rear door from the stage, where he kept his ice cream truck parked flush with the door, push us all in, and drive furiously to the pub. The police would be phoned, and when order was restored we would return to finish the night.

We returned one night to find two policemen had been stabbed and all the glass display cases broken. 'This is gang warfare,' one of the constables told us and warned us not to take sides. I didn't need to be warned twice.

Danger came from unexpected areas, this time--Palestine.

The 'Liverpool Echo' had a picture of two Liverpool soldiers that had been captured and hung by a Jewish terrorist group. This had triggered riots and many Jewish shops had their windows broken.

I arrived early at the Gordon Institute and met Teddy, a wonderful trumpet player, he was fourteen years old and Jewish. We stood chatting in the doorway when a motley group of locals came down the street, some of whom I recognised as our customers.

'Hey ! You two look Jewish,' one of them yelled, and they gathered around us. I was just hoping the door would open and give us an escape route. Things started to look bad for us when another figure appeared, a large burly Irishman; who was the brother of a girl I had been walking home. He was also one of the local gang leaders. I had never spoken to him, and always felt nervous about being seen with his sister.

He pushed his way through, 'What's this about,' he asked. One of the group explained that they figured we were Jewish. 'No, these blokes play in the band and this one goes out with Teresa, my sister.' Just then to our relief the doors opened. 'Thanks,' I whispered as I pushed my way in. He raised a finger and beckoned me over; I looked up at him. 'Just don't get her in the 'puddin club' he growled.'

The entrance fee was nine pence, and collected at the door by our leader's mother, who was just as courageous as her son. After the girls paid, they headed over to the stage and tossed their shoes over our wire barrier. As the evening wore on we had quite a pile, and I tried to keep them in some sort of order, otherwise it would be like a rugby scrum when they tried to retrieve their footwear.

Friday night was pay night, two pounds ten shillings for me. As the customers paid mostly is pennies, that is how we in turn were paid. An unwieldy pile of pennies wrapped in a page of the newspaper.

Three hundred and sixty pennies not only weigh a lot, but would fill both trouser and jacket pockets to the brim. I found I walked Teresa home a little slower with this excess weight, and hesitated to mention why, in case she mentioned it to her brother--this may have been too much temptation.

On arriving home usually about midnight, I would empty my pockets into a biscuit tin on the sideboard, drink half a bottle of milk, and refill the bottle with water, so no one would notice.

My Father had begun to take an interest in me... well, he acknowledged my presence. Previously, he ignored me most of the time, or said things like, 'What's wrong with your ears? You look like a Morris Minor with both doors open.'

I was probably doing too much for a sixteen year old and sometimes I would be quite depressed. One evening I was in this mood and confided to my father, I felt I may as well end it all. He glanced up from his newspaper and said, 'Oh, can I have your ration book.'

About this time I mentioned Teresa to him, but he said, 'Don't bring her home; she sounds rather common.' Next day, he gave me a book on sex, approved by the 'Boys' Brigade.'

The opening statement was...that a sex act uses the same energy as a five mile run. The suggestion posed was, why waste your energy on sex when you could run five miles, hereby not risking pregnancy or contracting a deadly disease. At sixteen that made sense, along with all the other fables we were told.

My father must have mentioned something to Mr. Potter our Boys' Brigade Captain, because he too, gave me a little book on sex; this again listed all the deadly diseases one could contract, and suggested taking cold showers to relieve unnatural urges.

Between cold showers and five mile runs, it left little time for a date.

Mr. Potter was what we would call today 'a fitness freak.' Apart from insisting that we stride out when we walked, he issued every boy who joined the Boys' Brigade, along with his uniform, two rubber balls, one to be gripped in each hand and squeezed in tempo with his walking pace.

He was a familiar figure in our area, as he was the bank manager. If he spotted me on the street he would yell, 'Are you squeezing your balls Scott?'

'Yes, Sir,' would be my startled reply.

All this, of course, though I didn't realise it at the time, was for the glory of the British Empire. At eighteen we would be doing Military Service and to fail the fitness test was, in Mr. Potter's words, 'a disgrace to the King and country.'

Thanks to five mile runs, cold showers, and much ball squeezing, I was pronounced A-1 and very proud I was.

Having had some flying training in the Cadets, I put down for air-crew and, as Mr. Potter said, 'England will always know some country that needs to be bombed.' However, I was to be disappointed; with the war over and hundreds of air-crew idle, one more eighteen-year-old was not needed.

My next interest was my drumming, and I knew the Royal Air Force had five bands. I applied and signed on for five years so I could attend the RAF School of Music in Uxbridge.

I was apprehensive about the three months basic training, but with my previous cadet training and with about one hundred eighteen-year-olds in the same boat, I enjoyed myself. No more boring work and with forty of us per building; never a dull moment.

Plus we had dances five nights a week on the station, which after my second week I was happy to be playing for, until I was transferred to Catterick three months later.

You make a lot of friends in three months, and I was sorry when we all had to go our different ways. We all liked our drill instructor, he was from Cornwall and his accent was very hard to understand. He never swore at us or used bullying techniques, and told me that he hated people that swore all the time, because it showed they had a very limited vocabulary. Very profound I thought.

Following basic I was assigned to my first band: The RAF Regiment Band at Catterick in Yorkshire.

Our main work consisted of playing for the ceremonial closure of RAF stations in the north of England. This we did month after month, same speeches, same ceremonies, same music and it always seemed cold and windy. Sometimes, I thought Littlewoods was not so bad.

Then our fortunes improved: we had a new director of music and we were going to Malta. 'Must be closing it down,' somebody said.

We flew into the island of Malta and what a contrast to the bleak Yorkshire moors, sand, sea, and sun instead of wind, rain, and cold.

Part of our indoctrination lecture was given by a young army intelligence officer, who informed us that some of the local people were hostile to the British. (What would Mr. Potter have said?) He went on to say he had reports of women of easy virtue, using their charms to seduce young soldiers into giving away military secrets. We all wanted to know their whereabouts... so we could avoid them, of course.

Sliema Bay was beautiful; and as soon as we settled in it was swim time. This was a new experience for us to swim in warm water, and was not going to be too hard to take.

Myself and Taffy walked to the town and the people seemed friendly, but aloof. Later we sat at an outdoor restaurant watching a wonderful guitar player and a flamenco dancer. The performance was enhanced by the beautiful chaperoned girls strolling the street, the warm evening and the star-filled sky.

When the music finished we told the guitar player how much we enjoyed it, and Taffy never one to be shy, asked if he could sing a song with him.

They discussed keys for a few minutes and decided on 'Come Back to Sorento.' The applause encouraged an encore and they did 'Lucky Me.' The audience in and outside the restaurant clapped and sang along in rhythm to this modern tarantella, Taffy singing in English, the audience in Italian.

Pleased with their reception they launched into another encore, this time

'Beseme Mucho.' A slow romantic ballad, Taffy singing a few words in Spanish this time, and directing them to a beautiful young lady escorted by Mum of course. I thought Mum may have been annoyed, but she loved it, and the young lady presented him with a rose, which drew applause and laughter from the crowd. Not speaking Italian, we missed the jokes but at least everyone was happy.

The owner beaming and laughing refused payment for our wine and sat with us; we asked if he would like our dance band to play on the Saturday evening and he was delighted but said he could not afford to pay much. We stuck our necks out and said, 'No problem.

On our return to camp we extolled the beauty of the girls and the taste of the wines to the rest of the dance band, infusing them with our enthusiasm.

Saturday night found our twelve piece combo crowded on the little stage, under the stars playing, 'In the Mood,' 'Over the Rainbow,' and tunes of that era to a delighted audience and, yes, Taffy sang 'Beseme Mucho.' But the young lady had another escort, a tall handsome male with Latin film- star looks.

Poor 5ft 3in skinny Taffy, with his mop of unkempt red hair, was I felt, outclassed. However, I noticed he was invited to his dream girl's table and lack of Italian or not, they were soon laughing and talking. He must have complained about the omission of a rose presentation, because next moment I saw the handsome man bow and present Taffy with a red rose. Again to much joking and laughter from the surrounding tables.

We played past midnight and returned to our base. Several hours later I awoke to the soft sounds of guitars. I looked out the window, and four musicians were leaning against the wall serenading us with wonderful Italian melodies.

Alex who had the bed next to me, decided to join them with his flute; we leaned out the windows and sat on the wall and steps, enjoying this impromptu concert from four guitars and Alex in his pyjamas.

Two months later we returned to the bleakness and cold of Catterick.

Sometimes, after a wet, cold parade, we would flop on our beds, and I would see Taffy, a far-away look in his eyes and a book open on his chest, with the petals of a pressed red rose peeping out.

Allan F Scott

The End

Cardington 1948

MY FIRST MENTORS

Arriving at RAF Cardington in 1948, I was apprehensive about the three months basic training to come. However: being eighteen the rebellious mode had started to insert itself into my personality. The reason--I was developing as a musician and being flattered for my ability as a drummer. I felt just a little bit special and I was not looking forward to being just one of the young sprogs in an ill fitting uniform, being shouted at and treated with contempt by any other sprog with two weeks longer service than myself.

On arrival, as we all filled in our personal history and indoctrination forms a pleasant looking Flight Sergeant strode into the room. 'Attention!' he shouted. We all stood.

'Not that type of attention, just listen, and please sit. Fill out this form concerning any special interests you may have. Such as playing football, rugby, field hockey, swimming, cricket or even musical skills.' Here, I pricked my ears up. 'We have a marching band and a dance band on the station. If you are accepted in any of these sports or musical activities, you will be excused guard duty and fire picket, but, you still have to attend all classes to complete your basic training.'

I filled in the form and it was securely clamped onto his clipboard.

'Scott?' I nervously stood up.

'Report to the band room at 1700 hours.'

The band room was not hard to find. I had already noticed the squeaks, wails and thumps that are the indication of this hive of musical industry, anywhere in the world.

I hesitated in the open door and the Flight Sergeant waved me in.

'Can you read this?' He held a march card up and pointed at a drum on a stand in the corner. 'Just do two three beat rolls, and I'll thump the piano.' As I played the introductory rolls he strode to the piano, and commenced playing The Thin Red Line. I drummed along with him.

'Good, that's fine. I'll give you the chits for your corporal. You'll only be missing physical training.' As I turned to leave he asked, 'have you done any dance band work?'

'Yes, I played in a big band for for two years,' I replied hopefully.

He nodded. 'Good, we have dancing five nights a week here and our drummer is posted at the end of the week. Come to the dance Tuesday night and sit in for a few numbers. If you do OK, you'll have the job for the next three months.

I arrived back at the green hut, my new home, and noticed my compatriots were all busy folding blankets and placing stuff into their foot lockers under the direction of an immaculately groomed and rigid Corporal.

'What's happening?' I asked the nearest fellow sprog.

'No talking,' the corporal swung in my direction. 'And where have you been?'

I pulled the two chits form my pocket.

'I don't need to see your last will and testament, just watch what we're doing because by tomorrow morning you will be expected to perform same.' He turned to the airman who was actually performing the tasks required to complete the making of a perfect bed and the arranging of a perfect foot locker. He gestured to the airman. 'Thank you, Olckers.'

'They are just two of the tasks you will perform on a daily basis. Do them as well as A/C Olckers just demonstrated and all will be well, if not--repetition is the best teacher. His eyes swept the room, as he turned to leave he gestured for me to follow.

Outside the hut he relaxed and sighed, 'chits please,' and pulled a pen from his battle dress pocket, glanced at the pieces of paper, initialled them both. and handed them back.

'So--no fire picket or guard duty. That will make life easier for you, but remember you still have to have everything else up to snuff or I can have your band duties revoked. Understood? Being in the band does not make you special or give you a position of prestige. To me, you are just another sprog that has difficulty folding a blanket, making a bed, standing erect, shaving, marching and knowing left from right.'

'Yes, Corporal,' and feeling quite deflated I slunk back into the confusion of bed making and locker sorting.

'That's our Corporal Truscott', my bedmate informed me, 'and he's from Cornwall, can't understand a word he says when he gets excited.'

'I had trouble when he wasn't excited,' I laughed.

He flopped onto his half-made bed. 'Seems a nice bloke though, looks like a movie star, jet black hair, beautiful teeth and brown eyes. Nice body shape and a tailored uniform' I looked surprised at his quick assessment of our Corporal.

'I'm a hairdresser, it's very important to read people in my job.' My friends call me Flash and he extended his hand.

'Allan,,' I replied.

'That's no good. You're from Liverpool so I'll call you Scouser.'
'Scouser, it is,' I grinned and returned to my blanket folding.

The following Tuesday evening found me scrubbed and polished, and with Flash for moral support heading for my audition. It went well, I played three arrangements with the band. One of them being Hawaiian War Chant which features a drum solo. I knew it well, and was given the thumbs up.

The dances were Tuesday to Saturday and the pay was 12 shillings a night. This tripled my weekly pay!

'Buddy Rich couldn't have done any better.' Flash commended. 'You look a bit square though, you need to look a bit more,--with-it.' I frowned at him, my Liverpudlian sensitivities being exposed. 'You have to look like Buddy Rich--what you need is a crew-cut.'

Flash's power of persuasion soon had me seated in the ablutions on an upturned red fire bucket, a towel round my shoulders, as Flash, clippers and scissors in hand slowly circled round me. 'Right,' and he commenced the operation. My head was tilted to the left, to the right, and lastly I was ordered to look up and straight ahead. All I was aware of was the quantity of hair amassing at my feet.

'That's it, what do you think?' He rotated me to face the mirror.

'It looks like an upside-down toothbrush.' I gasped.

Flash stood back admiring his handiwork. 'Think what you'll save on Brylcream.'

My new hairstyle was admired by all. Within a few days Flash had built a thriving business and performed his skills on nearly all 110 members of B Flight at the modest sum of six-pence a head. Plus he had a sweeper-upper and a shampooer complete with hand held dryer.

Corporal Truscott huffed and puffed the first time he wandered in to find this thriving business flourishing in Hut 22. Flash used his Cockney charm as he explained, it was done in our own time and everything was cleaned up each evening.

'You have great hair corporal, I could give you the latest style from London. Like this,' and Flash produced a glossy photograph from amongst his equipment. 'Plus it's free, for first time customers.'

'OK, but if you muck it up––there's three sacks of potatoes waiting to be peeled in the cookhouse.'

'Good, a shampoo first corporal, get that greasy stuff out of your hair.' He placed him in a chair by the sink. Flash winked at us as he rubbed the soap into our corporals hair. The hair was dried and the cutting commenced.

'Lots off the top, but little off the sides, moisten, dry, comb and brush, and voilá, the latest London style.' He turned his victim to the mirror. 'Really hip, corporal. Nothing to fall over your eyes and great for dancing.'

Our corporal looked impressed. 'Good work Flash. I like that and I only came in to get two volunteers for the cookhouse. You and you!' and he pointed at two sprogs lurking and smirking in the background.

Our mornings started at 0600 with our corporal pushing open the door and chanting. 'Wakey, wakey this wasn't how the British Empire was built, laying abed all hours of the day.' This raucous awakening was followed by him banging on our metal bedsteads with his pacestick, and out he would go.

I never heard him swear, or yell. He knew just the right words to encourage, shame or berate us future saviours of King and Country.

Three months later we graduated. We took up a collection for our corporal and having heard he liked to write, we bought the biggest dictionary we could find and with 110 signatures inscribed, it was my privilege to present it.

Later in the mess after a few beers, I asked our mentor, why he, unlike the other NCO's never swore, screamed or belittled the slower members of our flight.

'Well, if you have to stoop to bullying, threatening and profanity I think you lack one of the basic qualities of a real Englishman--a good vocabulary.'

'Plus--a good haircut,' Flash concluded.

Allan F Scott

The End

Catterick 1948

UNLIKELY FRIENDS

A barracks room in 1948, due to the two years compulsory military service, contained an amazing cross section of male humanity. My barracks room certainly did, but, we had one common bond, we were all musicians. Again an amazing cross section was evident.

Aspiring jazz musicians, brass band stars from the mills and mines of England and Wales, an accordion prodigy who played the clarinet as if he hated it, a star cornet player of Salvation Army persuasion, who, for the first time was practising profanity as a second language, an engine driver, who was a frustrated trombonist, symphony players who talked in hushed tones of the old masters, a tap dancer for whom the air force could not find a trade classification, but who was told, 'We'll put you in the band they're rather an odd lot.'

Lastly, those left over from the war years, who decided to stay in for a pension, and regardless of how uncomfortable our duties, would always rationalise: 'It was all pensionable time.'

Several of these bandsmen, as we were called were as old as thirty, to an eighteen year old, that seemed like a dinosaur.

One of these ancients was a graduate of the Indian Army, and not only was he the perfect bassoonist, but the perfect soldier. He even ironed his issue pyjamas to knife like creases, and frequently, when walking on the base, whether in civilian clothes or uniform, would be saluted by the recruits.

When this happened, he would stop them and say: 'You don't have to salute me, I'm just as common as you are.' Though his English was superior to ours, we pointed out, though correct, it was not... really the thing to say.

He would regale us with his experiences in the Indian Army, and told us he was in a mounted band, mounted on elephants! He continued, 'This was not a good idea, because a man can master a horse, but an elephant is big enough to have a mind of its own.'

'During a parade supposed to end in the grounds of the Taj Mahal, the elephants, which had not been fed for twelve hours, (for obvious reasons) had smelt the food tents and headed not only to them, but through them, helping themselves as they went, and scattering the upper crust of India in all directions. Our discipline was so strong we never stopped playing. Another time, I was about to play a bassoon solo with the band and I felt my instrument was not responding as it should. I removed the bottom section and a snake crawled out. But I didn't panic, I picked it up, put it in my case, played my solo perfectly, then released the snake into the garden.'

'Didn't you kill it?' someone asked.

'No all life is sacred, specially a snake that has an affinity for a bassoon.'

We did wonder if we were having our leg pulled, but I noticed anyone playing an instrument that involved tubing, took a few minutes, to surreptitiously look in both ends, before putting it to their lips.

My room contained about twenty beds, neatly arranged round the walls, with tall grey metal lockers between them. The area that contained the bed was called the bed space, and you were responsible for its cleanliness and the orderly appearance of your locker.

The bed space on my left was occupied by Peter Wolston-Croft, known as Crafty. We all had nicknames, that just happened, I can never remember anyone formally giving anyone a nickname, some of them went with your instrument, like mine, Sticks.

It was obvious that Crafty had a public school education, not only by his accent and vocabulary, but by his self assurance and aristocratic demeanour. Plus he had a degree in composition which he earned after four years study at the Royal Academy of Music. However: he did have an eccentric streak, which always puzzled us working class types.

We were allowed two photographs (specified respectable) on top of our lockers. Most of us had girl friends or pin ups, but Crafty had ...Lenin and Trotsky.

When questioned by the less worldly corporals, he would tell them it was Uncle Lenin and Uncle Trotsky. However, when the wing commander inspected, Crafty was ordered to remove them, as subversive material. Which he did, but not without protest.

Telling the Wing Commander that Lenin and Trotsky, were, until recently the heroes of the working man, and continued: 'Sir, one of whom, upon termination from the service... you will be.'

This statement produced a few moments of uncomfortable silence, and the Wing Commander turned to the Warrant Officer asking him if there was anything in King's Regulations forbidding photographs of political leaders on our lockers.

But before he could answer Crafty replied, 'No, Sir, I have checked, and it is permitted. Be it Winston Churchill or Mahatma Gandi.'

'Er...Quite,' the Wing Commander said turning away to inspect my area, dominated by Patty Page and Judy Garland. 'More like it,' he mumbled and headed out the door.

The Station Warrant Officer, looking on the verge of a seizure exploded, 'How dare you talk to your Commanding Officer like that?'

Crafty just smiled and replied, 'Freedom of speech, reinforced with a little education... Sir.' The Station Warrant Officer raised his arms like a frustrated Italian waiter, and too headed out the door.

We were still laughing and congratulating Crafty when the door opened and the doorway was filled by a large figure carrying a footlocker in one hand, tuba case in the other, a full pack on his back, on which rested his kit bag. Any one of these items I would have considered a full load.

He gently lowered everything to the floor, looked around and said:

'T'is dis be bandoyle am thunkin?'

'My God, we'll need an interpreter with this one.' Crafty groaned.

Our only other member from Newcastle came to his rescue, and they chatted away in native tongue. As Crafty put it.

I helped him sort out the bed next to me and put his stuff in the locker, but I noticed the tuba was placed very gently under his bed. Of course his nick name was Tubby, due to his size and choice of instrument.

Crafty aired his caustic wit at Tubby's expense many times, but either Tubby didn't understand or ignored him. Though, on one occasion Crafty noticed Tubby looking at the two political figures on his locker, and was about to launch into his dialogue on Communism, when Tubby said, 'Lenin and, Trotsky, you would have been very popular with my dad, he was a Communist.'

'I am sure I have nothing in common with your father,' Crafty snorted.

'Not anymore, he died two years ago in a pit accident.' Tubby replied.

The top of Tubby's locker was graced with a picture of the Colliery Brass Band, and a photograph of a buxom young woman smiling over the bell of her tuba.

This was Mildred one of the loves of his life, the other being his tuba. No ordinary tuba as he proudly told me, but a silver plated, presentation model made by the world famous Boosey and Hawkes of London.

The engraving on the bell read:

August 1947. Presented to Larry Mund by The Right Honourable Basil Morley for his outstanding musical dedication and performance 1946 and 1947 at the Royal Albert Hall, London.

'You were only sixteen' I said.

'Well, I started on cornet when I was four, and played ever since.' Tubby modestly explained.

We often returned to our barracks room cold, wet and dispirited after a long boring parade and bus ride. Everyone would have some complaint or other, but not Tubby, he would listen to our laments and proclaim:

'You buggers don't know when you're bloody well off.'

Then he would launch into a dialogue on the hard life of the miner, which he had been since he was fourteen.

This became routine, after moaning and groaning, we would wait for his repartee on the harsh reality at the coal face of Brandon Colliery.

We had, had an unusually frustrating day, waiting in the rain for two hours at the Air Port for a VIP to arrive. We played the National Anthem, and marched off, during which Crafty fell over a low chain we had been warned about many times by our stoic Drum Major. Even Crafty's mastery of the English language didn't help, when the Drum Major yelled: 'Stupid thing to do Croft!.'

We arrived back in our room flopped on our beds and the complaints came loud and long. Sure enough... 'You buggers don't know when you're bloody well off,' came from the predictable Tubby.

Crafty slouched in, still trying to remove the mud from his greatcoat and boots. 'Anyone who blows a piece of plumbing like that deserves to work in a pit,' and aimed a kick at the reclining tuba under Tubby's bed.

Tubby who to this point was ignoring Crafty, jumped off the bed and picked him up by the collar of his greatcoat and held him against the wall.

'Now you can kick me any time but you kick my tuba and I'll get very nasty with you,' and he added emphasis by banging Crafty's head against the wall, then releasing him to slide down, with a look of amazement at this attack on his aristocratic personage.

For the second time that day, Crafty failed to find a reply from his extensive verbal repertoire.

I lay back on my bed, boots hanging over the end, so as not to mark the blankets. On one side I had Crafty, the essence of depression, the other, Tubby, his usual cheeriness depleted.

I looked a Crafty and said, 'That was a rotten thing to do, you're the one with the education: What happened to... words will live, and violence will self destruct, as your Uncle Trotsky used to say?'

I saw a spark of amusement in Crafty's eyes. 'OK, I was wrong,' and he leaned towards Tubby, 'Sorry Tubby that was a stupid thing I did, I behaved very badly.'

I interrupted; 'The NAAFI is open, I'll buy you both a cuppa if you shake hands.'

Tubby shook himself and rolled off the bed, still looking very glum, 'God, I'm cold he mumbled.'

Crafty, imitated Tubby's lumbering walk, then his accent. 'You buggers don't know when you're bloody well off, I remember when I had to wait ten minutes in the rain for my taxi to the conservatory, it was sheer hell.'

Our down mood was broken and laughter replaced sullen silence, Tubby joined in, beginning to look like his old self.

We settled in the canteen, hands wrapped around our tea mugs. 'No practice for tonight,' Tubby said. 'Need some new stuff to work on.'

'You can use any of my books, but they maybe difficult for you.' Crafty replied.

'No, played most of those, nothing I can't whip through there,' Tubby almost yawned.

'You are not going to tell me you can play the Bach Variations on that pile of plumbing.' Crafty replied indignantly.

'Here we go again.' I softly murmured.

But Tubby, put down his mug and replied. 'You get your oboe, and we'll go to the bandroom and run through some of those duets you're always spouting off about.'

Off they went, contrasts in every way. Six feet placid and lumbering Tubby and five feet something Crafty, gesturing and almost running to keep up. I had a feeling only one would return.

But return they did, Crafty full of enthusiasm about the duets they had performed, then trying to push his way past Tubby through the door of the barracks room, something he always tried, I think unconsciously to do, but of course never made it and wound up wedged against the door frame, until Tubby squeezed past him.

Most afternoons and evenings, the sounds of oboe and tuba drifted across the field from our bandroom. We all had to admit, musically it was perfect, though not quite the sound Bach, Mozart and the other Old Masters, intended.

We had worked many weekends, and were due for a five day leave, Tubby was saying how he was looking forward to seeing, 'My Mildred,' as he called her.

'Be careful or you'll get hooked,' we warned. 'No I have the best contraceptive in the world... my tuba.' We waited for further explanation.

'We just keep it between us.'

'Bet it gets dented a few times,' Crafty said.

'Eh, Crafty why don't you come and stay at my place, your folks are in Paris,' Tubby said, ignoring our further advice on contraception. 'Bring your oboe, we'll amaze my folks in the brass band. Plus we can hitch hike in two or three hours.'

'Hitch hike,' Crafty echoed. 'Not sure if I like that, that's for down and outs.'

'Too bad, you can be down and out for once. It'll do you good,' Tubby replied.

The five days were over too quickly and I sat reading on my bed as my room mates drifted in, but I was really waiting for Crafty and Tubby, they arrived just before supper and the three of us headed into the mess hall.

Crafty was quite indignant, 'We had lifts on five lorrys, and not one of the drivers knew what an oboe was.'

'I'm sure they found out.' I said.

Tubby started laughing saying, 'Out would come his oboe, then a demonstration and a recital, all squeezed in a truck cab.'

'Would have cost them five pounds in London,' Crafty added, 'and all I got was two bananas and half a bar of chocolate.'

'You must have really impressed them.' I said.

He continued 'I had a great time with Tubby and his band. They played pianissimo all the time, so I would be heard. They play as if they were born with their instruments.'

'Or at least conceived with them.' I added.

'I even went down the mine on Sunday, that was frightening, you go down and down, it's dark, wet and hot and some places you have to crawl through, other places you have to press against the wall as trains of coal come past.'

Tubby standing behind him winked at us, as Crafty aired his knowledge of a working mine. Crafty finished his dialogue, looked around at us and said: 'You buggers don't know when you're bloody well off,' though we had heard it many times before, it still sent us into fits of laughter, specially coming from aristocratic Crafty.

A month later it was Tubby's turn to be treated to a home visit. I had heard them discussing it, but somehow felt it unlikely, due to what Crafty had told me about his home life.

His father was Sir Henry Wolston-Croft, now Air Commodore and Chief Padre for the Royal Air Force. His mother Lady Lilian Woston-Croft had been in the news for declaring as a mother– –'Compulsory National Service was a waste of the countries money, and that anyone forced into a vocation, would never do a good job, and quoted the unpopularity of the British Forces in many parts of the world.'

They don't want us there, our troops don't want to be there, surely a recipe for further violence, was a quotation from one of her many speeches.

It is time we put the British Bulldog back in it's kennel, she had concluded.

Thursday morning was leave day, for this weeks chosen ones, as they were called. I had used up my leave and was watching Tubby and Crafty sprucing themselves up. 'What train are you catching ?' I asked Tubby.

'We are being picked up at the main gate,' he whispered.

Crafty eyed him reproachfully.'Don't tell the world. I'm off to the band room for some music, back soon.'

As soon as Crafty left we started pulling Tubby's leg, telling him he didn't need to take his own mug or eating utensils and the toilet would probably be inside and he didn't have to wait for Saturday to have a bath. Don't forget your dinner jacket or to bow or salute when introduced to his father, or both if you want to really impress him.

Our humour was flowing freely, when there was a knock on the door, it opened and an assertive woman's voice asked, 'Band Quarters?'

'Yes,' several hesitant voices replied.

'Are you respectable?' The female voice continued.

'Yes,' we chorused and those lying on their beds stood up, she entered and said: 'I'm Lilian Croft, Peter's mother.' We must have looked perplexed and she continued, 'You know, Crafty.'

'Oh, Crafty,' we nodded. The sound of the familiar relaxing us.

'Please sit down,' she made it sound like and order, we obeyed immediately.

In her familiar surroundings she would have looked beautiful, but in the drab masculine greyness of our barracks room, she was stunning.

Light cream riding pants, highly polished brown riding boots, a green jacket and white shirt with a dark green tie. Her jet black hair parted in the middle and flowing to her shoulders. Her green eyes regarding each of us in turn with a humorous twinkle.

'How about a cup of tea chaps while I wait?' There was a scuffle as we all rushed to grab a mug. Then I remembered Crafty had a real cup with flowers on it. 'This will be fine,' I said waving it in the air, and rushed out the door to the mess hall.

I was eyed with suspicion by a group of burly infantry men as I put the small flowery cup under the spout of the urn, trying not to let it overflow.

When I returned she was reclining on my bed, surrounded by hypnotised admirers. 'Ah... thank you,' and she reached for her tea, continuing to hold court.

She raised her eyebrows,

'You are?'

'Sticks, Er...Allan,' 'I have heard about you all. Peter is quite the prolific scribe.'

I think we all felt a little over exposed with that statement.

The door opened and Crafty stuck his head round, yelling at Tubby to get a move on. 'Don't want to keep the old lady waiting.' He eyed us quizzically, when no one replied with the usual witticisms this remark would normally have provoked.

The circle of admirers parted to reveal Lady Lilian comfortably ensconced on my bed. Crafty froze, blinked, took a second look, realised he wasn't hallucinating. 'Mother, what are you doing here?' he squeaked.

'Our driver is sick so I thought I would give you a surprise.' She swung off the bed and gave Crafty a kiss on the cheek. 'You're Tubby,' he nodded his head, as if he wasn't sure. 'Let's be on our way, we'll be home for afternoon tea and thank you for tea.' I took the cup from her manicured hand, restraining the urge to bow as I did so.

We waved out our window, watched them climb into the blue Bently and laughed as Tubby insisted his tuba occupy a passenger seat, rather than be confined to the trunk. They drove off, Lady Lilian waving nonchalantly, Tubby making rude gestures from the rear window.

I felt I had a glimpse of an unobtainable world. I flopped on my bed which was still warm and retained the faintest aroma of her presence. I regarded a thin line of lipstick, which marked the rim of the cup still held loosely in my hand. I felt strangely subservient and depressed.

Sunday evening Crafty and Tubby floundered their way into the barracks room, and placed a large box of cakes and biscuits on the table. Someone arrived with a bucket of tea and we settled down to hear an account of the weekend.

'Crafty, how can someone as ugly as you have a mother like that?' Came from one side of the room.

'You should see his sister,' Tubby groaned, 'and sexy--wow! she sat on my knee when I was practising in the garden, and whispered that the vibrations from my instrument went right through her.'

'She wasn't talking about the tuba,' someone laughed.

'Hey, that's my sister you're talking about,' Crafty complained and continued.

'On Saturday night, mother had eight guests for dinner, and asked us if we would play our instruments, then oblige with a little conversazione in the Conservatory after dinner. And Tubby said, I don't like Italian food. I've never seen my father laugh so long,' Crafty chortled, the memory still fresh in his mind.

Tubby laughed, 'Funny thing I didn't know what he was laughing about. Until we played the Double Oboe Concerto, and some of the guests started asking questions about who wrote it, and when. I told them I really didn't care, who, or when. Then Crafty told me I should talk about Brass Bands or anything... even tubas. That is what a conversazione is. Every day I learn something new.' Tubby said shaking his head.

Tubby continued, 'Sunday, we had Sir this and Lady that and an Arch Bishop for champagne lunch in the garden, about twenty people, we pulled the piano onto the lawn for his sister, I got my tuba and we played waltzes and polkas.'

'Did she vibrate on your instrument?' came a Liverpool voice from the end of the room. 'Hey, that's his sister you're talking about,' Tubby yelled and continued: 'It was right grand, everyone dancing round the piano.'

Then Lady Lilian came out, hit a gong and complained, that though we had fresh strawberries, the real Devonshire cream was not available and we would have to do with ...tinned cream. The guests, all well into the champagne, groaned and shouted: 'Shame! Shame! Shame!'

Crafty climbed onto a chair, and in his best Newcastle accent shouted:

'You buggers don't know when you're bloody well off!'

"I was real proud of him," Tubby shouted, as he held Crafty up by the arm pits.

Allan F Scott

The End

London 1951

THE DINNER I ALMOST HAD.

When I became twenty-one I was told, 'You are free to do anything, go anywhere, live your own life.' This, in theory is fine, but I was in the RAF Music Service, that meant I had to live where I was told, do what I was told, plus only thirty shillings a week, did impose limitations on most exciting activities.

However, one activity I had yearned for was marriage. To be out of the barracks room environment, to wake in the morning to the smell of bacon cooking, hear the sounds of feminine endeavours in the kitchen, and arrive home in the early hours of the morning--as musicians frequently did--to be accepted into loving arms and a warm bed.

At twenty-one I didn't realise my imagination was based on fantasy, nurtured mainly, via a type of novel known as a, Bodice Ripper.

The sex education provided by my parents was a small green book, that today, reminds me of the leaflet and diagram provided with a tin of Draino: Three easy steps and all will be well.

My wife too, lacked any credentials for marriage, except for being female. We never discussed our marital shortcomings, mainly because of the language barrier; my wife was from Königsberg and my German was as bad as her English.

Our first apartment was in Maida Vale, London, the top floor of a three-story row house, overlooking a cricket ground. We even had a phone in the hall, at three pence a call.

For me it was bliss; here I was in the musical centre of London, close to all the jazz clubs, theatres, and concert halls. Plus I could be at RAF Central Band Uxbridge in an hour.

Due to my participation in anything musical that paid, meal times for us had not become routine. Eating was something we did in between what we really wanted to do. Until, one day, Ruth came home with a copy of Life Magazine.

Here an advertisement in glorious colour, was a roasted chicken, surrounded with corn on the cob. Ruth noticing my interest, boasted, 'we used to have that at home every weekend in Königsberg.'

We had a two-burner electric hot plate in the corner of the room and a washbasin with cold water, hardly a dream kitchen; but so far it had sufficed. Had we not let our culinary ambitions run amok, would have continued to do so.

Next Saturday morning saw me in unfamiliar territory--a deli. Here I purchased: A frozen chicken, four frozen corn on the cob, and for dessert, a tinned apple pudding.

Beginning to get the hang of this cooking business, I realised the chicken would not fit in our frying pan, so I spent next Sunday's gig money on an item called, A Self-Basting Cooking Pan. The lid illustrated a spectacular colour picture of a beautifully basted chicken.

Ruth decided, as I was playing on Sunday from 2-4 p.m., to have dinner early. So she was up before me, and as I observed from the bed--where I was pretending to be asleep--started working on the chicken. She turned, frowned at me and asked me if it had been cleaned.

'Just wash it under the tap,' I said. Then, by her gestures, I realised she meant on the inside. Here, I had to admit defeat.

'I'll ask Greta,' Ruth said. Down she went, chicken in hand, to our friends on the floor below.

I made tea and waited. After ten minutes or so, no Ruth, so I headed down to Greta's. Here they all were, sitting on the bed, talking and laughing, the chicken reclining in the middle.

'Well?' I said.

Greta waved the frozen bird at me saying, 'It was frozen so it must have been cleaned; all you do is put stuffing in.' Ruth knew, or pretended to know what that entailed.

'Toasted bread will do,' Greta shouted, as we headed back up the stairs chicken in hand. The chicken was stuffed and placed in the baster, surrounded by the corn cobs, then placed on the burner. The tinned pudding was put in a saucepan of water and placed on the other burner. Early dinner seemed well in hand, as we sat in our third story window watching a cricket match on the pitch below us.

Not knowing how little heat the burners gave, two hours seemed a reasonable time for the chicken to cook. After half-an-hour, the water surrounding the tinned pudding started to boil. This looked promising, but on inspecting the chicken, there was no evidence of the any self-basting occurring.

I had to leave for my gig, and prodded the chicken, just in case a miracle had occurred. Ruth glared at me, 'every time you open the lid you hold up the self-basting.'

I headed out, a drum case in each hand, and an element of doubt in my mind

'How's the chicken?' Greta asked as I slid my drums passed her open door.

'He's a lot better than I am, at least he's stuffed.' I moaned as I continued down the stairs.

The jazz club was as usual, for a Sunday afternoon, thick with smoke and the smell of beer. The hip ambience was complete when we added our vigorous flavour of jazz.

At our break time I said, 'No,' to the offered sandwiches, and explained to the rest of the group. 'My wife is cooking dinner.' They looked at me in awe and envy, because musicians' wives were not noted for cooking dinner.

Three hours later as I dragged my drums back up the stairs, I imagined I smelt basted chicken, but on passing Greta's ever open door, I noticed she had her in-laws in for dinner and a large roast was evident on the table.

Our apartment was tidied, the table laid. Ruth was lying reading on the bed and uttered teutonic grunts of disapproval as I slid my drums under it. The safe storage of my precious drums was an item of contention for Ruth, in moments of nocturnal passion, they would clang and rattle like a drum corps coming down the street. Next morning, if I met Greta on the stairs she would laugh and say. 'Nice drum solo last night.'

I looked hopefully in the direction of the cooking corner, and there was the pudding boiling away and the baster basting.

'How is it?' I asked hopefully.

Ruth shook her head and said, 'I don't think it's done yet.'

'But it's been seven hours now,' a note of irritation in my voice. I lifted the lid and she was right, it certainly wasn't the golden basted delicacy pictured on the lid.

Plus, to insult to my cooking knowledge even further she said, 'Greta says you have to boil that corn.'

'No you fry it, I saw it is a movie.'

I should have sensed Ruth was quite irritated, but I was tired and hungry and persisted in prodding the chicken as I criticised her efforts.

She growled, leapt off the bed, reached round me, grabbed the corn and proceeded to hurl it out the window with a strength and aim that would have done credit to a member of the Wehrmacht. Next the chicken was grabbed and bounced next to the corn on the cricket pitch.

I raced down three flights of stairs and across the grass to see my precious chicken surrounded by white clad cricketer's, one of them prodding it with his bat and looking up for the source of the missile.

'That's my chicken,' I yelled as I pushed the group aside, snatching it off the ground. I raced back upstairs and put it in the sink to wash it off.

Ruth snatched it up again and ran downstairs--me in close pursuit--to Greta's who was enjoying a quiet dinner with her in-laws. The chicken was plonked in the centre their family dinner, Ruth yelling,

'YOU can have the dam chicken!'

Followed by me yelling, 'No YOU can't!' and snatching it up again. (I have never seen four more amazed people in my life) But as I ran upstairs, Ruth reached through the banisters and grabbed it again.

This time she ran into the bathroom, by the time I reached the door she had locked it. What now? I thought. After a few seconds the door opened and a triumphant Ruth glared at me. I could see the window was open, I pushed past her and looked down into the back garden.

There, three floors down, was our landlord's dog enjoying a gift from doggie heaven. This time retrieval was not on my mind, and I returned chickenless and defeated.

Ruth was sitting on the bed crying and I felt like a real jerk. I put my arms around her. And to console her I said, 'We still have the apple pudding.'

I lifted the tin out of the pan where it had been boiling for most of the day, placed it on the dressing table, and sank the point of the tin opener into the top. What followed was like the engine room scene from the sinking of the Titanic.

Hissing steam gushed in all directions, I leapt back pushing Ruth onto the bed, as the molten apple pudding, sprayed the walls and ceiling.

By this time we had an audience. Greta and John were peering round our door.

'Anyone wounded?' John asked.

'Come and have dinner with us.' Greta said sympathetically
'What about this mess,' I whined.

'Leave it, it gives the room character,' easy-going Greta laughed.

Rather shame faced we joined the group downstairs. A glass of wine later, they started to give us a description of the afternoon from their angle The corn and then the chicken zooming past the front window to halt the cricket game. A few moments later the dumping of same onto their table by a furious young lady, lastly retrieved by an equally furious me a second later.

We erupted into laughter that lasted the rest of the evening. As Ruth and me headed upstairs, Greta giggled and pointed to the ceiling.

'Looking forward to the drum solo.'

Allan Francis Scott

The End

London 1952

THE FUNERAL AND THE CORONATION

To be part of a parade through London was always an exciting experience. Laughing pretty girls waving, people cheering. Students chanting, 'Throw it!' as they heckled our drum major to toss his six foot mace as high as physically possible, where it rotated and glinted in the rays of the morning sun . This feat always aroused cheers and applause as it was snatched from the air by our giant drum major, just a fraction of a second, before it contacted the ground.

But, today was a grey February day in 1952. A day that was the antithesis of the aforementioned. The Funeral procession of King George VI.

We had formed up early in the quiet London street, one of many military bands to provide a sombre musical contribution for this sad occasion. We were not alone, over 300,000 people lined the route that cold morning, to pay their last respects to a King that had endeared himself though the years, to us all.

The parade Marshall waved us into position and we quick- marched from the side street onto the parade route. We commenced our first slow march, drums muffled in black crepe, a cymbal struck with a soft mallet producing a sombre gong like tone every second bar. The tune, one of many historical funereally slow marches we would perform that day.

The sounds of the music and the rasp of leather soled boots on the sanded streets echoed off the tall buildings around us. The route lined with troops, rifles inverted and heads down stretched into the distance.

The strangest experience was to witness 300,000 people standing silently, as far as I could see. No shouts, no cheers. The pretty girls, tears in their eyes, watched sadly as we slowly marched passed.

I was a spirited twenty-two year old, usually ready with a joke or a witticism, but today as I glanced at my fellow musicians, no smiles, no mirth, or bandsman's banter, just a mood of mournful resignation.

It was not until June 1953 that we experienced an occasion of the same magnitude, the Coronation of Queen Elizabeth II.

A surprise, we were not marching in the parade, but would be the static band, placed just inside of the gates of Buckingham Palace. Why we as the RAF Central Band had this privilege I'm not sure, but myself, I'd rather be playing through the streets than standing many hours in one location. But ours was not to wonder why etc.

We assembled at 8 a.m. as instructed and were shown our exact position in the palace forecourt by a guards officer. Here we stood at ease watching the ever growing throngs, some had obviously been waiting all night, others just arriving with umbrellas at the ready. The more adventurous clambered up and onto the already crowded Queen Victoria Monument directly opposite the palace.

One young man climbed to the top of a large gatepost in front of the palace, here he evaded a persistent policeman by hiding behind the statue on top of the gatepost.

This whole 'Keystone Cops' episode was watched and encouraged by the happy throng on the street below, as the policeman having struggled to the top of the gatepost chased the alpiner round the top of the gatepost Their laughter and shouts of encouragement turned to boos as the policeman called in a comrade and the unintentional entertainer was removed from the top of the gatepost and led away.

Sounds of cheering echoed down Pall Mall and our director called us to the ready, but the cheering turned to laughter, as the cause was a young telegraph boy riding his bike leisurely down the Mall, and waving to the cheering crowd.

Our main function was to play the salutes as various members of the Royal Family drove through the gates to attend the Coronation Ceremony at Westminster Abbey. Lastly, the short version of the National Anthem as Princess Elizabeth departed via the gate and on to the Abbey.

By now it was about 10.30 a.m.and starting to rain. It was with relief that we were told to fall out and reform at 2.30 p.m. We stowed our instruments under an archway and headed for the nearest pub. Not for the beer this early in the morning, but a cup of tea and somewhere to watch the ceremony on one of the new television sets.

The second pub we tried had tea, sandwiches and a 14 inch black and white TV. What luxury. We sat absorbed as the ceremony unfolded before us via a small screen placed on top of the bar.

The Dean of Westminster lifted the Crown from the Alter and slowly walked to the Archbishop of Canterbury where the Archbishop took it from him and reverently placed it upon the Queen's head.

GOD SAVE THE QUEEN echoed throughout Westminster Abbey, the homes and streets of Great Britain, the Commonwealth, plus our little pub.

The great guns at the Tower of London roared and the cheers of thousands sent the pigeons soaring high above the city.

'You'll probably never witness anything like that again,' our drum major expounded. 'But we better head back, the Royal Air Force would not be very popular if we missed the Queens first homecoming.'

We edged our way through the crowds, Drummy all 6ft 5ins of him leading the way. As we formed up by the gate facing the crowd. We knew Queen Elizabeth--as she now was--would arrive at 4.30 p.m. One hour and a half from now. We played marches and waltzes, the crowd clapped and even danced. It was raining but no one seemed to notice.

Then from the distance, the sound that always thrilled me and made the hair stand up on the back of my neck. Hundreds of thousands of people cheering, with one voice, one message. The roar surged down the Mall towards us and at last the Gold State Coach drawn by eight beautiful grey horses came into view.

Attention! our drum major shouted, and as the first pair of horses entered the Palace gates the Director swept his baton down and we commenced the full rendition of the National Anthem--for the new Queen.

She glanced in our direction, smiling, young, with an aristocratic beauty that stirred even the most tarnished of Royalty viewers amongst our flinty bandsmen.

The thousands of people had moved down Pall Mall and filled every available space and were pressing against the railings of the Palace. 'We want the Queen,' the thousands of voices chanted.

After a short delay the doors and curtains on the Palace Balcony parted and the members of the Royal Family appeared. Lastly the Queen.

'Long live the Queen,' the thousands roared as she waved and smiled.

The gates were still open in front of us and this is where the thousands headed. I was looking for an escape route when a solitary policeman moved forward stood between the open gates and raised his arms. The multitude hesitated and stopped, and moved back to the railings.

'Long Live the Queen,' they chanted.

I was thinking, 'Long Live the Policeman.'

Allan F Scott

The End

London 1953

THE UNPREDICTABLE

The Lord Mayor's Show is admired for the beautiful gilded coach built in 1757 in which he rides, this pulled by six horses, the precision of the bands, and the surrounding pomp and pageantry.

As a member of the Royal Air Force Central Band, our day began at 6 a.m. in the quiet, early morning streets of Whitechappel.

Here the bus left us and we marched towards the city, other bands and troops would integrate from the side streets. The watchful eyes of the parade marshals, whose job it was to insure the sequence matched the printed programs that were being handed out two miles ahead of us, kept looking at their watches and clip boards.

We alternated playing with the bands in front and behind as soon as we reached the official parade route. The people cheered and the sun shone.

London was very good at this type of ceremony, they had been doing it for about six hundred years, so it was not likely that anything unpredictable would occur.

We had an hours break at Mansion House where the parade halted, for the Ceremony of the New Mayor of London. This took place inside the Guildhall.

We all dashed to the various cafes in the area for a quick snack, then formed up again to await the appearance of the Mayor. I noticed the coach and horses still parked against the curb, the postillions leaning against the wall enjoying a last smoke.

The parade Marshall gave the signal and we commenced the drum rolls for the next march. The boisterous sound of the trombones and cornets reverberated off the tall buildings around us, but the clarinets had suddenly stopped.

I glanced behind me. It was an unbelievable sight; the woodwinds were scattering in all directions as the riderless horses and coach bore down on them. As it careened through the rear of the band some musicians had time to leap out the way; some didn't. The horses ran down the slower movers, then onto the pavement and into the spectators. The two leading horses fell as they hit the side of a building, the other four tried to run but were trapped in their harnesses and by the coach behind them.

Confusion was rife, our director seemed frozen in a state of shock, the band stopped and the troops ran to help, adding to the confusion.

Our bass drummer was the first to recover, he shouted, 'We can't stop, the parade is behind us,' He gave the signal for the drum rolls and we started playing and marching again, clearing the road behind us.

He was given a special commendation for his quick thinking.

We had only three members that had to receive treatment, several spectators suffered minor wounds and the baby in the pram I had seen on it's side was fine. The horses too, finished the parade with no injuries.

I read this all with relief in the evening paper.

It had been so unpredictable.

Summer is the time for outdoor concerts in London. We would alternate with the Guards Bands around various locations in the city.

I looked in my diary for the week, and it read: Tuesday 12-1:30 Trafalgar Square.

I lived downtown and would use my car to take some of the percussion equipment, the large items would arrive on the truck with the bus and the rest of the band.

I parked my car as usual in the reserved area for Trafalgar Square, and the policeman put several red cones out to reserve parking for our bus. Then he went to turn the fountains off, as the wind often blew the spray onto the tourists, not to mention us.

The city attendant appeared from the storage area and proceeded to cordon off the band area with yellow ropes. He asked how many chairs we required and frowned when I said 'thirty-five.'

'The guards only need twenty-five,' he grumbled.

'Ah, but we are bigger and better,' was my flippant reply. Still frowning he carried the chairs out and I attempted to place them in some sort of stage order.

I looked at my watch and it was just after eleven. I had plenty of time and as the fountains slowed to a trickle, I leisurely removed my drums from the car, and set up between the two lions.

The usual brown bag crowd and tourists began to gather, several people asking what time we started. 'Twelve o'clock,' I replied and later heard this information being passed on to the new-comers as they settled themselves to enjoy the forth-coming concert.

I sat in the shade of one of the lions, feeling rather important in my ceremonial blues, and waited for the arrival of my cohorts. It was eleven-thirty. Any minute they would be here, and myself and the timpanist could set up the rest of our instruments.

Eleven-forty-five...I started to feel anxious: Maybe a breakdown or heavy traffic.

Eleven-fifty-five, and I told the policeman I had to leave to use the phone. He nodded and pointed out the nearest red booth.

When the corporal in our orderly room back at Uxbridge replied, he said: 'The band have just phoned about you.'

'I have been here since eleven-thirty.'

'Where is here?' he continued.

'Trafalgar Square of course,' I said indignantly. '

'Oh, that's why, you should be at St.Paul's Cathedral; Trafalgar Square is next Tuesday.'

'OH!' was the only humble retort I could manage.

If I had been a flute player, I could have surreptitiously slunk away, but having four drum cases to pack up and fit in my car was not going to go unnoticed.

I edged my way through the expectant crowd and was greeted by a smattering of applause as I approached my drums. I dismantled them as I explalined to the bewildered bystanders what was happening.

Two slightly tipsy Australians said, 'Tough luck mate, we'll give you a hand. Where you off then?'

'St.Paul's steps,' was my hasty reply.

'Great, give us a lift and we'll help you set up.'

As I pulled away I saw the attendant re-stacking the chairs and glaring in my direction, the policeman too, hands on hips followed my hasty retreat. They were not amused.

On reaching St.Paul's, I parked at the bottom of the steps, realising there was no way I could join the band unnoticed. Plus they were playing the third number on the program.

'Sounds fine without you,' one of my assistants remarked. We grabbed the cases and headed up the steps. My newly acquired Australian chums thought this lots of fun, and one remarked to our dignified director of music.'Found your drummer laying around in Trafalgar Square.'

I busied myself setting up the drums again, and gave my car keys to one of the Australians, asking him to park it, which he did two wheels on the curb at the end of the steps. He tossed the car keys to me and shouted, 'Bye Mate.'

The band finished item four, and the director nodded and said it was nice of me to pay a casual visit.

At the end of the performance, I was told to report to the office at nine tomorrow morning. Lastly I removed the parking ticket from my windscreen. As I was about to drive off I was advised by the band sergeant to keep a low profile, but keeping a low profile was not one of my attributes.

A few weeks later we were playing in Hyde Park, and being the xylophone soloist, I arrived early to practice my solo.

I had finished my warmup, was enjoying the sun, and watching the kids playing with their sailboats on the Serpentine. Suddenly, one of the little ones fell in backwards. Being close I jumped in to help, the water was only about two feet deep, but the child didn't know that and was really panicking. As I tried to lift him to the pathway my feet slipped on the muddy bottom, and I sat down which completed the soaking of my dress uniform. The mother rushed over scolding the child and thanking me profusely.

Being a percussionist I was at the rear of the band, and during the early half of our concert I would leave a little puddle as I moved from instrument to instrument. But I was beginning to dry out.

My xylophone solo was played from the front of the band, and I could feel the eyes of the director on me as I played my solo, and I avoided eye contact even during my encore.

I thought maybe he hadn't noticed, but during the intermission he beckoned me over, 'Good solos, but what happened to your uniform?' I told him the saga, but felt, he didn't believe a word of it.

Next morning I was told to report to the office. Here goes I thought, 'Back to Catterick.'

When I stopped in front of his desk and saluted he actually smiled, 'Very nice letter from that boy's mother, said he may of drowned if you hadn't been so quick. Pity we didn't have an Air Ministry photographer there,' he concluded.

'We could re-enact it this afternoon, Sir.'

'Steady Scott,' he admonished. This being his favorite reproach when he felt one of us youngsters was over stepping the mark. 'The band fund will pay to have your uniform cleaned.'

We had the funeral of King George and then the Coronation. Both very long parades, and were constantly warned about the Air Ministry photographers.

'Always check your dressing, you never know when they will photograph you.'

The photographs we did see, showed our dressing to be perfect and our director actually congratulated us.

Then came the Jewish Remembrance Day Parade which was always a week later than the November 11th parade.

A military snare drum, has hanging underneath it, two ropes that nearly touch the gound, called drag ropes. They are part of the ceremonial look of the instrument and had been used to carry the drum like a back pack on long marches.

We were marching down Pall Mall, six abreast, myself on the left flank facing the one traffic lane that had been left open. The cars slowly filtered by on my left side. Suddenly ... I felt myself swung round and looked to see my drag ropes caught on the rear bumper of a taxi. All I could do was chase after it and try to disentangle the ropes, and not drop my drum sticks as I ran behind it. Luckily, the traffic was not moving much faster than a walking pace, and I managed to unhook them and re-join the band.

As the director was at the front of the band I felt this potential tradgedy had gone unnoticed. Except for the members at the rear of the band, who thoroughly enjoyed it.

However, in the Daily Mirror next morning was a picture entitled, 'How to catch a taxi, Air Force style.'

In the office, the director prodded his finger at the picture, shook his head and said, 'You really are unpredictable Scott.'

Allan F Scott

The End

London 1953

CONVERSATIONS WITH WINSTON

Only three words in the title and already I'm exaggerating. So I'll confess that my side of the conversations consisted of saying: 'Yes, Sir.' However I did say it twice. The first time I was fearful and hestitant. The second time I was still fearful but not quite so hesitant, but then I was three years older.

I could have made history if I had just had a little coaching from Sir L or a crash course at RADA and waxed eloquently into an arictocratic repartee that would have left Sir Winston and his entourage gasping at my command of the English language. But I was ill prepared for either encounter. My creative juices squeezed from the fruits of my Liverpudlian education could only create: 'Yes, Sir.'

My first encounter was at Blenheim Palace. It was a Hunt Ball in the early fifties and I was with the RAF Dance Band. This was my first visit to this magnificant establishment and was impressed as our small buss drove through the gates and to the side of the building. I was the junior in rank, age and experience in the band. They were all Senior Technitions but I merely a Junior Technition. We unloaded our instruments, music,and with the aid of the driver, my drums. Cases in hand and hats under our arms we made our way through the deserted hallways to the ballroom and onto the low stage.

The hallway was lined either side with glum and resentful lookings busts of the previous residents dating back many years. Our sense of humour rose to the fore and each member of the band placed his hat on one of these unhappy looking creations. 'There that looks better,' our leader laughed as we continued into the ballrooom and started setting up the music stands and microphones.

Being the drummer I was still setting up after the rest had departed to the room set aside for our breaks and refreshments. We had been booked to 4 a.m. It would be a long interesting night.

I checked all the wing nuts, tom-tom positions and seat height until everything was tikerty-boo as Sergeant Fitzhenry used to say. 'You keep one eye on me, one eye on your music and the other for the ladies,' was one of his favourite quotes.

I nodded and smiled to myself, 'looks good,' I murmured, and headed in the direction of our refreshment room. I better remove my hat from the hallway was another thought and I turned in that direction where I noticed my hat sitting at a jaunty angle on the nearest bust. It was the only hat remaining.

I had taken a few steps in that direction when I heard voices and saw a small group of elegantly uniformed and tuxedoed guests approaching. The one gesturing with a cigar and expounding about a painting they stopped to admire, was unmistakeable, Sir Winston Churchill.

My self satisfied mood rapidly evaporated as I briskly climbed back onto the stage and became engrossed with my drum equipment. The recognisable voice rumbled closer then stopped. I heard a few tuts of displeasure and the group arrived in front of the stage.

Sir Winston still had his cigar in one hand but in the other was my hat! I turned to face them and stood to attention. His magnetic gaze took in the stage then settled on me.

Holding my hat between two fingers and then dropping it on the front of the stage like a doctor disposing of his rubber golves. He growled, 'Air Force--I think.' He turned away and each member of his party frowned in my direction as they departed.

My second encounter with Sir Winston was about three years later at the historic RAF Station of Bentley Priory. We were to play for a ceremonial parade and march past.

However: due to heavy rain it was held indoors, and having inspected the honour guard Sir Winston in uniform and walking with the aid of a cane slowly headed in our direction. My attention was drawn to his footwear, he was wearing brown suede shoes. I must have done a 'double take,' because the only other person I had ever seen sporting this type of footwear in uniform was Sir John Slessor, but, he was Marshall of the Royal Air Force.

Sir Winston may have noticed my fleeting glance, because followed by the inspecting party he stopped in front of me, looked at me and through me with those very blue penetrating eyes. He slowly looked down at my only medal, the Coronation Medal.

'You all got very wet that day I believe.'
'Yes, Sir.'

Our band-sergeant, weighed down with at least ten medals dating back to the days of the Royal Flying Corps was a little put-out. 'How come Sir Winston only spoke to you Scott?'
'Well ...We've met before,' I smugly replied.

Allan F Scott

The End

Malta 1954

MURPHY STRIKES AGAIN

We all know the adage, 'If something can go wrong it will.' But what could possibly go wrong with a parade through city streets, cheered by the residents on a sunny afternoon in 1954

The place was Valletta in Malta. The parade, in honour of the Queen and Prince Philip's visit. The RAF band was about sixty strong and would march trombones to the fore six-abreast. Behind us were several hundred troops, arms at the slope and bayonets fixed also marching six-abreast to give the parade a neat, orderly and powerful appearance.

We marched past the saluting base where the Queen, Prince Philip and the VIP's proudly saluted our efforts. We played, the crowds cheered, the sun shone and all was well on this beautiful Mediterranean afternoon.

Our drum major had warned us about circumnavigating the various statues placed in the middle of the wide boulevards, each created a large traffic circle. At his signal--a rotation of his mace--the band would divide. Three ranks would go to the left; three to the right. The bass drummer would go to the right and myself (the snare drummer) to the left. I was to listen for the bass drum and follow his beat until we all met up again on the other side of the statue and traffic circle. The troops were told to follow the same format taking their pace, if going to the left from myself, if to the right the bass drum.

We marched around three large monuments with no problem, the metronomic beat of the bass drum holding us in-step like a well-drilled chorus line. As our drum major said, 'the merging of the divided band and troops was a thing of great beauty.'

Ahead I saw the largest monument so far, with a mounted statue on top. The drum major signalled and we smoothly divided, cut to pianissimo, and listened to the fading sound of the bass drum. We kept marching.... and I began to feel that this narrow avenue had no intention of rejoining it's previously wide boulevard.

I tried to keep a tempo going, but between the distant spasmodic beats of the bass drum echoing off the surrounding buildings, and the wave of our director's baton, (who was hoping to save the day) plus, the whistling of the troops behind us, who thought their rendition of Colonel Bogie far more musical and rhythmic than anything we could muster at present, won over, and we all ground to a halt.

By now we were being observed by curious locals and small boys on bicycles who had been pedalling along with us. All wondering I'm sure, what half a band and masses of troops were doing all clustered in their alleyway. Our Director, now on the verge of a nervous breakdown, put his next pleading question to them. "Can any of you boys lead us to where the rest of our band might be?"

One happy little boy pointed, jumped on his bike and waved for us to follow. "Follow that bike," our band director shouted. We broke ranks and trotted after our new leader.

Whose intentions were good.... I think, but trying to get thirty musicians complete with bulky instruments and several hundred troops all with rifles and fixed bayonets to follow an energetic little boy on a bicycle through a maze of back alleys and yards--some complete with hanging laundry--was not a task I'd wish on any invasion force.

However, eventually led by our miniature guide, we burst panting and gasping from a dark and narrow alleyway. There was the rest of our band, followed by their contingent of troops looking cool, in step and organised. We scrambled into position, fell in step and resumed our display of military might and music for the British Empire.

Of course someone had to take the blame, it was put down to Illogical City Planning and a lack of concentration on the part of the snare drummer (guess who?).

Allan F Scott

The End

London 1954

FANFARE 1954

I was feeling very lucky. Our director of music had decided to add timpani to the fanfare trumpets of the RAF Central Band. The reason he gave was that not all guests warrant a fanfare, and during the announcement of their name, and title if any, a timpani roll would have to suffice. I think he had been watching the Ed Sullivan Show too much.

However, I kept my thoughts to myself as this meant extra pay, plus we performed at: Film premiers, Gala balls, Major sporting events, the Miss World Beauty Pageant, The International Motor Show, elegant dinners at The Savoy Hotel and the most memorable-- The Crufts Annual Dog Show at Olympia. The latter event involved 15,000 dogs who yowled and howled at the first sound of our fanfare trumpets. Their canine vocals drowned out not only our musical efforts, but, whom the fanfare was announcing. It led one Royal personage to remark, that the last time he heard anything like this, was on his last visit to parliament.

When a Royal is involved in a ceremony, nothing is left to chance, the Royal Rolls arriving the exact minute stipulated on our itinerary, even if it means other guests' cars being shunted into side streets to make way for Royalty.

The exit from any royal car is choreographed into several smooth and efficient movements on the part of the participants.

Well...usually it is, but tonight was a little different and my position facing the arrival point, gave me the full view of the forthcoming comedy, involving Princess Margaret and her new equerry.

It should have gone as follows: the Rolls Royce stops with the exit door for the Princess adjacent to the red carpet and the car door handle in front of the awaiting air force policeman. He reaches down for the door handle, opens the door with his left hand, takes one step back, then salutes with his right hand. As soon as the Princess has left the car, he takes a step forward and slams the door. This is all done without him bending or looking down at any time.

The Royal Equerry, who accompanies Princess Margaret, leaves the car at the same time, but from the door on the opposite side, he steps round the back of the car and follows her to the red carpet, where he stands five paces behind her, then, we play the Royal Salute, and he follows her into the theatre.

However, this being a new equerry, he must have neglected to read his instructions or was confused by them, because he tried to follow Princess Margaret out of the same car door.

The policeman who opened the door for Princes Margaret didn't see this, saluted and slammed the door on his plumed and helmeted head, knocking him back onto the rear seat. He recovered, and started to climbed out the door on the other side. The driver, having heard the door slam, began to drive off as usual, assuming that all had gone according to plan.

The equerry, by this time had one leg in the car and one on the road, and was trying to hold onto his sword and large plumed helmet whilst hopping down the street, which he did very well for a second or two, but then collapsed in the road.

The princess now on the red carpet stood waiting for the Royal Salute. By this time her Rolls-Royce had driven off, she glanced in our direction to see what was holding up the Fanfare, what she saw--was her escort for the evening on his hands and knees in the middle of the road.

I must give her credit for not showing any emotion, other than slightly raised eyebrows, whilst the eight of us were ready to explode. It's not easy to stand at attention, laugh and blow a trumpet at the same time. I just had to bang a little harder on my timpani.

It was May 16, 1955, and the reason for the Royal presence at the Odeon Theatre in Leicester Square, and us of course, was the Royal premier of The Dam Busters. A film about the RAF bombing raid of May 16th 1943 on the Moehne, Eder, and Sorpe dams in the Ruhr Valley, Germany. These dams held back millions of tons of water, needed to turn the wheels of German industry.

Nineteen aircraft had taken part in this raid, but eight were lost. They had done intensive training until they could drop their bombs over water from 60ft. Very difficult for a fully loaded Lancaster weighing 63,000 pounds.

We had moved into the orchestral pit as part of the Royal Air Force concert band, and were playing the now popular Dam Busters March as the surviving fifty or so crew members filed into their front row seats.

As the movie progressed, I notices several members of the RAF contingent leaving their seats, bent over, heads lowered and heading to the side door.

At the end of the movie, the lights went up, the audience stood and applauded, but only three members in Air Force Blue remained to acknowledge it.

We packed up our instruments and headed out for a beer before the pubs closed. Outside the pub you could hear the singing and merriment.

Inside, yes... the remainder of the famous Dam Busters Squadron. If you ignored the bright lights and the non-blacked out windows, it could have been 1944 again.

Allan F Scott

The End.

PS. The The Dam Busters March was used in many maternity wards to encourage any prospective mothers to get a move on. That's true, a nurse told me.

Switzerland 1954

VIP'S GIG.

As our eight piece RAF Dance Band arrived at Northolt I noticed a very smart DC-3 parked in front of the terminal.

'That's for us,' Fitz nodded at me. This was a hint to start unloading. I was glad to see an old friend behind the check in counter. I noticed he was now a corporal.

'Hey Wally, you're rapidly rising through the ranks,' I joked.

Wally pointed at his clipboard. 'You're in good company this trip. Have a word with Lord Tedder, he is Chief of the Air Staff. You too, could be an almighty corporal.'

'You're joking,' I laughed. He nodded his head and pointed at the list:

Lord Tedder.
Lord Brabazon of Tara.
Marquis of Milford Haven.
Squadron Leader Neville Duke.
Major Michael Lithgow.
Cicely Courtneidge and company. (3)
RAF Band Members. (8)

'All that history on one DC-3.' Wally observed.

I pulled the laden trolley across the tarmac to the open door of the DC-3. Then passed the cases up to Fitz, who was directed by a very smartly uniformed and attractive stewardess.

Back at the reception area, the rest of the passengers had arrived. I was wondering who was who on the distinguished passenger list, when Wally's voice interrupted my thoughts. 'All aboard for Zurich.' He winked at me, 'it's nice to order the aristocracy around. Have a good trip.'

We filed up the steps and the stewardess pointed to a seat next to a tall pleasant looking man, who I recognised as Neville Duke.

'You can have the window,' he said.

'Thank you, sir.'

'I can't hear on that side,' he added. I thought it sad that one of the worlds top test pilot and a fighter ace with 27 of the enemy to his credit, had trouble hearing. We soon fell into conversation and I congratulated him on his much publicised speed record of 728 MPH in a Hawker Hunter. I asked him about the other passengers.

He pointed at an elderly gentleman a few seats ahead of us.

'That's Lord Brabazon, he was the first person in Britain to be licensed as an Airplane Pilot and also the first to fly a live cargo flight.' He paused, and added, 'it was a small pig in a waste-paper basket--tied to a wing strut.'

'Don't tell anyone,' I laughed, 'or I know how they'll fly us next time we have to play for a mess dinner in Cranwell.'

'What's the joke, Neville,' Major Lithgow asked leaning across the aisle.

'This is Allan, he's the drummer with the band, and we've found a way to help transport command. Is that Cicely Courtneidge?' he asked. I nodded.

She turned, and noticed us looking in her direction. Stood up, and worked her way towards me. 'Are you with the band?' she smiled down at me.

'Yes, Ma'am, but Fitz is the leader, ' I pointed to him.

'I just need to talk about a rehearsal.' She nodded at the two officers and edged her way along the aisle to Fitz..

It was early afternoon when we arrived at Zurich. 'An hour to wait,' Fitz observed. 'Then, it's by train to Davos,' and he produced a handful of strange looking money. 'Been robbing the Monopoly game, 'Chirpy, our bass player laughed.

'Follow me,' and money firmly in hand Fitz led us up the stairs to a very glitzy restaurant. We sat side by side at the counter and looked at Fitz. The waitress approached. 'Tea for all,' Fitz ordered.

'English?' she asked.

'All except him,' Fitz pointed at Ron. 'He's Welsh.'

Ron shook his head at Fitz, 'don't tell her that, she'll expect me to burst into song.'

'Or give her a lump of coal,' Chirpy added.

Our server returned a few minutes later with a tray full of tea pots, cups, saucers, a large jug of boiling water, and a small bowl containing little paper bags, each one with a string protruding. We looked in the tea pots, then the cups, but no sign of tea. We looked at Fitz; he looked at the waitress.

'Tea,' she smiled, pointing at the little bags.

'Ahaa!' we voiced in unison. Ron tore one open, and the contents sprinkled the counter.

'Try this,' Fitz said, and took his nail clippers from his pocket. A few snips and he carefully emptied the contents of the small bag into the tea pot. By now, the water was only hot and the tea leaves floated to the surface. We were looking in vain for a sieve, and being observed by a smartly dressed man seated at the end of the counter.

'Tea,' he called to the waitress. In came the hot water, the cup, the teapot, and two little bags on a saucer. He smiled at us, and taking a bag by the string lowered it gently into the pot, added hot water and jiggled it up and down. We followed this procedure with bovinical interest, then burst into laughter. He smiled, and sipped his tea.

We argued the merits of our new experience as we piled onto the bus. 'My mum wouldn't like those,' Ron complained. 'She likes to read the tea leaves.'

Fitz added, 'we toss them on the roses.'

'I used to dry them, and smoke them in my uncle's pipe' I contributed.

'Just like a drummer,' Chirpy concluded. 'No wonder you can only go bang-bang.' Our arrival at the station saved me from being the butt of more, 'drummy-type' jokes.

The train journey was magic. I now understood what was meant by a 'Winter Wonderland.' The hotel was pristine and efficient, the rooms ready, our cases by the room doors.

We headed to the ballroom . Here, we were met by a robust and immaculately dressed man who informed us. 'I am the MC. As soon as you're ready we'll have a short rehearsal with Miss Courtneidge.' Fitz nodded and passed out the show music.

The dance over, I decided to have a bath and had noticed a bathroom at the end of the corridor. A small notice in our room told us the bathroom doors could be opened with our room key. I wrapped a towel round myself and walked to the bathroom. There was a small notice on the door that I didn't bother to read. I tried the handle, which seemed a little stiff. However, by putting my toothbrush in the finger grip of the key, I levered it open. It was cool white marble, with a very large tub. It was luxurious after the 'knees up' type we had back at Uxbridge. After soaking and scrubbing, I dried off and putting my key in the door tried to turn it. This time it resisted all my efforts, I tried again, my tooth brush broke.

I leaned out the window, ten stories up and no fire escape. So?

'You'll just have to sleep in the bath,' I said to myself. I settled in the bath using my towel as a pillow.

When I awoke, it was daylight. I heard a sound at the door and then a key jiggled in the lock. A young maid edged in, took one look at me in the bath, screamed and ran out. By now I was cold, hungry and disenchanted with my marble bath room. The door opened again and this time a man peered in. I think, he said, 'what are you doing here?' I climbed out the bath, picked up my key and indicated that it didn't work. He looked at the key number and pointed to the numbers on the door. Then pointed to a similar door on the other side of the corridor. 'The wrong door,' I whispered sheepishly. He nodded.

Gathering my towel, broken toothbrush, and what dignity I had left I slunk back to my room. To be greeted with, 'You must have had a good time last night, who was she?'

I escaped for an early breakfast.

From here it was an even more spectacular train trip to St.Moritz. The Palace Hotel was reputed to be one of the best in Europe, and tonight we would alternate with a Latin band.

We played the floor show, Cicerly Courtneidge and her team wowed them with comedy, songs and dance. When the Latin band struck up in the next ballroom, it was my turn to listen. I was fascinated at the percussion section. Then noticed a beautiful lady across the room as interested as myself. I made the international motion for, 'would you like to dance?' She nodded, I walked over and we moved onto the dance floor. I could see she was trying to figure out my uniform which had no rank or country of origin shown, just a pair of golden eagles on the high collar. She looked up at me, 'do you speak English?' she asked, in an educated English voice.

'No.... I'm from Liverpool,' I replied. She laughed so hard we had to leave the floor. I admitted, I was a mere Junior Technician, 'but I'm very talented,' I added.

'Indeed,' she grinned, and pulled me a little closer.

Allan F Scott

The End

London 1954

GIG AT TAGGS ISLAND

As it is today. As it was in 1953.

Taggs Island

One of my favourite people in the London music scene was Big Joe, he was always pleasant and smiling, played his sax and violin with skill and feeling plus was a major source of well paid gigs for me.

I had played for him several times in what he called his, 'Society Band'. We got on together musically and socially, very important, when some of the gigs, hunt balls, coming out parties etc. lasted six to eight hours. Most of them were on large estates, or the Café Royal in the West end.

London in 1953 was getting more crowded, but I always seemed to find a corner to squeeze my old Morris into. I would make several trips with my drums and be set up by the time Joe arrived. He always complimented me on my early arrival. 'So nice to see the drummer set up; now I can relax. Nothing more worrying than five minutes to go and no drummer.'

I noticed he was greeted by name by many of the aristocratic guests.

'Hi Joe, don't forget The Charleston.'

'Joe, Lili Marlene, for old time sake.'

'Big Joe, Gay Gordons at midnight.'

He kept a clutch of small file cards in his pocket and when certain couples arrived he would consult the card, turn to Ron (the pianist) raise his hand, fingers extended to indicate the required key, then play their favourite tune. Joe also had the ability to smile, then bow whilst playing his saxophone.

After my fourth gig, he asked me to see him before I left. I loaded my gear into the car and panted back up the stairs to the ballroom where Big Joe was sitting enjoying a coffee with the Maitre d'. Joe beckoned me over and waved me to a chair as the Maitre d' left, poured me a coffee then consulted his well worn diary.

'Five more gigs here in December for you.' He jotted the dates on a slip of paper. 'No substitutes though, when I book you, I expect you to turn up, not some young bebopper who can't play waltzes or polkas, and wears running shoes with his tux.'

'Of course Joe,' I replied.

'Good, and thanks for playing for the bagpiper during our break, he really appreciated it and I appreciate it. Now, here's a little extra for you, as you missed your meal,' and he slipped a ten shilling note into my hand.

'Thanks,' I murmured gratefully.

Joe leaned towards me, 'I have one of the highest paid New Year's Eve gigs in London for you, but,' and he looked around, 'you must promise you'll not discuss it with anyone. It is VIPs Only by invitation, even they don't know the location until the day before. So mums the word.' I nodded, intrigued.

'I'll tell you a few days before. However: you must be at the location by 6 p.m. and expect to play from 7 p.m. to 4 a.m. It's about an hours drive from town, and you'll have to stay the night.'

'Is it a hotel?' I whispered.

'You'll find out, all in good time. One more thing, we'll need two drummers because there is a floor show and a bagpiper for highland dancing. We play non stop, no breaks at all. You pick who you want as the other drummer, but make sure he's mature and steady. I'll give you an extra fee and you'll pay him. If he also plays piano a little, that would help, and he could give Ron a few breaks.'

'How much do I pay him?'

Big Joe grinned at me. 'You'll like this, I pay you a hundred and fifty, from that, give your man about forty-five. Plus Ron will give him the same and I know he'll be happy.'

I was happy too. That was more than four times the usual rate. 'Great,' I replied.

As I drove home, I was thinking who I knew that played drums and piano and would not be working New Year's Eve. Passing through Uxbridge I saw the sign, The Railway Arms.

Les Smart, had just a couple of days ago been complaining to me about not working at the Railway Arms over the New Year, because they were hiring a folk trio. Les played drums a little roughly I thought, but he played pub style piano and was also the bouncer. This is why I never told him I thought his drumming a little rough.

'Les is the man,' I said out loud. Problem solved. I didn't know him too well, but he had been an army boxing champion and top a notch swimmer. We met when I took swimming lessons and he helped me overcome my fear of water by showing me how to jump off the top board, sink, relax and float to the surface.

'Used to do it with a fifty-pound pack in the army,' he'd grin at me. Les had been a sergeant in the commandos for three years, he never boasted, he didn't have to, he just told the truth.

I knew he'd be playing for the brunch crowd on Sunday and that's were I headed for a late breakfast. His vigorous piano style rang through the open windows of the pub as I switched off the Morris and headed up the steps. He waved, thumping hard on the octaves with his left hand as I headed for a corner table.

I was enjoying my coffee, when Les's energetic playing ground to a halt and he rumbled over. I say rumble, because he'd start the conversation from across the room and continue until he plonked himself down next to me, beer mug in hand.

The patrons were mainly the church crowd, old, quiet, respectable, suits, white shirts, flowered dresses, big hats and sensible shoes.

'How many have you had to toss out this morning?' I laughed.

'Just that little old lady in the blue dress over there. Every week she wants The Robins Return. Drives me nuts, because she starts singing it no matter what I'm trying to play. I told her I'd lock her in the washroom if she didn't shut up. She nudged me in the back and said, Just make sure it's the men's.'

He gulped his beer, 'but good news, they want me to play over Christmas and New Year, just to 8 p.m. then the folksy group comes on.

My spirits sank when I heard this, but finishing at 8 p.m. I realised he could still make my gig later. 'How about this Les?' and I told him the situation.

'Quite the secret then,' Les whispered.

I nodded.'Yes, but here's how we can do it. I start playing at 7 p.m., then I do the floor show from 8 to 9 p.m. Straight dancing until later when the bagpiper comes on for an hour. Then more dancing until breakfast time. So--no rush for you Les, just come anytime after 9 p.m.' You can play drums for a time and piano when Ron wants a break. I'll pay you forty-five pounds and Ron will pay the same. So ninety pounds should make you happy.

'Sounds great,' he laughed. 'I just hope it is only an hour from town.'

'Big Joe will let me know a few days before,' I confided.

This arrangement in itself seemed very satisfactory, except for one detail. My current girlfriend, Sylvia, was expecting a New Year's Eve dinner in the West End and in a moment of male vulnerability and generosity, I had promised just that. Now I rationalised that with my large gig fee I could just change that to New Year's Day lunch in the West End.

However, when I broached the subject, hostility quivered via her body language like porcupines quills.

'You promised and I've already bought a beautiful green dress and matching shoes.' The hostility I could manage, but the tears and reproaches just shattered the wall of indifference I was trying to construct. 'I'll pay for the dress and shoes,' I said in a further explosion of generosity.

'Really,' Sylvia smiled up at me brushing her thick copper coloured hair from her tear stained face. I nodded, 'and what's more, we'll have a New Year's Eve dinner at a beautiful hotel, stay the night, and I'll just have to pop off for a few hours.' The encounter ended with smiles and promises, that I felt might require just a little juggling to fulfil.

Next time I met Big Joe, I wheedled out of him that the gig was in the Hampton Court area. Again I was warned not to divulge this top secret information. What, I wanted was, to ensure a nice room and dinner for two in a pleasant hotel in that area.

Next morning I drove around the Hampton Court district until I noticed The Sleeping Giant Hotel displaying a large sign outside offering, Dine and Dance on New Year's Eve. 'I'll just check the prices,' I thought. Noting, that when no price is mentioned it's usually rather expensive.

The desk clerk glanced out the window at my ancient 1936 Morris as he checked the reservation list. 'It is rather expensive,' he mumbled.

'No problem and I'll need a double room for the night,' I replied, trying to impart an impression of eccentric affluence. The clerk consulted another list. 'The dinner is twenty-two pounds which includes a bottle of champagne. A room overlooking the river is thirty pounds. There will be dancing to 2 a.m. in the lounge, which is just off the dining room. So it should be a wonderful evening for our guests.'

I tried to appear nonchalant as I slowly removed my cheque book from my inside pocket. 'You require a deposit I imagine?'

'Yes, sir, or you could post-date your cheque to December 15th then all would be taken care of.' Little did he know, what it took care of, was most of my bank balance.'

'Well, it should be a wonderful evening,' I rationalised to myself as I headed back into London. 'Sylvia and I could have dinner at five, I leave the hotel at six for - where-ever - to set up. I play for the floor show and some dancing until Les arrives about 10.30. Then I'll head back to Sylvia for drinks, dancing and a New Years Eve we'll never forget. Big Joe will have a drummer, Sylvia will be happy, Les will be happy. It just takes a little organising I concluded.' And I gave myself a self-congratulatory nod in the rear-view mirror.

A week before New Year's Eve, Big Joe phoned. 'Here's the address, write it down and pass it on to Les, but, it's still a secret.' I waited pen poised. 'It's on Taggs Island near Hampton court. Just follow the river road until you see a sign with lots of balloons on it, then turn left over the bridge onto the island. It'll all be lit up so you can't miss it. Give your name and the band name to the guard on the bridge and he'll direct you.'

'What's on the island?' I asked.

'It's a huge house, used to be the home of Fred Karno years ago. He discovered Charlie Chaplin and many other stars of the silent movies. They called it, The Karsino,' Joe laughed, 'it's just been done up since it was a factory for AC Cars during the war. You'll love it, people you only see in the movies and read about in the Tatler will be there by the dozen.'

'You better polish up your file cards,' I quipped.

'You bet,' Joe agreed, 'each one of those can be worth ten pounds a night.'

After he rang off, I checked the map and was pleased to see Taggs Island was only about two miles from my hotel of choice. 'What organisation,' I congratulated myself.

Les, when I saw him and passed on the secret information, was pleased it was not too far out and reckoned he could easily be at Taggs Island by nine-thirty. 'It'll give me an hour to check the girls out before I have to play,' he rationalised.

'That will be great,' I grinned, 'but don't forget, I'll have been playing since seven and if you finish the night out I'll make it fifty for you.'

'Even better,' Les nodded.

'Yes--and here's why,' and I told him how Sylvia would be waiting anxiously for my return to The Sleeping Giant, to enjoy the promised champagne dinner and my excellent company far into New Year's Day.

'You're so organised,' Les complimented me. 'But, is this OK with Big Joe?' 'Sure, Joe will be socialising once the floor show is over. As long as there's a drummer he'll be happy. Then you just play a few waltz's to get Ron away from the piano for awhile and it'll be 4 a.m. in no time. You can have a few hours sleep, breakfast, then drive home.'

'See you on Taggs then,' We shook hands and parted, both obviously content with the mutual arrangement.

With four drum cases plus our suitcases stowed on the back seat, Sylvia and I rattled along the River road in the direction of our hotel. All had been forgiven, and she gave me a quick kiss as we arrived outside the hotel.

'What a posh place,' she observed, 'must be very expensive.'

'It is, but it's only once a year,' I coolly stated. This warranted another kiss, just as the doorman opened the car door.

'Any luggage,' he asked grinning at us, then stepped back when he saw the six cases on the back seat. "Just these two,' I said and pointed.

The desk clerk was all smiles and gave me the key with a flourish, pressed the desk bell and announced, room 304 to the porter. Sylvia nudged me as we stood squeezed in the elevator. She was looking at a framed poster next to her. 'Look Danny Brooks is playing here tonight, that will be great!'

I liked Danny and had played with him several times, but he was one of those good looking men, with perfect teeth, curly black hair that always stayed in place and a ready smile for everyone. As if that wasn't enough, he had a perpetual suntan and glowed with good health. I asked him about the suntan and he said, 'you have to have a Grandpa from Trinidad to get that.'

Lastly, he was a great piano player and sang in the Nat King Cole style. My only consolation was when I introduced Sylvia to him a few months ago, then nervously asked what she thought of him. She shook her head, 'he's too-o-o perfect.' I remember thinking that I'd never met a woman that I felt was to-o-o perfect, in fact, the more perfect, the more I would be smitten.

'So women are different,' I was thinking as the elevator wobbled to a halt at the third floor.

Sylvia was ecstatic with the room and its view over the river. 'Just beautiful,' she sighed as we gazed at what I thought was rather a forbidding, fast moving, body of dark water. 'Let's have a drink before dinner,' she suggested.

'It's only four o'clock,' I remarked.

'Well, a walk in the grounds then, and you should book our dinner early if you've got to leave before six,' she observed.

As we settled in the lounge after a rather short exploration of the grounds, mainly due to the icy wind blowing off the river, I noticed in each corner a photograph of Danny smiling out at us. The grand piano was set in the corner adjacent to a small dance floor or cuddle pad as we used to them. Set on top of the piano another sign proclaimed. dancing with Danny Brooks from 5 p.m. to 2 a.m.

'Let's see if we can have dinner at five,' Sylvia suggested as we sipped on our martinis.

The desk clerk held several lists scrutinising them carefully. 'Well, the five o'clock sitting is for the Hampstead Retirement Home, but, we could squeeze you in if you don't mind sharing a table.' I had no alternative but to agree to this exciting opportunity. 'Sure, that's in about thirty minutes,' I replied as I backed into the lounge trying to smile as I approached Sylvia. 'All fixed up,' I said 'Wonderful,' she purred, 'you are such a good organiser I'll just have time to change into my new outfit. I'll be back in no time.'

Sylvia returned and performed a delightful pirouette showing off her new dress and shoes. However, behind her and through the window I noticed two small buses with Hampstead Retirement Home printed in large letters on their sides. The ramps were being lowered and the wheelchairs slowly eased down the incline, to form a line rolling towards the hotel entrance.

'I think we better move to the dining room,' I suggested.

'I bet we'll be the only ones there at this time,' she laughed and continued. 'See!' as we surveyed the empty dining room.

'You must be the Scott party,' the waiter moved towards us. 'And the only party,' Sylvia grinned. The grin faded as she noticed the line of wheel chairs squeaking through the door.

'We'll put you in the corner at the small table and you'll only have to share with two people,' the waiter smiled and pointed at a table in the bay window.

I was afraid to look at Sylvia, not sure how she would accept the unexpected guests at our romantic New Year's dinner, or as she put it later, 'New Year's Eve fiasco.' I took her silence as acceptance, but, on glancing at her it was incredulity that registered.

Two wheel chairs bore down on our secluded table, 'I'm Betty and this is Fred,' a large woman in a blue dress expounded.' Fred too was quite large and gestured to Sylvia. 'You are?' His whisky loaded breath rasped in our direction, and Sylvia jolted back in her seat.

'Sylvia and Allan,' I replied hoping to at least melt some of the ice that was descending on our table.

'Married?'

'No,' and I glanced at Syliva who appeared still in a state of shock.

'Just foolin around eh,' and he nudged Betty with an enormous elbow.

Betty laughed, 'you young people think you invented sex.' and they both burst out laughing.

I was thankful to see the waiter hovering above us. 'You all having the standard dinner? he asked.' Sylvia and I nodded. Fred and Betty wanted a detailed account of everything available.

This rambled on for what seemed an eternity and I put my hand on Sylvia's hoping to at least get a sympathetic squeeze, but it was retracted faster than a fiddler's downbow.

I tried to be pleasant and asked if they had booked early for dinner.

'No, even a few days is chancy at our age.' Fred laughed and nudged Betty again and I noticed they both had large drinks in their hands.

'How long have you been married?' I asked.

'We're not married,' Betty replied indignantly and this is my first New Year's Party without Horace.... my husband. Seven months ago he passed on. She fell silent then started to sob, spilling her drink on Fred's lap.

'Have another drink Betty, it'll cheer you up.' Fred boomed at her.

'Do you think that's a good idea?' I asked as discreetly as possible.

'You stick to your foolin around, we'll stick to our booze.' Fred's voice grated in the confines of the bay window.

I stole a glance at Sylvia and she was radiating a smile developed through many years of night club hosting. I followed the direction of her pleasurable interest and there was Danny Brooks waving and exuding his charm from the piano bench.

Sylvia stood and eased herself round the table. 'I must say hello to Danny,' she snapped icily.

'Ho, Ho,' Fred stage whispered. 'I think you've lost her.'

'He's just a mutual friend.' I replied.

'Never have a friend that good looking,' Betty added. 'You'll lose all your girls.'

'I'll just say hello too,' and I squeezed past Fred and followed Sylvia.

'You better perform damage control, that little girl of yours doesn't seem too happy to me.' Betty observed.

'Well, look at you two,' Danny laughed as he tinkled on the keyboard. 'You're starting early.' I needed Danny's sense of humour. It balanced Sylvia's lack of same.

Sylvia glared at me. 'It's already too late for me, I've had one drink, then we were invaded by two ancients in wheelchairs, one sobbing and the other pissed and now Allan's off for four hours.'

Danny tried to keep the mood light and asked if we wanted to stay and watch the diners perform the Lambeth Walk, adding–-'in their wheel chairs. They lost two waiters and a bus boy last year. So this year, they'll all perform in a left hand circuit.' Sylvia still didn't smile.

'Come on, cheer up you two, you'll just have time to grab a wheel chair for the next dance.' Sylvia still looked as unhappy as a Liverpool docker on a wet Sunday morning.

'I'd like my dinner before I go,' I complained.

'Forget it, I'm not going back to those two.' Syliva proclaimed.

'We'll have it in the bar then,' I suggested. 'Then I'll head to Taggs and be back to see the New Year in with you.'

'If... you can spare the time,' she growled.

Danny shook his head, 'Sylvia, sit here next to me and I'll play anything you like.' He eased several inches along the bench and Sylvia slid next to him, 'plus we can watch all the fun from a safe distance. You can have a late dinner with me in the bar, by then Allan should be back, exhausted from giving his all to the beautiful Starlets on Taggs Island, and pockets bulging with crisp pound notes.' He grinned up at me and at that moment I had more affection for Danny than I did for Sylvia....At least he made me laugh.

I patted him on the shoulder and said, 'look after her for me Danny,' ignored the beckoning waves from Fred and Betty then headed into the bar for a quick sandwich.

Being alone for dinner was not in my plans and I hoped Sylvia would mellow, if only a little, and join me. But when

I peeked in the dinning room she was contentedly squeezed on the end of the piano bench and trying to sing along with Danny's rendition of This is a Lovely Way to Spend an Evening. 'I hope it is,' I murmured to myself.

Having changed to my tuxedo, I trotted into the dining room for a last farewell. Danny was singing Straighten up and Fly Right and waving his arms in imitation of an errant pilot in trouble. Sylvia was convulsed with laughter and barely nodded as I waved good-bye. 'So much for good planning.' I groaned.

I had only been on the road for a few minutes when I saw the balloons and a red sign. I turned the corner, in a few minutes there was the bridge. Two lights glowed above the ramp. As I slowed, two uniformed men stepped forward. One with a clipboard, the other with a large flashlight.

'Name, sir, and please open the trunk. The other man moved to the rear of the car.

'Scott, and there isn't one, it's all on the back seat.'

'Ah, the band, turn right and you'll be directed to the parking,' he turned to the next arrival.

It was rather a rickety bridge, and it protested as I rumbled across. I looked down at the black swift moving river thinking how bleak and sombre it seemed. But the huge house with its bright coloured lights and smoking chimneys elevated my mood. As I carried my first case in, Big Joe waved and smiled across the lobby, my spirits rose and I cheerfully set up my drums at the rear of the stage as I had so many times before in so many locations. The rest of the band arrived and the usual musicians' banter ensued as Big Joe gave us the sequence for the first hour or so. This involved picking out the arrangements from the appropriate folder and placing them in order on the music stand.

Big Joe boasted he had over two thousand arrangements in his library, which fitted into four large and very heavy cases, which Joe handled with amazing ease. 'Never been stumped yet,' he would proclaim. The floor show was a separate folder and was a matter of following the indicated sequence. The drum folder always had a queue sheet for dance's kicks, rolls for the magician, bumps for thc comcdian and so on.

Big Joe called us into a huddle. 'No inappropriate remarks, no ogling the girls-sorry--ladies, and no drinks or smoking on the stand. See me for your cheques before you go, I'm not sure how much they'll be, it'll depend on when we finish.' He glanced at me, 'is your back-up drummer all set?'

'Sure is, he'll be here soon and I'll look after him.' Ron leant towards me from the piano, 'I'll get Les to play for me later on when it gets a bit rowdy, he's a bit of a rough player, but, later on nobody'll notice.' Ron winked and sat down.

The guests started to arrive, some I recognised others I had to ask Joe about. But they all looked very prosperous, happy and spiked for pleasure.

By the time the floor show was over and I was wiping the perspiration from my face I realised I had almost forgotten about Sylvia. The audience was good, laughing at the right moment and if asked to participate, did so with great enthusiasm I looked at the wall clock almost hidden behind the balloons, it registered 10.15 p.m. 'Great,' I thought, Les should be here anytime then I'll continue until 11.30. Les can take over for the rest of the night, after all I will have done four and a half hours non- stop. I wondered if I would have to pry Sylvia away from Danny, but I'll suggest a bottle of champagne in our room to see in the New Year. 'That should do it,' I thought.

The balloon covered clock registered 10.45 p.m. and still no Les. I felt an internal squeak of anxiety, and checked with the wrist watch in my pocket.

I noticed a tapping from the window behind me. I turned round and pressed my forehead to the misty glass. The apparition that appeared on the outside of the fogged window nearly knocked me off my drum stool.

It was a dripping, nearly naked, except for a pair of soggy underpants and a plastic bag round his neck--Les. He was gesturing at me and pointing. I blinked my eyes, thinking due the stress of the evening, I was hallucinating. He waved again and began jumping up and down.

I looked over at the bass player. 'Play a bit louder, I have to leave for a minute.'

Ron and he looked puzzled as I squeezed past onto the dance floor and headed to a side exit via the kitchen.

I squinted through the mist rolling in from the river and saw a grey figure still peering through the window. 'Les, ' I called, 'what happened to you?'

He trotted towards me. 'You didn't tell me about the bridge, you turkey,' 'What about it?' I asked.

'They raised it at eight o'clock, so no press or party crashers could get in.' Les's voice shook with cold. 'Let me find somewhere to dry off and get my clothes on.'

'Right, Les follow me,' and I led him back through the exit door and into the room where I had stacked my cases. I had noticed shelves loaded with table clothes. I took one and handed it to Les.

'Dry off for a start, and I'll put your underpants on the heater.' He undid his bundle and removed a rather crumpled tuxedo, and with teeth still chattering proceeded to get dressed. I felt silence on my part the best option.

Les combed his hair and started to laugh, 'Jesus, I thought I could just swim from bridge support, to bridge support, but the drift wood was wedged all the way along and I didn't want to get swept under that, so I drifted with the current till I was clear and then headed right across. Still, here I am reporting for duty minus my under underpants,' and he gave me a mock salute. We both started to laugh. I was the first to stop, as my mind caught up with events. 'Will they lower the bridge so I can get off?' I squeaked.

'No way, it's locked up.' Les made a key turning motion with his hand. 'How do you know,' I asked.

'There's a big sign by the ramp,' Under no circumstances will the bridge be open before 9 a.m. tomorrow.

'I didn't see that,' I complained.

'It would be facing the wrong way for you to see it.' Les explained. But on the invitations it says in big red letters. Bridge closed from 8 p.m. to 9 a.m.

'How do you know?' I queried.

'There were four guests in the Sleeping Giant trying to get a room because they couldn't get over and had nowhere to stay. That's when I pricked my ears up, but I thought, they'll let band members over. But no--I drove to the end of the bridge which had a steel gate and two guards with instructions, that not even the Queen would be allowed over. So then I had to drive back up the road, pull off, and hide my car in the bushes. I hoped to find a boat, but no luck. Anyway it wasn't as bad as I thought.'

'What were you doing in the Sleeping Giant.' I asked.

'It was only 8.30 so I thought I'd say Hi to Danny Brooks. He was playing there. I wound up playing a couple of songs so he could dance with his girlfriend.'

I knew the answer, but I asked anyway. 'Did she have beautiful copper coloured hair and a green dress?'

'Yes, gorgeous! Have you met her?' Les asked.

'That is my Sylvia,' I replied indignantly.

'Well... don't worry she was enjoying herself, but you better get over or she might wind up Danny's Sylvia.'

'What do you mean, get over to her, you don't think I'd try to swim in that?' and I pointed towards the river.

'Well, I did and I didn't have a beautiful girlfriend waiting for me. Just the hope of a hundred pounds. Here--roll your clothes up, put them in this plastic bag, tie them round your neck, creep down to the river, quietly slide in and just back stroke till you reach the weeds on the other side.'

'But what about my car?' I asked, starting to grasp for any straw, that may abolish what by now seemed a very hazardous exercise.

'Here take these,' and Les tossed a set of keys at me. 'My car is about two hundred yards from the bridge.'

'I may drown in that current, and it's freezing.' I protested.

'That's ok I have another set of keys.' Les laughed. The sound of the bagpiper warming up stopped the conversation.

'The piper is about to go on,' I warned. 'He'll need me,'

'No he wont, he'll need me,' and Les pushed past me to the door.

'A faint heart never won a fair maid!' he shouted over his shoulder.

'You didn't say anything about suicide,' I shouted back. It was then I saw a half bottle of scotch on the shelf, obviously stashed by one of the staff. I took several sips, and then a few more. I started to feel, maybe I could do this, after all I had had a dip in the Serpentine last summer.

The sound of the piper backed by Les's drumming echoed through the hall as I started to take my clothes off and put them into the plastic bag along with the car keys and my wallet. My shoes and underpants I kept on.

I edged open the door and was met with an icy breeze. 'Just go,' I whispered and checked for any sign of the guards. 'Good no one about.' Moving quickly into the bushes I removed my shoes and dropped them into the bag. Well one shoe went into the bag the other fell onto the wet grass and slid down the bank into the river. I tried to grab it, but missed, and I too started to slide on the muddy grass. When my rear end hit the water, I forgot all about the shoe and clawed madly up the bank, the bag held in my teeth. I caught a glimpse of the white inside of my shoe as it was swept away slowly rotating in the current. 'I must be mad I thought, I'll die in that water, plus I can't even see the far bank.'

I hopped back across the gravel road and pulled the door handle, it was locked. 'Why didn't I wedge it open?' I berated myself. 'Now what?' I sighed.

Creeping along the wall hidden by the dripping bushes, I could hear the whoops and yells of the highland dancing. Les was sitting at my drums pounding away as I tapped then banged on the window to attract his attention. He turned and pressed his forehead to the misty glass, saw me and gave the thumbs up sign then waved. I realised he thought I was on my way. I tapped even louder shaking my head, and did a key turning motion with my right hand. Lastly I raised both arms in a gesture of frustration.

Les nodded and pointed at his watch, raised his right hand and extended his fingers three times. Which I sensed, meant fifteen minutes. I gave him the thumbs up and he went back to accompanying the piper with both hands and great vigour.

I crouched in the bushes by the locked door for what seemed the longest fifteen minutes of my life. I was muddy and wet from the waist down. I hugged the wet plastic bag, stood on one foot, and waited patiently for Les to appear.

The pipes and drums ceased, the yells stopped and Les appeared at the door.

'What's the matter?' he grinned giving me a clean tablecloth to dry myself off.

'Where's your other shoe,' and he began to open the plastic bag. I gestured towards the river. He tutted, 'the first rule of a good infantry man is to keep your boots on,' and added 'there's food and drinks for us across the hall.'

'My underpants are covered in mud,' I groaned.

'Give em here.' Les took them rinsed them under the tap and hung them next to his on the heater. I dressed minus my shoes and underpants. Les ran back to the ballroom and minus shoes I too headed for a coffee and sandwich.'

It was the best coffee I'd ever tasted. Mainly because the alternative would have had me somewhere in the middle the icy, foggy ,Thames trying to reach a wet, slippery, muddy bank and hoping I would have the strength to climb up it.

I looked at my watch, it wasn't working after its dunking in the frigid water. The clock on the wall said: 11.30.

Sylvia! I better phone her, but what to say. Just then Ron came in, 'Les is playing piano for me, they'll need you on drums for the latin set.' I rushed to the front hall and grabbed the phone and book.

The Sleeping Giant was living up to it's name and it was about ten rings before it was answered. I recognised the voice of the desk clerk.

'I need to talk to Miss Rogers she's in room 304,' I panted. 'Well, sir, she's not there at the moment I can see her on the dance floor from here.'

'Great, get her for me...Please,' I added.

'Hello,' came the familiar voice.'

'It's me, still on Taggs Island, and I can't get off, they've pulled the bridge up.'

'Really, how's Les going to get over to you?'

'He swam here,' I made the mistake of saying.

'Well, you can damn well swim back.' The phone clunked into silence.

I ran back to the ballroom and Les waved from the piano bench. Then started pounding away as I settled on my drum stool. By the second samba I had started to warm up and glanced at Les who burst out laughing as he observed my harrowed state.

The last waltz was at 3.30 a.m. which due to our marathon performance seemed to come quite quickly. Les and I found our room, which was at the top of the house of course and had a view of the dreaded river. 'I see the tide had changed,' Les said.

'How can you tell?' I sighed.

'I just saw a shoe float past. You could catch it if you ran down and jumped in.'

'Thanks a lot Les, but I'll fight the urge and go to bed instead.' Les was laying back laughing at his own joke.

'OK, he continued by tomorrow morning you'll have a nice new pair of shoes: black, drummer/non-swimmer for the use of.' We laughed at his use of military terminology.

Les was true his word. Next morning by my bed were a fairly new pair of black shoes, size seven. 'Where's my old one?' I asked Les.

'Well, I had to make an exchange,' he frowned.

We had breakfast with the rest of the band. Big Joe thanked us and passed out the cheques. I gave Les the promised forty-five plus another five for his, beyond the call of duty, arrival. Ron gave him his forty-five.

As we drove over the bridge I stopped and looked down at the fast moving black water. 'Want to have another go?' Les laughed.'

'Maybe after I've seen Sylvia, I'll just jump.'

We found Les's car in the bushes and he drove off towards the city.

It was nine-thirty by the time I drove into the Sleeping Giant parking lot and headed for the reception desk and my-never-used room key.

It all looked rather sad as the cleaners disposed of the debris from the previous night's party, the new calendar on the wall behind the counter read: January 1st 1954.

The room was as I had left it, minus Sylvia. I shaved and put on my suit and headed for a least a second coffee, maybe a second breakast, as I'd paid for it.

Sylvia and Danny were lined up at the buffet. They both waved and Danny pointed at a table in the corner already possesed by Sylvia's coat draped over a chair. I assembled my breakfast and joined them.

Danny looked at me, eyebrows raised. 'Well, you had quite the saga last night. What happened?' Danny looked serious but amused. Sylvia looked indifferent but not amused--maybe, vengefully content would be a better description.

I related my story, and flaunted my new shoes. At the point in my story where I hovered on the river bank, cold and fearful, I put my hand on Sylvia's, she glanced up. 'Thank goodness I had Danny to look after me, I was nearly abducted by two men in wheel chairs.'

'Well--Happy New Year to us all!' I voiced.

As I settled the bill at the desk and sadly counted the few remaining notes in my wallet, a small man in a tuxedo and brown slippers asked the clerk if there were any shops open today.

'I need a shoe store,' he uttered in an aristocratic voice. 'Can you believe it? Someone stole my shoes during the night on Taggs Island and left me just one muddy shoe .' I hastily moved my feet round the corner of the counter.

Danny smiled at him, 'I saw a one legged man waiting outside for a taxi a few minutes ago.' Our aristocratic shoe seeker bounded to the entrance.

Sylvia frowned at Danny. 'Did you really?'

Danny smiled, 'No... but why let the truth get in the way of a good story.'

We burst out laughing, Sylvia put her arms round our necks pulling us to her.

'Bloody musicians! I'm going to find a nice quiet bus driver and settle down.'

Allan F Scott

The End

London 1955

WE CALLED IT PANTO

Recently, I was showing an American friend some of the photographs from my playing days in London, two pictures aroused her interest. They were of a group of actors, on stage in theatrical costume.

'What's this, a play?' she asked.

'No, this is what we call Pantomime in England,' I replied.

She peered closer at the photograph. 'Quite a hodge podge even a donkey, and ballet dancers. Was it a comedy?'

I told her if she really wanted to know, she better make herself comfortable, because there is no short explanation of Pantomime. She sat down and I continued.

'Traditionally it is a Christmas Entertainment, intended particularly for children, and peculiarly British, during which good always triumphs over evil. The first performance of a panto was Robinson Crusoe, performed at the Drury Lane Theatre in London, during Christmas of 1781. From here it spread to most of the London Theatres, and then to the provinces. By 1800, Panto was emerging as a distinct form of theatre, and today, around two hundred theatres in the UK run a six week pantomime every Christmas.

'The performance always contains songs, dancing of all types, jokes of the corniest variety, slapstick, and lots of audience participation, consisting of booing and hissing the 'badies,' cheering the 'goodies' and sometimes, throwing cotton balls or some other harmless missile at the actors.

'As a child, in that two hours, you ran the full gamut of your emotions. Then there was always the Grand Transformation Scene. Which left you gasping and amazed, as to how in a few seconds, (if the puffing stage hands pushed the revolving stage fast enough) aided by drums rolls, smoke, and flash powder. The whole world changed before your very eyes.'

My friend remarked, what nice legs the lady in the centre of the photo had, and was she a dancer? 'No,' I replied, 'this is a bit complicated, and I should explain the main characters in the panto, are standard regardless of the story.

'The lady you are looking at, is actually the Prince, who is a woman dressed as a man. The older lady next to her is the Dame, who is a man dressed as a woman, and frequently acts the roll of the Princess's mother. This star part is usually given to a well known comedian and requires singing, dancing, slapstick comedy, roller skating, gymnastics and ham acting of the worst sort.

'The Princess is a woman, dressed as a woman, the epitome of feminine virtue, true, loving and beyond reproach. (Another fictitious aspect of pantomime.)

'However, she always gets her Prince. Then you have a duo comedy team, an evil magician with a wicked associate, a fairy complete with magic wand, a corps de ballet recruited from the local ballet school, and lastly, either a horse or a lion containing, two long suffering student actors, or maybe a bear, containing, one long suffering student actor.'

When I worked as a pit drummer for these shows, we would have four rehearsals then forty-eight performances. It was interesting to see how differently the audience reacted to each performance.

The most important part of comedy is the timing, and the actors would experiment with this, and sometimes change the dialogue to suit a topical situation of the day. So even into the last week of the panto, it was never boring.

A few weeks before Christmas I carried my drums and accessories into the theatre and started setting them up in the pit next to the electronic organ. Just the two of us-- how electronics had changed things.

I noticed a pretty young lady sitting just above me at the end of the stage, reading a very thick book with great intensity. I tried to catch her attention by making more noise than usual as I set up my percussion instruments, but she gave me a look of complete indifference and returned to her book.

During the forthcoming rehearsal I tried to see her role in the show, but ... no sign of her. I rationalised she must be at least an understudy for a principal part.

The twenty minute break was announced and I pretended I needed something back stage; as I passed her, I made a very original statement. 'Must be a good book.'

Not even looking up, she said, 'It is,' and I continued to be ignored.

Later, Brenda (I now knew her name) was called to the front of the theatre by the producer, and I reached up, took the book and read the title. Method Acting by Konstantin Sergeyevich Stanislavski. Lower on the page it went on to say, he was the founder of the Moscow Art Theatre in 1898.

I was looking forward to seeing Brenda perform during the dress rehearsal, but she just walked around with Stanislavski under her arm.

For dinner I went to the restaurant across the street, and there she was... sitting alone, in the corner reading. The restaurant was quite busy and I asked if I might sit at her table. She shrugged, nodded, I sat down. Then forced the conversation, by asking if it was a novel. She looked up saying, 'No, it's Stanislavski's book on method acting.'

I tried to look surprised, 'Not the Konstantin Sergeyenvich Stanislavski, who rose to be short order cook at Fred's Fish and Chips.'

'No,' she laughed.

'Then he must be the one that founded the Moscow Art Theatre in 1898.'

'Right on. How come a drummer knows that?' She was still laughing.

'Percussionist please,' I replied.

'I've got to be off to change,' she sighed, and headed out the door.

We finished the dress rehearsal and the producer leaned over the pit rail and said he was not happy with the donkey dance sequence. 'We need more wood block in time with the donkey's feet.'

'Well, it's difficult because I have to follow four feet instead of two.' I replied.

'OK,' he replied. 'We'll have the rear feet do the same steps as the front feet.'

After a few attempts and much puffing from the two internal members comprising the donkey, we had it down to perfection. The producer was happy, smiled, looked up at the stage and voiced. 'Great work donkey people, I know how hot and uncomfortable it is when you're bent over wearing that heavy outfit--especially Brenda in the rear, where you can't see.'

The donkey unzipped in the middle to reveal my beautiful book reading beauty, panting, perspiring and bedraggled.

The producer leaned over to me and whispered, 'She really is the best donkey's arce in the business.' I looked up and replied, 'She should be, she studied under Constantin Sergeyevich Stanislavski.'

In all walks of life we experience Murphy's Law, but in theatrical performance every precaution is taken to foil Murphy.

Every facet of a show is rehearsed to eliminate anything going amiss. But we all knew if something can go wrong--it will.

This year's panto was Aladdin, complete with a Genie, who appears when Aladdin rubs his magic lamp. There is a drum roll, a puff of smoke and the Genie materialises on stage, which usually draws a startled gasp from the audience.

The magic is performed, via a spring board and a one way trap door in the stage floor, that can only be opened from below.

Sitting in the pit I was privy to the whole amazing episode... night after night.

I would hear the Genie run along the passage, which ran parallel to the pit, jump onto the spring board and bedong! he was projected upwards through the trap door onto the stage.

I would commence the drum roll on hearing him begin his run along the passage, the on-stage effects man poised ready with a flash and smoke, waiting for my cymbal crash, which I hit, when I heard the Genie bounce on the spring board.

We were playing the spooky incidental magic-forest music. I was watching the stage when I noticed the trees were not arranged in their usual formation.

I heard the running feet and looked at the Genie's usual arrival point but it was obscured by a tree.

Drum roll, bedong! from the spring board followed by another bedong! and a painful groan from the other side of the wall. Cymbal crash, flash, smoke, the tree twitched ... but no Genie.

A quick thinking stage hand, in jeans and a T-shirt, looking rather out of place in a magic forest, rushed on-stage and pushed the offending tree to it's correct position.

There was much shouting from the passage next to me, and I heard the running feet again, though I noted it was an apprehensive run, much slower and almost hesitant.

Aladdin being a pro, had not stopped rubbing his lamp but did look a little bewildered and stared at the empty space on front of him.

A stage whisper from the wings 'he's trying again.' This was for Aladdin's benefit who continued rubbing with greater vigour.

I was doing the drum roll again, readying for the cymbal crash at the sound of the spring board, but it was a rather anaemic bedong! as if the 'Genie' was not sure if he wanted a second attempt to materialise.

Cymbal crash, flash, thick smoke. It cleared, to reveal the head and shoulders of our Genie, turban askew, protruding through the floor.

Aladdin put his lamp down and dropped to his knees and pulled the bedraggled Genie through the trap door. At this point the Genie usually said. 'Your wish is my command Master.' But all he could muster was -- 'What the hell happened?'

The audience, who of course, didn't know this was not part of the regular routine, laughed and clapped loud and long, until the groggy Genie had to take a bow.

Back stage after the show, the producer voiced that maybe we should keep this in, as it got more laughs than the contrived comedy. The Genie refused, stating that it took away the magic of the moment.

But I knew, and we all knew, that whenever a Genie spoke of a magic moment, this would be, THE ONE, we would remember.

It would be unfair to blame Murphy for every unexpected event, and for the following, I had no further to look, than myself.

I had a phone call from John, who was much higher up the ladder of success than myself, and I was always happy to fill in for him on any occasion.

He had a six week Pantomime gig, and asked if I would play for about ten days, as he was to tour with a London Orchestra.

A week before he left, I watched the show four times to familiarise myself with the music and the effects required. John left knowing his job was in good hands, and said he would phone me, when he arrived back in London, in about ten days.

I fitted in fine, and probably not many of the cast realised they had a different percussionist in the pit. However, the two comedians knew, because I had to watch them for all the slapstick comedy, and it takes a while to catch every fall, slap and bump they do in their routines. Later they came over and said, 'you did a good job, how long are you with us?' I explained that John would be away about two weeks.

They said they liked John, but he was a bit stuck up sometimes. 'How do you mean?' I asked.

'Well, we wanted him to help us get a few laughs, but he said that wasn't really his job, so we gave up on him.'

'What did you want him to do?' I asked, my curiosity aroused.

'Well, you know the scene in the bakery where we throw dough at each other, and then flour bags.' I started to laugh immediately, because it was the funniest slapstick scene in the show, finishing with them and anyone else on stage covered in flour.

'So..,' he continued, 'We wanted to throw a couple of dough balls at the drummer. He keeps them until our backs are turned, then he throws them back at us. The kids love it.'

They looked at me eyebrows raised, but I was laughing already.

'Sure I'll do that,' I said.

'Great we'll give you a cape to put over your tuxedo, it can be a bit messy.'

All went well, the kids loved it, they loved it and I enjoyed trying to play and catch the dough balls. Even more throwing them back.

A few weeks later my phone rang, it was John back from his tour and saying he would be able to play that evening. Plus, if I liked to meet him after the show, he would pay me for the two weeks.

'Great,' I said, 'I'll see you about ten-thirty,' and I hung up knowing I'd done a good job. At the pub, I ordered a beer and meat pie to celebrate my forth coming paycheque.

A few minutes later the cast started to drift in, and I had a feeling of nostalgia, as I realised I was no longer a member of this theatrical family.

My comedian friends bustled in, saw me, pointed and started laughing in fact laughing so much, they had difficulty in talking.

'What's so funny?' I asked, beginning to feel it concerned me, more than I wanted it to.

They flopped down next to me, looked at each other, which created another outburst. 'Come on then,' I said. Pete the tall straight man of the pair, continued,

'God, you should have been there.'

'Where?' I asked.

'At the show.' Harry the small rotund member of the duo replied.

'You mean you didn't know?'

'Know what? ' the pitch of my voice raised with curiosity.

Pete looked at Harry, 'He really must have forgotten.' More laughter.

'Well John played the show tonight, but you didn't tell us, and we can't see over the foot lights. So we did our usual routine, winding up by throwing our dough balls, at who we thought was you, and waited for you to throw them back.

'The next thing I knew a drum stick hit me and then another; I looked behind me and there was John half hanging over the footlights covered in flour, yelling and hurling all his sticks and anything else he could reach at us.

'As the curtain came down, we realised what had happened and we've been laughing ever since. But the manager told us the least we could do, is pay for him to have his tuxedo cleaned. But it was worth it.' More laughter.

Up to this point I had found their laughter infectious, but the infection ceased immediately, as I realised the situation I was in.

This was hardly the time to accept John's pay cheque, and I was debating beating a hasty retreat, when the door opened and a pale, flour stained, obviously not amused John appeared. This brought on another burst of laughter from my compatriots, which did nothing to ease the situation.

He approached our table reached into his pocket, pulled out an envelope and in a cold firm voice said: 'Here is your cheque Allan, and thank you.' Reaching into a paper bag he added, 'these are yours too,' and he dumped two big hunks of dough covered in flour on my head.

All I could do was blow the flour out of my eyes, try to smile and shrug at the comedy duo, now sprawled over the table, helpless with laughter.

The beefy barman had witnessed the assault, but without knowing the events leading up to it. He rushed over, grabbed John by the collar and seat of the pants, and ejected him out the door and onto the street.

My companions, now in a state of collapse, looked at my horrified expression and Pete said: 'Don't worry, it just wasn't his day.

Allan F Scott

The End

London 1955

TAXI! AIR FORCE STYLE

An aspiring actor once told me, it's hard to get your picture in the paper, then if you do, it's usually for the wrong reason. He was right about the last bit.

London 1955. The event was the Jewish Armistice Day Parade. This was held a week after the standard Armistice Day Parade, on a Saturday, and we always got paid thirty shillings. Why? I'm not sure, but both were very sad and serious occasions.

We were marching down Whitehall towards the Cenotaph followed by the parade participants. Not all the avenue had been closed to traffic and we had a single lane of vehicles moving slowly towards us, and past us on my left side.

Our military snare drums had two white ropes looped beneath them. They were called drag ropes and hung almost to the ground, to be used only when not playing, so it could be carried over your shoulder.

It was a bright November day and I was playing away, glancing at the crowds, and the pretty girls. Maybe, not concentrating as I should have been, when, I was vigorously jerked around behind a taxi. The drag ropes had caught on the rear bumper of the vehicle as it past me in the opposite direction. I had no choice but to run after it, at the same time try to remove the ropes from the bumper. I heroically decided, if he speeds up, I'll just let the drum go.

However, the taxi stopped and a capped head appeared out the window.

'What's yer doin mate,' a cockney voice shouted.

'I've got my drum caught on your bumper.'

'Got it off,' the voice continued.

'Yes,' I panted.

'Good. No charge for the ride mate,' and he was gone.

My antics drew a round of applause from the crowd, and much banter and laughter from the band. Our band director, being at the front of the band, and much to my relief, knew nothing of this near tragedy.

However, next morning I was called to the office and asked why, I had been fooling around on such a serious occasion?

'What me?' I asked.

The Wing Commander waved the newspaper at me and pointed at the incriminating photograph.

The title: 'Catching a taxi, Air Force style.'

Allan F Scott

The End

London 1955

SEEING IS NOT EVERYTHING

The News of the World newspaper in 1955 was a must for Sunday morning reading in England, and probably still is. All sorts of scandalous news, rife with moral turpitude, filled these fascinating pages.

However, ignoring the latest indiscretions of the aristocracy, my attention was drawn to a small article headed, Jazz pianist arrested and charged.

It went on to say, 'Mark Bass, of Ealing, was arrested riding a bicycle, while intoxicated and under the influence of drugs.' This was not earth shattering news in itself, except for one thing--Mark Bass was blind!

When the judge asked him to account for his delinquent behaviour he replied,

'I was on a gig at Ealing Town Hall and couldn't stand the bass player, so to cheer myself up I had a few drinks and smoked a reefer.'

The judge replied, 'Everyday I meet people I can't stand, but I don't go out and drink and take drugs.' To this, the accused replied.

'You should, it would cheer you up.'

Mr. Bass was fined five pounds and given a year's probation.

I had seen Mark Bass play many times, and though he never reached the musical heights of George Shearing, (one reason being the account just quoted) he was just as capable and attended the same school of music as Mr. Shearing in London.

George Shearing was now at the top of the Los Angeles music scene. Had a very caring wife and manager. He and his quartet were toasted as the new sound. While Mark's moment in the sun, was riding a bicycle round a traffic circle, with a beer bottle in one hand, and a reefer in the other .

Another reason I was drawn to the story of this evil doer, was--because I was booked to play in a trio with him over the next several months. I wondered if I would be musically compatible, or would my drumming bring on another round of boozy-bike- riding and reefer smoking.

Later that week I spoke to the agent who said, 'Mark is a great bloke except you have to watch him; if he doesn't like the band, he just disappears at the first opportunity. So keep an eye on him, especially during the breaks. By the way, you live close, could you pick him up for the gig?' Sensing my hesitation, he added, 'you get a double transportation fee of course.'

Mark's house in Ealing was a typical terrace house facing onto a traffic circle, and I noticed a bicycle parked in what passed for a garden in a terrace house.

I could hear a piano as I approached the door, his mother opened the door and led me into the front room. Mark stopped playing and I introduced myself. He shook my hand, then gently reached and touched my face, moving his hand to the top of my head. 'Glad you're not tall; I hate having to shout up in the air. You're from Liverpool,' he had picked up my accent, which was not too hard to do. 'I like Liverpudlians, not so full of themselves as Londoners.'

He wore a tuxedo under a dark overcoat and with the dark glasses looked every bit the jazz musician. He followed me out the door, his hand on my arm.

I pointed at the bicycle.

'Is that the famous bike of News of the World fame?' I asked.

'Sure is,' Mark grunted.

My curiosity got the better of me and I continued, 'How do you ride if you can't see?'

He let go my arm, 'Easy,' he said, and grabbed the bike, pushed it out the gate, and slid onto the saddle in one swift movement. On to the dark street he went, just missing my car. I started to panic thinking already he was absconding. 'You don't have a light,' I shouted after him.

'I don't need one,' he yelled back.

Then I saw how it was done, he peddled with his right leg while his left foot touched the curb and round the traffic circle he went. 'That's great,' I yelled, 'but we have to go.'

His mother appeared, carrying what looked like a deflated football.

'Your hat Mark.' He put on this ridiculous piece of head gear, it was the type worn by the lower ranks of soccer fans.

'What's with the hat?' I asked.

'Oh this one is easy to find and no one will steal it,' he replied.

"It's not very cool," I observed..

Mark pulled it to his ears saying, 'I used to wear a black beret like Dizzy, so did all the other guys in the band, and I kept coming home with the wrong one.'

'Well, you're safe with that one,' I retorted and led him to my car.

'Pretty old car,' he said as I eased him into the passenger seat.

'It's like your hat; no one will steal it.'

'Hmm,' he grunted. 'Engine sounds good; don't forget to turn right at the next corner,'

'Are you sure you don't want to sit in the back seat?' I countered.

'Only if you're girlfriend's there,' was his snappy answer.

We headed into Regents Park and located Winfield House, which in earlier times, had belonged to Barbara Hutton and was no basement jazz club; in fact, it was the new home of the American ambassador.

I was trying to locate the rear entrance but got caught in the traffic heading to the front, which for this occasion had been decorated in regal style, complete with red carpet and awning to the front entrance.

I tried to drive past, but two white gloved American service policemen stepped forward, one saluting, the other opening the passenger door.

I jumped out to assist Mark, as this would be very confusing for him, and eased myself in front of the policeman. I took Mark's arm and led him along the red carpet. I looked back. One policeman was in the car, the other pushing it to the side to make room for the other arrivals. No words had been exchanged, but I could almost hear them think: Another pair of eccentric Englishmen.

I found the ballroom and led Mark to the piano, which was a large grand.

He sat down, and I could see, after noodling a few notes, he was content.

'Stay here Mark, while I get my drums in.' This involved about four trips for me, and this time I would find the rear entrance. Being saluted four times, would be just too much.

The policeman must have noticed the drums on the back seat, and my car had been relegated to a dark corner of the lot, soon to be filled with Rolls, Bentleys, Jaguars, Cadillacs, making my 1936 Ford 8, seem like a collector's item. Plus, Mark's hat which I noticed he dropped and I had neglected to inform him, had been found and was on the hood. I resisted the temptation to hang it on the hood ornament of the nearest Rolls.

I weaved my way through the kitchen, cases in hand, and set up in the ballroom close to the piano.

Our group was a great success, due mainly to Mark's musical predominance, enabling us to handle any request. Even if the title was in question, Mark would ask the requester to hum a few bars, then he would be on his musical way.

I only had one anxious moment, when, during our dinner break, Mark vanished.

I knew he was known by many of the Americans as he played at their clubs and for their functions around London. So I asked someone who looked like a General, but turned out to be the Mess Sergeant.

'Sure, he always plays the one-armed bandits during his break. He'll be in the main hall.'

When I came in earlier in the evening I hadn't noticed the machines lining the entrance way, but there they were, about twenty-four on each wall of the elegant carpeted entrance. At the far end was Mark, surrounded by guests, as he carefully manipulated the handle, his head pressed against the colourful whirring machine.

As I approached, he moved to another machine and was followed by his entourage all holding plastic cups full of quarters. "What is he doing?" I asked the nearest guest.

'He listens to the machines, and he can tell which one is ready to pay off.' Above the whirring of the machines and the chatter I shouted, 'Time for the piano man.' 'Not yet,' someone in the group shouted, he's on a roll.'

Next second, with a whirr and a clatter, a cup full of coins spilled out of the machine. By this time I was next to him, my hand on his arm, and I whispered.

'Just one hour to go,' and I gently edged him through his admirers.

By 1.30, I had my drums and Mark, whom, I had to drag away from the machines, stored in the car.

The London mist had covered my windows with a moist haze. I kept a wet sponge to hand for just this situation. In the dark corner of the parking lot, I started wiping them down.

Unknown to me, Mark had rolled down his window and as I applied the wet sponge with great vigour, it hit him directly in the face.

'Quite the storm brewing,' was all he said, as I tried to control my mirth.

On the trip through the Park, I let him change gears, as I did feel guilty over the sponge incident. But, then he wanted to steer, and held tightly onto the wheel as I tried verbally to direct him round the Inner Circle of Regents Park.

'OK, let go now; we're coming to the end of the park.' I tried to sound calm, but I was becoming a little nervous, as he was obviously finding this very exciting and hung onto the wheel with grim determination.

We meandered over the fortunately deserted traffic lanes as we both gripped the wheel with mutual animosity, until all I could do, was switch off the engine, and we coasted to a halt after bouncing one wheel onto the curb.

I was saying a few choice words to him when there was a sharp knock on my window. I looked up, to see the unmistakable outline of a bobbies helmet.

'What is going on here?' was his first question.

Mark grabbed my arm and whispered, 'Don't forget I'm on probation.'

'Well, I was just teaching my friend to drive a little,' I said, trying to keep my voice steady and pointed at Mark.

'It certainly was a little,' the officer replied.

'Step out the car, please,' I stepped out as instructed and went round to help Mark. I felt like an errant school boy as the policeman surveyed us.

'Why have you got dark glasses on, when you are supposed to be learning to drive?' he said looking at Mark and licking his pencil, readying himself to make a suitable entry, in the recently produced notebook.

'Well...I'm blind,' Mark said. This stopped the pencil-licking.

'And you?' the bobby asked staring hard at me.

'Oh ...I'm fine.'

'You're fine, and you're the one who drove onto the curb,' he continued, a note of sarcasm creeping into the voice of authority.

'Well, I had to stop and couldn't get my foot on the brake.'

'And why was that?' his voice took on a patronising note.

'Well he had his foot on it,' I replied, pointing at Mark.

'I was trying to find the accelerator,' Mark interrupted.

'HOLD IT!' yelled our interrogator.-- 'Now let me get this clear,'--he leaned forward and looked closer at me.

'You--are teaching a blind man, who is wearing dark glasses, to drive round the Inner Circle in Regents Park at two o'clock in the morning.'

'And you?' he said looking at Mark, 'being legally blind, are learning to drive while sitting in the passenger seat, sharing the steering wheel and gear shift, your feet between those of the instructor. How do you think that will sound in Magistrate's Court on Monday morning?--Is this a regular Saturday night out for you two?'

'No, we've been playing at Winfield House, and we're just on our way home.' I said, hoping to curry some sympathy.

The constable looked up from his notebook. 'The band at Winfield House, I was in there having a little sustenance, a few hours ago. In fact, you played a request for me, A Nightingale Sang in Berkeley Square, I asked a waiter to ask you.'

'Very nice song,' Mark said.

The Bobby slid his notebook back in his top pocket saying, 'Great blokes those Americans, really look after us Bobbies.'

He looked thoughtfully at Mark. 'Wonderful piano playing, but aren't you the one that was charged with riding a bike, smoking a reefer and being drunk.'

'I'm afraid so,' Mark agreed, thankfully with a tone of humility.

The constable adopted a serious expression and hands on hips, leaned towards Mark. 'So--you've gone from riding a bike round traffic circles in a drug induced state, while imbibing in alcoholic beverages, to driving a car... side-saddle in Regents Park.

Quite the achievement for one legally blind. Now...I'm going to ignore these pranks on several conditions,' and I held my breath while he continued. 'Firstly,' and he nodded at Mark:

'You sit in the back seat with your arms folded, and you,' he nodded at me, 'keep both your hands on the wheel and both feet on the pedals.

If I see you again in Regents Park, these are the seating arrangements I want to see--or it's to the Magistrate's court we go.'

'Yes, constable,' I sighed with relief, and hastily edged Mark into the back seat, burying him in my drum cases.

Our next gigs were in what Mark called, 'my stomping ground.' Gerard Street in Soho. Today the health conscious person would find it unbelievable to experience the conditions we worked in.

The Delta Jazz Club, as it was pretentiously called, was entered via a set of stone steps leading down into a long low basement room. At the far end was a small stage containing a piano of doubtful lineage, on the right a wooden barricade dominated by three raised barrels, two containing beer and one cider.

Adjacent to the bar was a folding table containing two electric hot plates, which should have been used independently, but by replacing the frequently burnt fuse with a guitar 'A' string (which glowed as brightly as the hot plates) both hot plates became available. This was laughingly called, 'the cuisine area.'

Here the proprietor's mother would cook a never-ending stable of sausages, insert two between two pieces of bread and serve with a grubby hand on an equally grubby plate, to anyone with two shillings and sixpence. The sixpence was the deposit on the plate, and when returned, would be dropped into a barrel of dirty water to be as we joked, sterilised. Nothing could survive in that water!

For us, a free meal was included. Guess what that was?

I used to save the sixpence and feel happier eating off one of my cymbals.

The beer barrels above the bar were labelled Mild and Bitter. Each barrel had a length of hose hanging from it that enabled the server to pour directly into the glass. To stop the flow he would insert his thumb into the end of the hose, bend it over and clip it with a clothes peg. On busy nights he just kept his thumbs in until a beer was needed.

By nine o'clock the smoke was so thick it was impossible to see the end of the room, by twelve o'clock it was impossible to see the floor or anything else, which was probably just as well.

Before starting a tune, Mark would rock to and fro, creating the tempo, a look in my direction he wanted a fill in, a look to the ceiling was for inspiration, when he hunched up, something was not pleasing him.

Mark, a cigarette hanging from his mouth, the ash being pounded into the keys as it fell, and stomping his feet he emitted verbal grunts as a musical phrase excited him. He rode the wave of his musical ecstasy, chorus after chorus into the night.

We frequently had musicians who wanted to sit in with us, some good, some bad, and Mark had various techniques for dealing with these musical social climbers. If he like the player, he would accompany with great sensitivity, rocking to and fro, and grunting his approval whenever a particular phrase pleased him.

These would be the magic moments, the never repeated spontaneous creation of swinging jazz.

The next group would be the 'tryers' as he called them, usually and understandably, modest.

Mark would begin in a sympathetic vane, but as boredom took over, he would lapse to using one hand, the other covering his mouth to stifle a pretentious yawn, leaning in my direction as he did so.

Lastly came the group known as the 'play actors.' They usually had a good education, and having reached the level of a doctor or lawyer could not understand, why we working class types could play jazz, while they couldn't.

Frequently a 'play actor' was accompanied by a clique of friends who assumed that if they owned an instrument, they must be able to play it, and so encouraged and pushed them onto the stage.

From here on, what happened depended on Mark's mood and the attitude of the aspiring soloist. A well mannered player would only have to know the title of the song and the key. Mark would play a suitable four-bar intro and follow him, regardless of bars missed, wrong notes or invented middle eight's.

To the listener, it could be an entertaining performance. However, one, showing signs of belligerence, such as yelling a key in the same mode as calling a waiter, or stomping in the tempo without any consultation, could expect may types of pianistic sabotage.

A four bar introduction, a half-tone higher than usual, leaving the victim examining his instrument and wondering why it sounded so good in his living room, but not here.

A subtle change of key at the middle eight, putting the soloist in a different key than he started in, or missing out one beat every four bars, leaving the player completely out of rhythm; in this, myself and the bass player had to be fellow conspirators.

Furthermore injecting at every opportunity the notes of an entirely different song, confusing the would-be 'Benny Goodman' to the point where he couldn't remember what song he started in the first place.

During a break, after a particularly destructive performance, I told Mark I felt he was a bit harsh. 'Look blokes like him always blame the pianist; why not give him good reason.' With that he bit furiously into his sausage sandwich.

'The late shift,' as we called it, was from midnight to four a.m. following our earlier seven to eleven gig. This gave us an hour to get some fresh air , 'Very bad for you,' Mark assured me.

We wandered down Gerard Street, Mark asking me if so and so was standing on the corner, or requesting a commentary on the local ladies. He seemed to be known by many of them and after they shouted his name, it was up to me to guide him in their direction.

His greetings to them were the same as I had received on our first meeting, starting with touching the top of the head, except he went into more detail with them, running his hands over their body, while they stood giggling and laughing.

He complimented them saying: 'Just as beautiful as ever Martha, everything in the right place,' and so on, sometimes spending our whole break visiting one of his amours after another.

Martha was his favourite and he used to ask me if she looked as good as she felt, I, of course not wanting to disillusion him, had to confirm that she did.

One night we had nearly completed our nocturnal tour when a burst of female laughter attracted his attention. 'That's Sarah, I bet,' he said, pulling me in that direction. 'She has just been on a wild trip to Spain with a Duke; She is beautiful.'

'Here put these on,' he whispered, removing his dark glasses and thrusting them in my general direction. I took them and put them on.

He yelled, 'Sarah,' and a very beautiful sun-tanned lady sauntered across the street in our direction. 'How was the Duke?' he asked. 'Like this,' she replied, extending her little finger so

Mark could feel it. This was greeted with much laughter. 'Good job you weren't paid by the inch,' Mark laughed.

'This is Allan from my trio.' (By now I had the dark glasses on). 'He has the same problem as me; good job one of us knows the way around.' He enforced this statement by tapping his white cane on the curb.

I extended my hand, and patted her on top of her head, 'You're taller than you sound,' and I ran my hand down her well-endowed bosom, (I was beginning to get the hang of this).

I continued my explorations, reaching her rear end, which she wiggled in a most delightful manner. 'Well, what do you think, do I pass,' she giggled.

'I think you are just beautiful.' I said removing the sun glasses and beating a hasty retreat down the street. I looked back to see Mark covering his head as she yelled and swung at him with her hand bag.

'That is a rotten trick you Polish piss artist,' were the last words I heard form this Aphrodite of the night.

I was laughing so much I had to sit down as soon as I rounded the corner.

A few seconds later I heard Mark's cane clicking on the curb. 'Fine friend you are, leaving me like that,' he complained.

'Well I didn't think she would take it out on you.'

'Well, she did, and I was scared; I didn't know if it was a chair or her hand bag she was hitting me with, you should try being blind.'

'I did and it was lots of fun,' It was my turn to dodge as Mark swung his cane in the direction of my voice.

Mark was looking most unhappy and continued, 'She used to give me a discount, now she said full price--if ever.'

'Sorry about that, but why did you get a discount?'

'Because she didn't have to put make up on,'

'See all the perks you get being sight impaired?' I said trying to cheer him up. 'Plus you have a wonderful girlfriend that looks after you like a mother; isn't making love with her better than all these other women you have momentary pleasures with?'

Mark looked heavenward as if seeking forgiveness for his mortal sins.

'Yes, it is magic with her, sometimes I see stars.'

'That must be wonderful,' I replied, feeling a twinge of romantic nostalgia.

'Not really; it's when I bang my head on the bed post!' Mark was back to his impossible self.

Allan F Scott

The End

Le Mans 1957

MY FIRST GRAND PRIX

I had seen races at Brands Hatch and Silverstone, but in 1957 the thought of the Le Mans Grand Prix seemed so much more exciting and exotic. The only real way to go was by road and ferry of course.

With the paper work from the 'AA' in the glove compartment, my friend Ray in the passenger seat as navigator and my suitcase tied on top, we were off--my 1938 Ford giving its all as we sped towards Dover. The speedometer climbed to 40 mph. a velocity that always produced a shout of approval from Ray, and providing we were not impeded by a hill or a high wind, that is where the needle hovered.

We followed the signs to the ferry terminal and joined a lengthy line-up of Bentleys, Jaguars and several Austin Healeys. Our paper work checked, and a sticker that reminded me to drive on the right in Europe fixed to my windscreen, we approached the he ferry ramp. Had two acts of fate not plotted against us, I'm sure we would have smoothly glided up the ramp and onto the car deck.

However, due to a very high tide, an almost vertical ramp reared in front of me. I held back waiting for the car ahead to move and leave me room to have a run at it. When the car in front was halfway up, I built up speed and bounced over the ramp flap onto the ramp. I was congratulating myself we would make the car deck, when the car ahead stopped. I tried to dog-leg up the ramp but to no avail. We slowed and stopped, Ray pulled hard on the hand brake and I pressed on the brake pedal. Much to my relief we didn't roll back. The car ahead started to slowly move, I eased up the clutch and Ray slackened his grip on the hand brake. But, it was not to be; our engine stalled, I pulled the starter and we repeated the process, it stalled again. The deck officer waved us forward, but all he heard was a feeble hiccup from my old Ford.

'What's the problem?' he asked.

'Ramp's too steep,' I replied and I noticed Ray was sitting very low in his seat.

The officer pointed. 'Hold it there, I'll get the two behind you to move back down, then you back down, turn on the dock and head up the ramp––but backwards this time. Use reverse and you'll have a lower gear ratio. You'll make it in reverse,' he assured me.

'I'm sorry, I'm holding everyone up,' I ventured in my subservient Liverpudlian accent.

The deck officer smiled down at me and whispered: 'I love it when I see these rich old codgers in their Jaguars gnashing their aristocratic teeth in frustration. Nothing makes me chuckle more than a fellow scouser pushing them back down the ramp with an old Ford.'

Ray and I joined in his laughter, the Jaguar behind tooted.

'Can't wait to give that old tooter the good news,' our deck officer winked and headed in the offender's direction. Slowly, guided by the officer the three cars behind us gingerly backed down the ramp, and onto the dock.

I acknowledged his wave, and we slowly backed down. I did a tight circle and waved on by the officer, started to reverse up the ramp. I wasn't trying for speed, in fact, the officer walked past us to assume his original post at the top of the ramp and we triumphantly chugged to a halt next to him.

'Congratulations, you've made my day,' he said, and waved at the applauding passengers leaning over the rail on the deck above us.

We decided it was beer time and headed into the lounge. 'Nothing tastes as good as a beer after a nerve wracking experience,' Ray sighed, I agreed. Our officer joined us and I bought him an orange juice, with a little vodka added, just to kill the bacteria.

'That was a bit tricky,' I said sipping on my beer.

He nodded, 'Good practice for you, now you know what you have to do when we arrive at Calais.'

'But then it'll be easy, because it's down the ramp.' I laughed.

'No!No! he replied seriously, 'France is a lot higher than England, really, really a steep climb.'

'I better have another beer,' I moaned.

'You'd better,' and he winked at the barmaid.

It was early evening when we arrived at Le Mans and having been warned about the lack of accommodation, we had sleeping bags and were prepared to rough it outdoors by the race track.

The road was rutted and bumpy, and as if that wasn't bad enough, it turned into cobbled streets as we drove into the town.

Then as if by magic, it was as smooth as silk.

'What a great road,' I commented.

'Sure is,' Ray agreed. 'What are all those straw bails for on the corner?'

'Maybe Friday is market day,' seemed a logical reply.

It was then I saw a blur in my rear view mirror. It shot past. Then another.

'Holy smoke,' Ray yelled, 'what were those?'

'Someone is in a hurry, and here's more.' Zoom! - zoom! and they whizzed past us, my old Ford vibrating in their slipstream.

I looked at the next cluster of straw bails and the famous bridge over the road.

'You know, I think we're on the race track; you must have missed a sign back there,' I complained to Ray. At that point a large lorry loaded with vegetable crates and exuding clouds of diesel fumes growled past us, the driver waving out the window. Next an Austin Healey, a red MG. All I wanted to do--was find an exit and park.

I carefully edged my way to the outside of the track and when an opening appeared in the straw bails I headed quickly through it. I breathed a sigh of relief as a large green field lay ahead. 'Now what?' Ray asked.

A small uniformed figure at the far side of the field was waving a flag in our direction. We bounced over the grass towards him, and with an assertive wave of his flag we were directed to a point on the grass, and coached in line with military precision.

Ray and I were still laughing at the adventure as I pulled my suitcase off the roof. 'You two made it,' said the owner of a green Austin Healey who wandered over. 'Saw you, getting on the ferry,' he grinned. 'A very tricky operation.'

'Not only that, we've just done a few laps of the track to warm up.' Ray nodded at the stranger.

'You are crazy,' the Austin driver proclaimed. 'They have more accidents the night before, than in any of the races. It's open to anyone till nine o'clock, so the local hotrods have dinner, a bottle of wine, then drive the track as fast as their old jalopies will take them.'

We enjoyed the food and the circus atmosphere that prevailed throughout the night. There was everything from a merry-go-round, to a contest for a naked lady who could sit the longest time in a bathtub full of snakes. One lady contestant was quite gargantuan, we decided the snake should get first prize!

Next morning, we stood next to the grandstand and watched the famous Le Mans Grand Prix start. The drivers lined up like marathon runners, ran to their cars, jumped in, started up, and away they went.

For the first twelve hours or so of the 24-hour race, the cars sounded like the finely tuned mechanical marvels they were. But, then problems became evident, oil leaks, exhaust pipes falling off, gears grinding and the beautiful paint work becoming scarred and scraped.

It was sad to see these supercharged pure-breds driven to near destruction in only 24-hours. As Ray said, with great conviction. 'It's done so people like you and I can enjoy the latest in motoring technology and drive safely on the highways and byways of the continent.'

'Plus backwards up ramps,' I added.

'That too,' Ray concluded.

Allan F Scott

The End

London 1958

THE END OF AN ERA

There was a well worn phrase applied to pit drummers, as we were called.

One eye on the music, one eye on the conductor and one eye on the stage.

The performers brought their own music, tattered and covered with ten years of drummer's scribbling, and frequently illegible. Then during the rehearsal you would add to these scribblings, with your own coloured pencil of choice.

The act that brought to mind the End of an Era was called, Night and Day. A dance act in the Fred Astaire and Ginger Rogers mode. She was white, he was black, and it is not hard to imagine the title of their theme song..

As the conductor passed out the music he said, 'Quite tricky for you, all drums in the middle.' He was right, the drum rhythms had to fit the dance steps all the way, plus several times the drums played a rhythm, and the dancers would repeat it.

After a few stops and starts, I realised this was going to take some time to smooth out. So I suggested to the dancers that the three of us should have a run through after the rehearsal, and not take up the whole orchestra's time.

They were delighted with this idea, and when the stage and pit emptied they knelt at the edge of the footlights and introduced themselves.

'I'm Elsie, and this is Percy, thanks for doing this.'

Two hours later we finished, it was a wonderful experience for me, and we hoped a series of perfect performances would result.

On stage Night and Day looked like two movie stars, he tall and handsome in white tails, she petite, blond and beautiful in a flowing black dress, which when discarded for tap routines showed off her beautiful long dancers legs to full advantage.

I imagined them driving off into the sunset in a white convertible, but was surprised to see them--board a number 8 bus one night.

The three of us had a good time and quite a rapport developed between us. Sometimes I would change the drum solo, and Percy would follow it every time, give me a wink and do his solo which I had to follow. The spontaneity inspired them both to laughter, which the audience picked up on, and applauded wildly.

During our nightly after show visits to the pub, I learnt a lot about Elsie and Percy. They met during the war when Elsie was with ENSA entertaining the troops, and Percy with the US Air Force.

She had been doing her dance act at a US Base, during which she asked members of the audience to join her on stage to try their skill at tap dancing. Percy volunteered, and proceeded to steal the show.

He became a regular visitor to her little Curzon Street studio, helping her with the lessons and trying to make little Cockneys into the next Bojangles. Several months later they were married and decided to go professional after the war.

It had been thirteen years now, and as they confessed, felt they were getting a little over-the-hill for this life. Plus theatres, were being turned into dance halls, super markets and bowling alleys. Now they were lucky to work one week out of every month.

As we said our 'Goodbye's' in the pub after the last show Percy gave me his card. Very elegant it was, with a picture of them both dressed to the hilt, waving from the rear seat of a white Rolls convertible. The address and phone number was on Elgin Avenue.

Several months later I was driving in that part of London. I suddenly thought of Elgin Avenue. I retrieved the card from the glove compartment and checked the address. I could phone, but no phone booth was in sight.

I left the car and walked to their address, an old three story row house that had been fashionable in the early nineteen hundreds. I saw apartment three was in the basement. Looking down through the railings I could see a light in the front room.

'Well here goes,' I thought, and applied the knocker several times. After a few minutes, I heard footsteps and the door opened a few inches, 'Yes,' a voice said, it was Percy.

'It's me Allan.'

'Oh, Elsie, it's Allan!' he shouted into the void behind him and Elsie appeared. 'Come in, but it's a bit untidy at the moment.'

Percy opened the door into the front room, cold and dark as only a London basement can be.

They led me into the kitchen and Elsie put the kettle on a rather dilapidated old gas stove; the flame flared for a moment and then died.

'I think there are a few pennies by the meter,' Elsie said.

'That's OK I'll get it,' and I took a shilling from my pocket, sliding it into the slot and heard the satisfying clump as it was accepted by the meter.

'Not much in furniture at the moment I'm afraid, but you can sit on this,' and Elsie pulled one of several orange boxes stacked against the wall up to the rickety table.

Percy joined us, and laughing said, 'Welcome to the Savoy.'

'Are you moving?' I asked .

'No, I know it looks a bit bare, but we live in the kitchen and use the front room to practice in.' I glanced in the direction of the front room, I could see it was devoid of any furniture. Just a well polished floor.

I tried not to show my surprise at the sparse surroundings. The bedroom door was open and I could see a large mattress covered with a brown blanket on the floor and a mirror leaning against the wall. The only sign of domestic creativity, two more orange boxes placed at the sides of the bed, these covered in red table cloths.

The kitchen door opened on to the back yard, a large portion of which was taken up by the sturdy, red brick, outdoor toilet.

Apart from several pots and pans hanging from nails, the only other item in the kitchen was a large dented zinc bathtub also hanging from a large nail.

While we talked, I noticed how impoverished Elsie and Percy looked, she in a shapeless old dress, he in threadbare trousers and a blue pullover, worn through at the elbows.

They went on to tell me all the theatres on the circuit they used to work for had closed. The only work they had, had in the last year had been private parties, to which they had to take their own records, eliminating any interaction with a live drummer, which had been a big part of their act.

'No fun anymore,' Percy said, Elsie nodded her head sadly in agreement.

'No--more money in bowling alleys,' Percy glumly added.

Elsie lit up, as only people with theatrical training can do.

'Percy is going to be a bus driver,' and she leant across the table and took his hands in hers. Looked into his eyes and said: 'He will be the best damn bus driver in London.'

It wasn't what she said, but the pride with which she said it, that I will always remember. She was a very special woman, and I had witnessed a very special moment.

I felt it was time to leave and we exchanged, 'Good Luck' in both directions.

I sat in the car looking at the laughing immaculate couple pictured on their business card. They did look like millionaires on a vacation.

But my inner voice asked, 'Have I witnessed the end of an era—–or the end of an illusion?'

Allan F Scott

The End

Edmonton 1965

THE HOUSE SITTER

Edmonton in 1965, was becoming a very prosperous city. Construction was booming, and people had started to arrive from all over the world.

I was playing at the Old Bailey, a local cocktail lounge, during our break a young man chatted to us and said how much he enjoyed our trio.

He went on to say he had been here only two months and loved the unrestricted way of life. Expounding further he said he was in construction and what a pleasure it was to work in Canada.

The young man introduced himself as Dave. I used to see him zipping around town in a very tired-looking yellow Volkswagen, and assumed he was... a construction worker.

About a year later we met by accident and he told me he was going to Bermuda to be married and would be away two months. On his return they would be having a house party, would we like to play for it?

'Sure, as long as it's a Sunday,' I replied. He pulled his diary out of his briefcase and gave me a date about twelve weeks away.

Dave told me his future wife was the daughter of his governess, but they hadn't seen each other for two years, though they had corresponded regularly.

This should have given me a clue, as it is not usual for a construction worker to have a governess, let alone use the word.... correspond.

Later towards the end of the summer, I had a phone call, 'Dave here.' I had to fake for a few minutes, while I tried to recollect who Dave was.

When he mentioned the house-warming, it clicked, 'Oh, that Dave,' I said.

'We have the party set for Sunday and we will have two dance areas; one in the house and one by the pool. It will depend on the weather which we use.'

'Why don't you just pipe the music from the house to the pool, then you can use both areas,' was my smart idea. 'If you have room,' I added. I heard him chuckle. 'We have room enough I think.'

It was not easy to find the address as it was on the outskirts of town, by the river, and as far a I knew had not been developed. But then, I saw the balloons, tied to power poles, leading to a distant point on the horizon. The next sighting was a security guard, who stopped me and asked, 'You have an invitation?'

'ER....No, Dave just phoned me,' and I loosened my coat so he could see my tuxedo.

He wasn't impressed and asked if I was an entertainer.

'Well, yes I am in the band.'

'Mr.Maclean has given us three names, you must be one of them.'

'Scott,' I said. He looked at his watch and made a notation on his clipboard.

'You will turn left at the main gate, use the tradesman's entrance and park in the designated area.' And he waved me on.

As I reached the main gate, I saw Dave's yellow Volkswagen parked just inside. 'I'll park next to him,' I thought, but I had hardly put my front wheels through the front gate, when a whistle blew and a guard came rushing over.

'Round the side, tradesman's entrance,' he shouted.

This was not the little intimate party I had expected; I had hoped to see a friendly Dave somewhere.

I carried my drums through the already thriving kitchen into the large foyer. I saw a grand piano in a room big enough for a night club. Here I set my cases down and returned for three more.

I had just finished setting up my drums when a tall, sun-tanned distinguished lady in a flowing, flowered dress swept by. 'Make sure you remove those cases before the guests arrive,' she snapped, then left a typewritten letter on the piano, and was gone.

The letter was the order of dances, including two breaks for us. Nothing was to be left to chance. By now I needed moral support and was pleased when the other two members of our trio arrived.

They had not, unlike myself, had the experience of playing for aristocracy and were feeling, and looking a bit put out.

'Jesus,' Ernie our tenor man grouched. 'Park here, use the back door, check your shoes are clean, leave your coat and case in the store room. It was easier to get into the maximum security than here. It makes me nervous.'

'You're nervous, I'm Jewish,' Max our piano man said, 'and what's that funny red flag with the little Union Jack hung everywhere.'

''That's the Bermuda Flag,' I said. 'After dinner and before the speeches it will be marched in, and we play the anthem.'

'I don't know the Bermuda Anthem.' Max said in a worried voice.

'It's easy.' I said. 'It's in G flat major and seven-eight time. I just beat seven in and away you go.'

'Right I'm off,' Max said heading for the door, where he nearly collided with the tall lady, who was sweeping through again.

She looked down at him, 'Make sure you get all those cases away, and you have the flag draped correctly over the piano.'

'Certainly, Commandant,' was Ernie's disgruntled retort. She gave him a withering look and swept out again.

Max retreated to the safety of his piano bench and began reading the dance sequence. 'What's this about honouring the Queen if we have to use the main corridor,' he said, pointing at a paragraph, at the end of our instructions.

'You have to bow discreetly, as you pass her portrait,' I said. 'It would be on your way to the washroom.'

He eyed me in disbelief and Ernie added, 'When you're in the washroom, you have to turn to the portrait, pull your fly up with your left hand and salute with the right hand. Don't get it mixed up, or it could be very painful.'

We followed orders, as Ernie called them, starting dead on six p.m. with a waltz, playing at first to an empty room, and then as the guests arrived, to a very full room.

We ignored the program to insert a request, and the commandant swept in.

'Please stick to the program; you'll confuse the guests if you deviate.'

Not wishing to be a deviant, Max modulated to the song on the program.

We were just wondering if we were at the right party, when Dave appeared bearing a drink for each of us. 'Sounds great,' he said. We relaxeds, sipped our drinks and chatted, then--in came the commandant.

Max and I immediately started playing, but Dave put his arm round her and said, 'I'd like you to meet my wife.'

'Well...fancy that,' Ernie exclaimed at an attempt at politeness. Later Dave took us on a tour of the house: Eight bedrooms, library, two kitchens etc. but the most interesting facet, was that the house was built round the heated swimming pool and hot tub, plus the master bedroom had a rope from it's balcony, from which you could swing right into the pool.

Everything was electronic, the front gates, the pool covers and the spotlights located all round the house. All operated from a small panel by the front door.

As ordered, we finished at 11 p.m. and Dave took me into his office to write a cheque. He handed it to me saying how pleased he was that the house was finished, and was treating his wife and staff to a ski trip next week. As a 'thank you' for all their hard work.

'How would you like to house sit for us?' he asked. 'I'm not too happy about leaving the place empty. Plus you have the new pool, you can have friends over, practice and I'll pay you of course.'

'Sounds great,' I said.

'Fine, that's one thing less to worry about. My wife will tell you about everything, if you can be here about nine on Saturday morning.'

'Great,' I said, with more enthusiasm than I felt. Remembering his wife--the commandant.

The following Saturday I drove up to the front gate, pressed the button, that said Press. The gates swung open and this time I parked at the front door. Feeling rather important.

A female voice from a speaker above the front door said, 'Could you park at the side Mister Scott, we are expecting our taxi.' 'Here we go again,' I thought, but at least she called me Mister.

As I reached the front door it swung open and the voice said, 'We are in the kitchen Mr. Scott.'

I headed along the hall, this time ignoring The Queen and into the kitchen.

Madame Commandant positively beamed at me when I entered, exclaiming, 'We are so delighted you are doing this for us.' She emphasised us by raising a large rotund, striped ginger cat in my direction.

I was just wondering if I should shake paws with it, when Dave stuck his head round the door.

'Taxi is here. Oh, Hi Allan, has Margaret filled you in?'

'Of course I have Dear,' she said, as she place a list in my hand.

'It's all there,' she whispered. 'Marmaduke's food is here,' and she opened a cupboard to reveal many varieties of pussy cat treats. 'He'll come when he hears the tin opener.'

She gave me a smile, that guaranteed my obedience, kissed Marmaduke on top of his head, placed him in my arms and walked out the kitchen door.

Marmaduke touched my nose with his, gave me a round eyed look of indifference, rotated in my arms, jumped to the floor and too walked out the kitchen door. I followed and watched the party load into the taxi, marshalled by the commandant.

Dave waved as the taxi negotiated the driveway, and they were gone.

As I stood in the empty kitchen, realising, the entire house was empty, I had moment of panic. A series of hypothetical, what ifs, ran through my mind. 'Smarten up,' my inner voice said--'and read your list.'

'Tin opener, I'll try that.' I pressed the button and the utensil buzzed aimlessly, as no tin was in place. Immediately Marmaduke slid round the kitchen door, tail erect, expectant and wide eyed. 'Caught you!' I laughed. If only I could manipulate the commandant like that I thought.

I was still toying with this delightful fantasy, when a buzzer sounded in the hall, and a light flashed next to the wall phone. I picked up the phone and a voice said. 'Safeway delivery.' I looked at the wall panel trying to find a button inscribed Gate, then the voice said, 'Gates must be stuck again, I'll climb over.'

From my position, I could see the top of a truck and then a man's head as he climbed on the hood, a large box in his arms; then I saw it, Gate.

Quickly I pressed the button, but by then, the man was half over the gate and as it opened, he was suspended and wedged against the wall, body one side of the gate, arms containing the box hanging to the other side.

I opened the front door, shouting, 'Hang on! I could see he was not amused, and I pressed the Close button. The gates then pushed him back onto the hood of his truck where he sat glaring at the front door. So I opened the gates again, and I saw the box pushed inside by a snow covered boot. An engine revved and he was gone.

Marmaduke sat on the steps watching this episode and I said, 'Don't tell the commandant.' He ignored the front door I held open for him, and entered via his cat door. 'OK, ignore me, but wait until feeding time.' I said, and closed the door.

By the third day I felt I had control of everything. I could operate all the alarms and flood lights, open and close the gates, slide the covers off the pool and hot tub, at the touch of a button.

Marmaduke appeared at the sound of the opener, and he only had one further disappointment when I opened a tin of beans by mistake. But he did have a habit of appearing outside the French windows, just when I thought he was safely locked in for the night. It reminded me of Alice in Wonderland. Suddenly he would materialise, paws and nose pressed against the window.

'Serves you right.' I would yell at him. But how did he do it?

I followed him, he would jump on the kitchen counter and crawl into a tube, that I thought was for garbage disposal, and slide down into the garden.

I was now thirty-seven, a dangerous age for men, because you keep falling in love and hoping the next romantic affair, will realise all your fantasies.

'Your last kick at the matrimonial cat,' as Ernie used to say.

This week was no exception, I felt I had met the ideal woman, a violinist in the orchestra.

I asked her over for dinner, and what could be more romantic than an evening spent in the pool and hot tub, the overhanging trees beautified by the recent snowfall, under the twinkling stars of an Alberta evening.

Anne was to arrive about seven, so I tested the lights and gates, to avoid any mishap in this area. I set the hot tub temperature, placed a bottle of champagne and a plate of strawberries in the snow alongside the tub. Lastly I ringed the tub with candles. I stepped back to view my creativity and had to admit even Hollywood would have difficulty to outclass this web of seduction.

Anne arrived, and I skilfully opened the gates and flicked on the flood lights as she parked her car. I had cold chicken and white wine set in the enormous dining room overlooking the river. I could see Anne was relaxed and enjoying herself.

'It's pool time,' I said. 'You put your swim suit on and I'll meet you at the pool. A good swim and then the hot tub.'

I ran upstairs and into the master bedroom, put on my swim trunks and to impress her, I was going to slide down the rope and swing into the pool.

I tossed the rope over the balcony and swung above the pool, sliding down the rope as I did so. 'Hi Anne,' I yelled. Hoping to create an impressive splash.

'You better take the cover off first,' she yelled back. I looked down, not at blue water but a yellow plastic cover.

My Tarzan impression came to a sudden halt, as I realised my predicament. My ego diminished as I slowly and painfully climbed back up the rope, huffing and puffing as I struggled to climb back over the balcony.

I was muttering obscenities as I trotted downstairs, found and pressed the button for Pool Cover. I heard Anne whoop, then a splash as she dived in.

It was starting to snow as I joined her. I watched her effortlessly stroke the length of the pool, putting my self-taught backstroke to shame.

'I'll check the hot tub,' I softly murmured.

Everything looked just as romantic as I had left it. Anne will love this, and I slid down to the seat level; the hot foamy water rising to my neck. My feet gently touched the bottom and I leant back.

What's this? Something touched my feet. I made a tentative prod with my big toes, and yes, there was something on the bottom. I took a deep breath and submerged, my hands exploring round my feet. I made contact, gripped what ever it was, and pulled it to the surface.

My heart stopped --it was Marmaduke! And a very soggy, dead Marmaduke at that.

To say I had mixed emotions was putting it mildly. Whilst, I felt very sorry for the deceased, he didn't contribute anything in his present state, to my planned romantic evening.

Anne would be here any second, waving a dead pussy cat at her and saying--'Guess who I found in the tub?' Might spoil her relaxed and sensitive mood.

I jumped out the tub, Marmaduke under my arm, rushed to the trees and straddled him across a branch six feet in the air. There he rested like an overfed leopard in the Serengeti.

My sombre mood was broken, when I heard Anne approaching.

'Looks beautiful, why so glum?' she said and started to rub my back as we slid into the warm soapy confines of the tub.

Her presence and the champagne soon dispelled any thoughts of the inanimate Mamaduke. The snow increased, the drifting flakes enhancing the romantic setting even more.

Next morning, my plan was to bury poor Marmaduke and prepare my tale of woe for the commandant. Maybe.... breaking it to Dave first.

Anne and I had just finished breakfast, the phone rang: 'Dave here, we'll be home in about an hour. How's everything?'

'Oh great, I'm tidying up, and I'll leave the heat on for you.' I did a hurried check round the house and rushed to the pool area, but with the heavy snow, it was impossible to locate Marmaduke's resting place.

'Phew,' I sighed smiling at Anne as the gates closed behind us.

Later that evening Dave phoned and thanked me for doing such a good job, and asked if I had seen Marmaduke, 'Not this morning,' I said.

'Oh... I guess he'll be hanging around the house somewhere,' and Dave hung up. Not realising the truth of his last statement.

Later in the week Dave appeared in the lounge and came to chat to us during our break.

'You'll never believe this,' was Dave's first statement. 'I located Marmaduke. He was up a tree, frozen. I found him when I decided to cut the branches round the hot tub. When I put him on the ground, he looked like a miniature sphinx; frozen solid he was.'

'Well, fancy that,' I said, repelling a sudden attack of honesty.

I was saved from clearing my conscience by Max tapping me on the shoulder. 'Time to play again.' We walked to the stage. 'What was that about a cat?' Max asked eyebrows raised.

'Oh, it's hard to explain,' I replied, as I sort comfort and security behind my drums and we started our first number.

It was a slow blues Max had written, and as yet untitled. We finished to mild applause and clinking glasses. 'I should give that a name,' Max said.

'How about.... Blues for Marmaduke,' I suggested.

'Great,' and he announced it over the mike.

In the corner I saw Dave, he nodded and laughingly gave me the thumbs up sign. I waved back, relaxed, and had a feeling of closure. Marmaduke's unexpected rise to pussycat heaven would be musically celebrated, at least three nights a week in the Old Bailey Lounge.

Allan F Scott

The End

Edmonton 1968

MR. PERSUASION.

In any career, I'm sure one looks back with almost contempt, at the steps of the ladder climbed to reach ones present position.

I was now timpanist with the Edmonton Symphony Orchestra and Professor of Percussion at the University of Alberta. No more late dances, or sweating in a pub for twenty dollars, no longer did I have to haul my drums through the snow to the back door of the Legion, and worse, out again at one in the morning when it was twenty below zero, returning home smelling of stale beer and smoke. All my moving was done by orchestral assistants, and I was enjoying a vocation that was both dignified and prestigious. Gradually the phone calls petered out from my compatriots of former days, because; I said, I am now a timpanist.

Most of them thought that was an East Indian religion, one friend suggested I meet his mother, who had just become a Mormon.

Then came the call from Mr. Persuasion, as he was known. Who, in previous years I had worked for many times. Usually with regret. He aspired to be a trumpet player, had a big band which he loved to front, cigar in one hand, trumpet in the other.

No one had ever heard him play the trumpet and with a big band and three other trumpets, all he did was put it to his lips and mime when the other three played. If a solo was called for, he would puff on his cigar, point at the other trumpeters and say to the nearest saxophonist, 'Got to give these kids a chance.'

When he phoned me, I explained I was now a timpanist. 'Great,' he said, 'very healthy, but I have a great gig, one hundred and fifty dollars for twenty minutes, that's more than you'll ever get banging drums in the Symphony.'

'Timpani,' I replied.

'Sure,' he continued, 'you'll be playing with Canada's new top country singer.'

'Anne Murray,' I asked, my interest aroused.

'No, Susie Edson, she's taking over from Anne Murray.'

'I don't know her.'

'You don't know Susie Edson, where have you been?'

'Well...ER.. working with the Symphony,' I almost apologised.

'I told you that stuff is not good for you.' Mr. Persuasion snapped back.

'I've got Matt on piano, Bob on guitar and the other Bob on bass. Just like old times, and all you have to do is play for about twenty minutes in the intermission... four or five songs. That's it.'

'The intermission of what?' I asked, beginning to feel it was too good to be true.

'The indoor rodeo, biggest show of the year at the arena and you will be part of it. Plus walk away with one hundred and fifty dollars, that's more than three hundred dollars an hour! For that I could get Buddy Rich.'

'Buddy who?' I laughed beginning to be swept along by his enthusiasm. 'OK, when is it.' I could hear Mr.P. flicking through his diary, then he said:

'The last Friday and Saturday of the month.'

'That is two nights then?' I questioned.

'Of course, Saturday is already sold out.'

'So it is one hundred and fifty for two nights?'

'Yes, but only twenty minutes and can you leave your drums set up. Just zoom in and out, unless you want to watch the rodeo.'

He put on his British accent saying, 'You can have the Royal Box and bring your favourite concubine.'

'Great,' I replied, 'I'll phone your wife later.'

However, later I phoned Matt, our piano man to see if he had been given the same spiel as myself.

'Yes, Mr. P does go on, but it's a gig. So I'll see you on Thursday,' 'Thursday, I echoed.

'Yes, for a rehearsal,' Matt replied.

'He didn't mention a rehearsal,' I said indignantly.

Matt sighed, 'We have to have a run through, and it's only four songs, about twenty minutes should do it.'

This mythical twenty minutes had now self-multiplied three times, and I was developing a sense of foreboding about the whole situation.

Matt's cheery voice continued, 'what is twenty minutes?'

'Well, I have to drive there and set my drums up.'

'Oh for Pete's sake, I'll drive and help you with your drums if you stop whining, since you became a drummer in the symphony we don't see you anymore.'

'Timpanist,' I said indignantly.

'Excuse me while I get on my knees, see you Thursday.' and Matt hung up.

When we arrived about seven on Thursday I was glad of Matt's company and the extra pair of hands, and of course, nobody knew anything about a band, or where we had to rehearse.

We cornered a man in a yellow jacket that boasted the word, Security.

'It will be a room with a piano,' I said as pleasantly as possible, considering I had dragged three large drum cases half way round the arena.

'Oh, that will be the staff lounge, way up there,' and he pointed up a series of never ending cement steps that faded into the roof.

Matt and I huffed and puffed our way up to a room reeking of last nights beer and smoke, but giving us a birds eye view of the arena and containing a piano that looked as if it had been used for target practice by the Edmonton Oilers.

Matt tried a few chords, groaned, saying, "well I guess they'll have a good one for the show."

The Bobs arrived puffing and panting:

'Why don't we just go on the roof,' guitar Bob gasped.

'No way I'm bringing my bass amp up here.' Bass Bob added as they piled next to the piano.

'It's only twenty minutes,' I said, trying to cheer them up. '

'Hell, it took me twenty minutes to get up the stairs,' Bass Bob snorted glaring at me. Ten minutes later we were set up, Matt noodling on the piano, while explaining it was unplayable. Both Bobs trying to tune to the unplayable instrument.

The door opened and a very pretty young lady complete with guitar, cowboy boots and a wide brimmed hat entered, followed by an older and angrier version, obviously her Mother.

'Can you believe it?' angry Mother growled, 'nobody knew who we were or where to go.'

'Same thing happened to me,' I said, trying to sound sympathetic.

'Yes, but your only the drummer.'

'Timpanist,' I replied. This statement was greeted with an indifferent shrug.

'You must be Susie, welcome to Edmonton,' Matt said ignoring the irate Mother, and turning his charm on the sixteen year old prodigy.

'Let's start, four or five numbers won't take us long.'

'What! we intend to do an hour at least,' Mother growled. 'We didn't come all the way from Toronto for four songs, my daughter has just done a recording with twelve top notch songs on it.'

'Let's have a look at the music then,' Matt said, ignoring Mother and extending his hand to Susie. Susie and Mother looked at each other, then at Matt.

'I don't have any music,' Susie replied.

Matt looked from one to the other. 'You must have the guitar parts for the songs on the record.'

Susie shook her head, 'no we just did them in the studio, it took us three days.'

'Well that doesn't help us,' Matt was now frowning and looking at the Bobs.

Guitar Bob, tranquil as ever said, 'Susie, you play the chords and I'll write them down.'

'That will take for ever,' Matt interrupted.

Bob shrugged asking if anyone had a better idea. We all looked very blank.

'Susie, sit here, so I can see your left hand. The rest of you may as well go for coffee and bring a few extra back.'

'I'll stay and put my feet up,' Mother said. Bob rolled his eyes at me as we retreated out the door.

Matt and I spent half an hour looking at the steers and horses, I aired my knowledge, by explaining the steers were the ones with the horns.

Matt pulled a face and said, 'I grew up in rodeo land, these small steers are to be used for team roping.' He continued, 'two cowboys have to rope the steer while at full gallop. One puts a lasso around the horns or neck and the other puts his lasso round the hind feet. They wrestle it to the ground and hold it there.'

'What are these, with horns as wide as a London bus?' I asked, making sure I was standing at a safe distance from the corralled animals.

'They are beautiful, Texas Longhorns, King of the cattle.' Matt expounded.

He slapped one on the rump and ducked as the horns swung a few inches above his head.

'Wow they sure move quickly,' I gasped as I jumped back a few more feet.

'They will be using them to demonstrate a round-up in the rodeo.' Matt continued, 'you watch the way the horses weave in and out and avoid those huge horns and then edge them into a corner.'

I interrupted Matt's reverie, 'better get back with the coffee.'

I edged in the door balancing the coffee and doughnuts on a cardboard plate, several pedantic guitar chords was the only sign of activity that greeted us.

Bob, pen in hand was methodically transcribing each chord. 'Here Matt write those out for piano and bass. Allan you can fill in once you hear them.'

Then he continued listening to Susie. Mother was still asleep spread over two chairs. I looked at my watch it was nearly nine o'clock.

I was just estimating how long before we could actually try anything, when the door burst open and a puffing young man asked if we were the band.

'No, we just come up here on Thursdays for a sing-a-long,' Matt said.

'Well the boss wants you in the arena in twenty minutes for a run through, be by the 'A' entrance at nine-thirty.' He left as quickly as he arrived, preventing us getting any answers to the obvious questions.

'Here we go again,' and I started to carry my so far un-played drums down the stairs, followed and helped by Matt and Bass Bob.

The 'A' entrance was where this all started, it seemed ages ago.

We had no sooner put down our equipment, than a man wearing a cowboy hat and a name tag pronouncing him 'Hank' rushed up to us.

'Are you the band?' We nodded to confirm his suspicions.

'Well climb on this,' he said pointing to a flatbed trailer.

'What for?' Matt asked.

'That's where you'll play from; when you're ready, we'll tow it into the centre of the arena. Be as quick as you can, because we're running behind schedule.'

'What about the piano?' Matt asked.

'That's on it's way,' and Hank pointed at two burly helpers pushing a dolly, on which the Rodeo Bernstien, wobbled precariously.

'Did you carry that down those steps?' I asked in amazement.

'No, we used the elevator, goes right to the staff room.'

Our quartet eyed him, and each other in disbelief.

By now the helpers were heaving our gear onto the flatbed and I was trying to set up some resemblance of a drum kit, the two amplifiers, and the last item, the piano, was lifted on the rear.

'Pull,' Hank yelled at the burly assistants, now two on each shaft, and we moved to the entrance, but as the arena floor was covered with turf and straw, it was uphill and our flatbed ground to a halt.

'We'll have to get a tractor,' Hank yelled and rushed away.

Then a voice, loud and clear boomed over the sound system, sounding like the Wizard of Oz. 'Where is the band, it should be playing in the centre by now. Get moving.'

The tractor arrived, Hank backed into the shafts, and the connection was made.

'Let's go,' and he goosed the engine. We went over the bump with no problem, but the piano didn't. It toppled off the back leaving Matt, who had decided to inject a little humour by playing Happy Days are Here Again pounding an invisible keyboard.

Much yelling, and the piano was hoisted back, Hank yelling at Matt to, 'Hold on to it!' We stopped in the centre after a bumpy ride, during which we had to hold onto everything.

The lights went out and the voice from above said: 'Tomorrow the lights will be out, but when a spotlight hits you, that is your cue to start playing.'

We obliged with just piano and drums, no power for the guitars.

'What about the guitars,' the voice boomed.

Matt dropped to his knees and assumed a position of prayer.

'We need power o'Lord, give us a cable.'

'Hank,' the voice boomed, 'take ten minutes and sort this out.'

We explained to Hank we needed a power cable hooked up, and Susie needed a microphone, and by the way, where was she?

'She is going to run on, when she hears her introduction music,' Hank said.

The voice boomed from above: 'Take the band back to the entrance and try again.' Hank went into reverse and tried to back us towards the entrance, but he was a miserable failure as a backer-upper.

The voice of wrath from above confirmed this, yelling, 'Forget it Hank, lights out.' We were plunged into darkness, still moving backwards, until we felt the crunch as we hit the barrier. Now we were all hanging onto our equipment, as it rattled around sounding like a hardware store in an earthquake.

'Right band to the centre,' the voice of wrath rising above our confusion , and Hank crunched into forward gear. Again we rattled over turf and sawdust to the middle.

Two running figures appeared out of the darkness each holding a yellow power cable, then tossed them to me, the only person not needing one. I disentangled myself and passed them to the two Bobs. Who immediately started vamping the intro music. I joined them, Matt joined in and we had sound. Umpa - Umpa - Umpa...we played wondering what was going to happen next.

A small white figure clutching a guitar and wearing a large white Stetson appeared running in our direction.

'Where are the steps?' she yelled and disappeared round the other side.

The spotlight hit us, just as we were hauling Susie onto the flatbed.

'No!, No!,' the voice from above boomed, 'you must be ready when the spotlight hits you.'

It is impossible to argue with a disembodied voice, so we ignored it and went back to Umpa-Umpa again. This is when we discovered Susie didn't have a mike, even if she had we still hadn't decided on her first song.

Another figure appeared holding a microphone, Susie grabbed it and broke into 'On the Road Again.' We all slid onto our musical positions and the voice from above announced. 'That sounds great.'

She was coming through the Arena's sound system, while our sound came from the amps on the flatbed.

It sounded like the Mormon Tabernacle Choir accompanied by a pub trio, but at this point we really didn't care.

The voice from above cut in, 'tomorrow you will have twenty minutes, then you will be whisked off before the round-up begins.' The voice continued, 'just remove the cables for now and we'll run the steers round so they can get used to the size of the arena; and Hank, hold the flatbed in position until the round-up is finished.'

I looked behind me, to see about twenty Texas Longhorns pursued by several whooping cowboys bearing down on us.

They split into two herds as they raced passed our flatbed, sawdust and turf flying in the air. I could see the cattle were going to miss us, but the horns were a different story, they swept off the music stands, amps, and straw bails that countrified our flatbed.

We huddled in the centre ready for the return stampede and back they came, dragging off any item they missed on the first run.

Hank appeared from under the wagon, wiping sawdust off himself, he was shaking his fist in the direction of the control booth.

We heard a God like chuckle: 'Sorry about that band, they were just supposed to trot out. Now Hank get the flatbed out of there, pronto.'

Hank shook both fists to the heavens as we bounced into entrance 'A' again, followed by several helpers carrying the items that had been swept from our precarious stage.

As we regrouped, I said to Matt. 'We should try for a gig at the Pamplona Bull run in Spain.'

'Sure pushing a piano down the street chased by fifty angry bulls, that would get my picture in the paper.'

'Fame comes in mysterious ways.' I laughed.

I looked at my watch, it was nearly eleven o'clock.

'That's the longest twenty minutes of my life,' I complained.

'We're off,' the Bobs growled, Matt and I nodded in agreement.

Friday night, the parking lot was filling up as I drove in. I parked and joined the rest of the quartet on the infamous flatbed. Matt was securing his music with bull dog clips to the piano.

'What if the piano falls off again?' I asked.

'Then, I won't need the music.' Matt laughed.

I noticed the piano was firmly held in place with two thick ropes, and the straw bails had been tied down.

'Nothing being left to chance tonight,' Bob guitar said as he handed me the song order. 'We'll just keep playing Country Roads if anything goes wrong.'

'Sure I'll just sing it if I get a longhorn up my tom-tom,' I laughed.

We sat on our flatbed for about an hour, quietly going through the songs Bob had so laboriously transcribed. Susie arrived and we had a pianissimo run through the program.

The spontaneous rehearsal was interrupted when Hank arrived and hooked up his tractor. 'See you later Susie,' we chorused.

'I hope so,' she laughed, waved and was gone.

Hank looking calmer than on the previous evening, and announced that the order had been changed. Instead of the Round-Up. we are to be followed by Steer Roping. Should be no problem, one steer comes in and out we go.

We were towed into the darkened arena, two figures ran out, power cables in hand. Clicked into sockets, little red lights on the amps glowed.

'Three-four,' Matt shouted and we began to vamp the introduction music, Umcha - Umcha - Umcha, echoed round the arena. The audience began to clap in time to our efforts.

The tiny figure of Susie appeared, ran up the steps, grabbed the mike off Bob, spotlight on, and the sounds of Country Roads filled the arena. Followed by wild applause.

The red light from the control booth was the cue for us to end and Hank to roll us out. Lastly the arena was plunged into darkness

All had gone like clockwork, but Murphy struck again, and the tractor refused to start.

The lights came on to find us still in the same place, I looked behind just in case we had the invasion of the Longhorns again, but just one bewildered little steer trotted out.

Our tractor finally started and commenced to push us back.

It was then the two cowboys galloped out .

One ran parallel to the steer and dropped a rope around it's neck.

The steer put on a burst of speed and ran round the far side of our flatbed.

Now we had a cowboy, rope in hand on one side, and the very upset steer on the other side of us, the rope performed the same function as the horns of the previous night, knocking over the amps and straw bails, we either ducked under it or jumped over it like a boxer doing skipping practice.

The other cowboy saved the day by putting a rope around the steer's hind feet, jumping off his horse and holding it until we disentangled ourselves.

The audience thought this was part of the show and we rolled off to quite the ovation.

Much to our amazement the Saturday night show went off without a hitch (no pun intended) and with much relief we unloaded our instruments from the flatbed.

The opulent form of Mr. Persuasion, cigar in hand materialised just as we finished.

'Great job boys,' he beamed. 'I told you twenty minutes, here are your cheques.'

'Great,' Matt said, taking the envelope, 'now about the other five hours.'

The two Bobs advanced on Mr. Persuasion: 'Yes, and my damaged amp, broken music stands, plus the six hours it took to write the music out.'

'Boys, please, Mr.P. whined. I was just going to offer you the Monster Truck Derby Show. Two hundred dollars for thirty minutes.'

Four voices shouted in perfect unison: 'NO WAY!'

I added, 'You can get Buddy Rich.'

Allan F Scott

The End

Edmonton 1970

NEVER TOO LATE

JACK.

Three words, I kept muttering to myself as I drove at five-thirty in the morning along Kingsway, to the Edmonton Municipal Airport, my inner voice replied with another three words, Let's go home.

It was a bright sunny morning in June, and the instructor had informed me it was ideal flying weather,when he phoned me the previous evening.

'Does it have to be so early?' I asked.

'Well, we can go later, but the air gets rough later in the day, and I think you would be happier with a smooth ride, for the first few times at least.'

This convinced me...earlier would be better.

I poked my head around the door of the deserted office and was slowly backing out, thinking... good I can go home When I was startled by a voice from behind. 'You must be Scott, beautiful day, let's go.'

My first impression of Jack was how young he looked, but I had reached the age of forty, and was realising that most authority figures had started to look young.

I followed him out the rear door to where a beautiful red and white Cessna was parked, gleaming in the morning sun, drops of dew twinkling on the polished wings.

'First: we do a walk-around, check the tires, oil, look for dents, chips off the propeller and make sure all moving parts are moving freely. See these!' and he waved several strips of red painted wood at me.

'These are the cause of more accidents than you can imagine, they're used to wedge the elevator and ailerons to stop them moving in the wind when the aircraft is parked outside. Guess what?' I couldn't guess what, and he continued, 'some people actually forget to remove them, and wind up in the fence at the end of the runway. Can you believe it?'

I was stuck for a reply to this--my first question. But, I was an expert at the non-committal reply, and nodded my head while mouthing, 'No.'

'Climb in the left seat and fasten your seat belt.' Jack hopped into the right seat and gave me a card labelled, Check List.

He asked me to read this out loud, and at about item twenty, the engine sprung to life. At last, I was looking through a whirling propeller.

'Now, the radio and really listen.' I pressed the button and really listened but not one word of the staccato instructions made sense. Except, permission to taxi.

'Do you drive a car?' Jack asked.

'Sure,' I replied, 'a Firebird.' Hoping this would impress him.

'Nothing like it. Put your feet on these pedals, fold your arms. All the steering on the ground is done with your feet.' With this he advanced the throttle and we started to move. 'Turn left past the hanger onto the taxi strip.'

As soon as I felt the need to turn I moved my hands to the yoke. 'Feet only, arms folded,' he said and tapped me on the hand with a rolled up newspaper.

After twenty years of driving with ones hands, it goes against all instincts to steer with the feet. So along the taxi strip we waddled.

'Hold it straight,' Jack complained and continued. 'Your brakes are just ahead of your toes on the pedals, one for each wheel.'

My mind was just analysing this information, when Jack continued. 'Stop at that white line.' My car experience took over, my right foot reached out to the brake pedal, and we did a very tight circle. 'Not quite what I had in mind,' Jack said, 'but it does keep the traffic controllers on their toes. Now refold your arms and remember, you have a brake for each wheel. Now follow the C taxi way until I tell you to stop.'

One observation I was making to myself, was how bumpy it was on the taxi way. The instrument panel jerked up and down and the whole machine rattled like my first car.

'Stop at the white line, and set your brakes.' This time I performed with a little more expertise.

'Now continue reading your check list.' I read up to item sixty, and we were still on the ground, but now I was instructed to turn towards what was called the active runway, and stop at yet another white line. During these manoeuvres Jack was chatting away on the radio. He hung up the mike, and told me to hold the yoke... gently.

'Turn onto the runway and keep the nose wheel on the white line. When the airspeed indicator reaches 50, start to ease back the yoke.' Here he tapped the dial with his newspaper, to make sure I was looking at the right one.

We rumbled along the runway until the dial read 50, and I gently pulled back as instructed. Suddenly, the rumbling and rattling stopped and I felt the gentle pressure on my lower back as we left the ground.

I was in the world of flight!

I had a moment of ecstasy before Jack tapped another dial. 'Try to keep to that line on your artificial horizon and you will be climbing at 15 degrees and this dial tells you your climbing speed of 700ft a minute, lastly your airspeed indicator reads 80 mph.

This was fascinating. 'One more thing,' Jack continued, 'always look out the window, because you're about to fly into the top floor of the hospital, and they won't like that one bit.'

'I've got it,' Jack said in rather a bored voice, and I released my vice-like grip in the yoke.

'That's the most important lesson so far. It's correct to check the instruments, but not if it involves flying into hospitals. Always one eye out the window.'

I was beginning to understand his method of instruction, he sets you up for an embarrassing situation, then explains how to recover, it certainly puts the point across.

He pointed at another dial, 'That is your compass, now press your left pedal gently and turn the yoke until it reads 100 degrees. Good, now ahead is Cooking Lake, which is a practice area. Now, fly towards it.'

I was beginning to enjoy this, the lake ahead reflected the morning sun, and I could see the earthlings below us... driving into town.

My reverie was interrupted, 'What is our altitude?' This was one dial I knew; the altimeter. '4000ft' I said. 'And how high above the ground are we?' Here I was stumped.

Jack reached across and showed me a map. 'Cooking Lake is 2419ft above sea level, so that means we are about 1500ft above the ground. Always check that and you won't try to land below ground level. It would ruin your whole day.'

I was still trying to read the small figures on the map, when Jack's voice interrupted. 'Better look out the window.' I was left wing down and starting an unintended turn.

'Concentrate, level out, and climb back to 4000ft.' I was down to 3200ft and hadn't noticed.

'Now, where is the Edmonton Airport?' he continued in rather a bored voice.

'Behind us,' I replied.

'Are you sure?'

I turned to look, but all I could see was a thick mist behind us. 'You came on a heading of 100 degrees, so to return you would add 180 to that figure and get what?'

This was like being in school again, 'Er... hum, 280 degrees,' I replied while trying to keep level.

'OK, remember that, always know where you're going, then you can figure how to get back again, using the reciprocal heading.'

An hour of climbing, turning, then descending, and it was time to head for home.

'Heading,' Jack said and I turned to 280 degrees, feeling quite pleased I had remembered the number.

'Notice any other aircraft?' Jack asked. I looked around.

'No, nothing I can see.'

'There are three Cessnas to our right and a D.C.3 about 2000ft above us. Always be aware of other traffic, it could spoil your whole outing if you bump into someone.'

By now I could see the outline of Edmonton through the morning mist. Jack was talking on the radio and looking out the window. 'I've got it,' he said and I noticed he was flying parallel with runway 16, where the adventure had started.

'We are on the downwind heading, we will make a left turn onto base leg and another left onto final. This is a left hand circuit, and we are required to be 1000 feet above ground level until we start our turn, then we begin a gradual descent. Traffic control told us we are number 4 for final, so we should be able to see three aircraft ahead of us.'

I looked ahead and saw three tiny models, the sun glinting on their wings.

The radio chatted away, and I heard Jack give an equally unintelligible reply.

'We are cleared to land, descending at 500feet a minute,' he tapped the dial, 'and at 75mph. I will trim out,' and he moved a small wheel I hadn't noticed before. He took his hands off the yoke. 'See... these aircraft are so stable they fly themselves. If all fails, hands off and they will correct themselves... as long as there are no heavy winds... and you have enough altitude of course.'

He replaced one hand on the yoke the other on the throttle and we glided to the runway, and touched down with a gentle bump.

'All yours," he said, and using my feet, arms folded, I gingerly turned off the runway and taxied to the Flying Club. Stopping with a jolt at the indicated yellow line.

Jack looked at me, a humorous glint in his eyes, 'Fine see you Thursday, unfasten your belt, open the door,' then with a bored sigh, ' better unfold your arms first.'

SOLO

We had done about ten hours of various manoeuvres, some very pleasant, like 180 degree turns, some quite frightening, like power on stalls, leading into spins, and the ultimate nerve test, power failure landings.

Here, the instructor will throttle back the engine without warning, and you are required to find a suitable area to land. This is done when you least expect it, usually, when you are just relaxing and enjoying the scenery. Then, splutter...splutter.. off goes the engine, I look at Jack and he seems oblivious to the situation he has put us in.

He raises his eyebrows, turns away, I and my dilemma are ignored. My mind races to visualise the instructions in the manual for this situation.

Head into the wind and look for a flat area, lower the flaps and slow to about 75 mph. His previous forceful instructions were beginning to sink in.

'That looks good,' I say out loud. Hoping for confirmation from my indifferent instructor. He starts looking at his newspaper and yawning.

Down we go to about 100ft, me wondering if the field I choose, is really as solid as it looks. The newspaper now rolled up, taps the airspeed indicator, Jack restores the power. 'Keep your nose down until the airspeed builds up...good, raise your flaps... lean forward.'

Lean forward...was something he said towards the end of the lessons, and had started to puzzle me.

'Why the lean forward?' I asked 'When I can see the perspiration through your shirt, I know it's about time to quit.' He was laughing, but added, 'don't forget your heading or it'll be dark before we get home.'

I had now about twelve hours of instruction and was beginning to feel at home in this environment, plus even understanding the Air Traffic Controller's instructions.

Jack would give me a heading, fold his coat into a pillow and take a nap, (or pretend to), while I navigated the blue skies above and around Edmonton.

Today after about twenty minutes Jack talked on the radio. Then turned to me, 'do a short field landing on runway eleven and pull onto the taxi way.' Now what have I done? I thought.

I landed as requested, even with a cross wind, left wing down into the wind, thus keeping the aircraft on the centre line.

Jack roused himself, opened the door, climbed out saying, ... 'It's all yours, do a few circuits and if you don't bend it I'll buy you a coffee.'

I pressed the mike button and told the controller I would be doing 'touch and goes.' Back came the wind direction and force, barometric pressure, active runway and which taxi way to use.

I was alarmed to hear the runway had been changed, which meant I had to taxi to the far end of the air port. Why does this happen to me? and I bounced along the never ending taxi strip.

Arriving at the runway threshold I did my run up. Everything sounded and looked good, the needles all in their correct positions. Changed my radio from ground to tower. Pressed the mike button and announced, 'VGF ready to go.' Heard a few jumbled words and looked towards Jack... but all I saw was an empty seat.

Then the calm voice of the controller, 'VGF cleared for take off.'

Here goes, and down the runway I headed. Off the ground in no time, and climbing to 3000ft. No one tapping the dials, or giving a perpetual barrage of criticism. How good it felt.

Then the seeds of doubt; do I really know what I am doing? What if my radio went dead? Stop worrying and look for other aircraft.

After three successful landings and take offs, I was feeling quite confident, and decided this would be my last landing for the day.

I was given clearance, and told 'You are number three for runway 34.'

I could see another Cessna, but only one. I asked about number 2 and the controller told me it was a Hercules, doing a straight in approach.

So he would be flying towards me.... then I saw him, a great lumbering monster gleaming in the morning sun, probably at twice my speed. As he descended towards the runway, I followed at what I thought was a reasonable distance, but noticed how bumpy the air was.

He landed, I landed, usually I just let the Cessna run until it slowed enough for me to turn off the runway.

I was admiring how gently the Hercules had touched down, when suddenly it reversed it's propellers and stopped on what could have been a dime. It was here that the turbulence hit me, and was enough to bring me to a dead stop, in fact I felt the nose lift and feared I might be standing on my tail. Then slowly he turned onto the first taxi way for the terminal.

I headed in the direction of the Flying Club. Taxied to the hangar and climbed out. I was feeling like Charles Lindbergh when he landed in Paris, but I didn't have twenty-five thousand people to greet me. Just Jack, leaning against the office door, hands in pockets, but he was smiling.

That was better than twenty-five thousand people for me.

When I entered the office I was greeted by a small round of applause from the office staff, and presented with a certificate stating: I had Flown Solo and Unaided for twenty-five minutes. I felt proud enough for it to be twenty-five hours.

'Come on Wilbur, I'll buy you a coffee,' Jack said, and we headed into the cafe, Jack performed as promised and produced two coffees.

'Now, a few points, always keep well behind and above the aircraft ahead of you on final, then you have time to go round again––if anything unexpected happens.'

'For example, you were too close to the Hercules ahead of you on landing, didn't you feel the turbulence?'

'Yes,' I replied, my newly found ego beginning to diminish. 'But it wasn't that bad,' Jack tapped the table with his spoon and continued.

'How would a passenger feel, being bumped up and down a hundred feet above the ground?'

'Nervous... I guess,' was my uncertain reply.

'Right, plus they would be making a mental note to fly with someone else next time.' He learnt towards me and tapped the table again.

'So what have you learnt today?'

Trying to inject a little humour, I replied, 'The aircraft is a lot lighter without you in it.'

'Good, and did you notice, how little runway was required for take off?' I nodded and Jack continued.

'Would you paddle behind the Queen Mary in your kayak?'

'No of course not,' I said.

'So why fly behind a Hercules in a Cessna 150, it is just as foolhardy, and the ground is a lot harder than the water.'

'What should you have done?'

Sinking lower in my seat I replied, 'Gone round again keeping well behind and above the Hercules flight path.'

'Ahaa, now you know,' and Jack settled back in his chair.

Then continued, 'always fly as if you have your dream girl with you on your first date, then maybe, she'll want to go with you again.'

Feeling as if I had endured enough criticism for one day, I skilfully changed the subject.

'Are you married?' I asked.

'Not really I am just waiting for a divorce, then I hope to marry my dream girl.'

He glanced up, 'and you?'

'No, I've been married twice, but neither worked out.'

'Always third time lucky,' Jack said with laugh.

'No thanks, I'll just keep paddling behind the Queen Mary!'

We headed back to the office, Jack giving me a playful push as we navigated the swing door.

'What are you two looking so happy about about?' the pretty young lady behind the counter asked.

'We were talking about paddling,' I replied.

'OH...sounds kinky to me,' and she exuded her charms and smile in Jacks direction. It was my turn to nudge him in the back.

'Mr. Scott,' and she resumed her professional voice. 'The Chief Flying Instructor wants you to have a check ride with Miss Hansen before you continue the rest of the course.'

'Fine,' and I looked at Jack, who also resumed his professional status.

Clear of the office, I asked. 'Why, and who is Miss Hansen?'

'Just so the CFI. can have an independent view of your progress. As regards Miss Hansen, you'll wish you were paddling behind the Queen Mary.'

Jack was leaning against the club door, as I glanced behind me and exited the wire gate, he was still laughing at his own joke.

A feeling of foreboding, replaced my previous elation.

MISS HANSEN.

The weather report this morning, stated, fog, clearing later in the day.

It was correct, and as I walked through the wire gate to the Flying Club, the hanger was just a grey silhouette, hardly visible in the morning mist.

The clock on the deserted office wall read seven-thirty, and I was just pondering the implications of the fog on my forthcoming check flight, when I smelt the comforting aroma of a cigar.

My gaze moved in the direction of a cloud of smoke, rising above a typewriter on the secretary's desk. The other half of the desk was occupied by a pair of reclining black and white cowboy boots.

The boots contained a rather attractive lady, blond hair tied in a pony tail, the cigar held jauntily between her even white teeth. She was observing me whilst rocking back and forth in the secretary's chair.

I was trying to ascertain her age; --a thought that always enters the male mind when meeting an attractive woman--but it was difficult. I smiled inwardly as I realised she appeared to me, as a cross between Julie Andrews and Humphrey Bogart.

'You must be Miss Hansen,' I ventured. 'Yep,' this information was uttered between teeth finding retention of the cigar, more important than verbalising.

'I'm Scott,' the cigar tilted up a few degrees. 'Yup, log book,' I rummaged through my briefcase, found it, and went to move around the counter to pass it to her.

'Just toss it here,' and she raised her arms above her head, I tossed it and she caught it neatly in her right hand.

'Only sixteen hours, well I won't be too hard on you.' She tossed it back and I missed, it landed on the floor like a discarded trashy paper back.

'Will we be flying this morning?' This I said to cover the embarrassment I felt as I retrieved my log book from the corner.

The cigar was removed and she flicked the ash into the trash can beneath her, the cigar was replaced and Humphrey Bogart replied, 'For me it would be difficult....for you impossible. You can wait in the class room and study your ground school, I'll call you if it clears.'

The cigar tilted almost to the vertical, indicating I was dismissed.

'Is the coffee on?' I asked and started to move behind the counter.

‘That is for staff only, the cafe opens at eight,’ and the cigar tilted in the direction of the door. I was dismissed for the second time in as many seconds.

As I trudged up the stairs, I thought, How come I pay good money to be treated like a school boy again?

I read my manuals until I felt the cafe was open, then joined the group of mechanics seated at the bar in their oil stained blue overalls. I finished one cup and was just debating another, when Miss Hansen’s head appeared round the door.

‘Scott let’s go, too much coffee and you’ll want stop at Cooking Lake for a pee,’ and she winked at the cashier as I fumbled for my twenty cents, and tried to ignore the chuckles from the mechanics corner.

I grabbed my case and scurried after her.

‘What is that for?’ and she pointed at my case.

‘It has my books and map.’

She swung her pony tail as she climbed in. ‘You wont have time to read, and if you need a map to find Cooking Lake, you better stick to your bike. Drop it back in the office.’

When I jogged back, she was sitting in the right seat adjusting her safety belt. ‘Right, you’re the boss, carry on as if I’m not here,’ and she continued, ‘I’ve checked the fuel and done the walk around. Everything looks just fine.’

‘Thank you,’ and I climbed into the left seat, pulling my check list out of my pocket.

‘What is that?’ she asked, eyeing it like a fly in her soup.

‘The check list, I replied, my finger poised over item number one.

‘Check list, and this is your twelfth flight?’

My finger retracted immediately.

‘Put it away and you’ll be amazed how well you remember without it. Plus, I want both eyes looking out, front, side, back and up. Right let’s go.’

I primed the engine, it started immediately, the tower information was quick and clear. ‘Got that,’ and I nodded.

'Check all your moving parts as we taxi, set your altimeter, radio volume, compass and keep looking around.'

When we do our final run up, check the magnetos, carb heat, mixture, flaps, doors and seat belts. That is your last chance and remember, no loose items in the back.

When I reached the active runway, I started my run up, turned off one magneto and checked the dial to note the drop in engine revs. Here I was interrupted by a sigh from my mentor. 'You don't have to look at a dial to know the engine is slowing down, listen to it, feel it. Those dials can be as reliable as my alimony,' I changed the radio and rolled to the white line as instructed. All was clear, front, behind, up, and to the sides. I waited nervously for my clearance.

'VGF clear for take off,' came the reassuring words of the controller. 'About time' my mentor muttered.

It was still a wonderful feeling to leave the ground, and I climbed at the prescribed 700ft a minute. All the needles in the right places.

'Climb to 5000ft,' Miss Hansen instructed, Edmonton disappeared in the mist behind us. I stuck to my heading knowing it would take us to Cooking Lake.

'I've got it,' and she put her hands on the yoke.

'Now, you know Edmonton is behind us, and you are hoping Cooking Lake is ahead of us.' She nodded her head in both directions, her pony tail swinging to and fro.

'This bit of information could save your bacon one day,' She trimmed the aircraft and proceeded using only her feet.

Pointing at a small circle drawn on the map, she continued: 'What do you see?'

'A radio tower 235ft high, CHQT.'

'Right now, look at this dial and set it to 1110.' I did as instructed and the sound of Marty Robbin's El Paso filled the cockpit.

'Nice,' I replied, nervously, feeling her use the pedals to keep us on course.

'See this dial,' and she pointed at a dial on her side of the panel. 'This is an automatic direction finder, and the needle will always point at that tower, as long as you can hear it. Now follow the needle and watch what happens.' I took the controls and wobbled a bit as I changed direction.

'Keep the needle straight ahead and don't loose altitude,' After a few minutes the needle flicked back and forth, then swung in the opposite direction.

'Now that means we have flown over the radio tower and are now flying away from it. OK, I've got it.' She took the yoke again.

'Look at the map, now what heading would you take for Edmonton?'

'Three hundred degrees,' I answered using a pencil as a guide.

'Good, now your heading to Cooking Lake?'

'One hundred degrees.'

'Fine, if in doubt use a radio tower, and remember a thumb length is about ten miles on this map. So how far is Cooking Lake?'

'About twelve miles,'

'And how long should that take?'

'About seven minutes.'

Sure enough in about seven minutes Cooking Lake appeared below us. I was beginning to realise this lady knew her stuff.

'Look above, all sides and below, especially below.' She instructed.

'Not good enough, bank right over so you can see below. I've got it,' and she turned the Cessna on it's side.

'Now you can see below.' I didn't have much choice, because my nose was pressed against the window. 'Your safety belt is not tight enough, no refund if you fall out.' I hastily pulled my belt until it hurt.

She placed her cigar packet on the ledge in front of me saying. 'Watch what happens to a loose object.' She applied full power turned into a bank and kept increasing the angle until I thought we would be inverted, she pointed at the packet as it slid to the lower side of the ledge. Then she increased the bank even more, suddenly as if tossed by a giant's hand, we flicked over onto our other side.

'Power on stall,' she yelled above the roaring engine. Then she throttled back and pulled up the nose until we ran out of airspeed, the stall warning ringing loud and clear, the nose dropped and down we went.

With no engine noise, just the sound of the wind, she leaned towards me and said very softly.

'Power off stall, a spin and three rotations.'

Cooking Lake rose to meet us. We rotated three times, levelled out and she restored the power.

'Well, now where is the cigar packet?' and she eyed me quizzically.

I remembered it shooting past my right shoulder at one point during these vigorous manoeuvres. I looked under the seat, behind me and shrugged in defeat.

'Now what if that had been your briefcase, and became stuck under your pedals? Never any loose stuff in the cockpit.'

She gave me the Julie Andrews look, and pulled the cigar packet from her shirt pocket!

I was impressed, how did she manage to catch it, while all that was going on? I never saw her take her hands off the controls.

The next hour was spent doing stalls and slow flight, being told to listen and feel, don't look at the dials, relax, learn to feel it in your bum. I thought of a witty retort to that statement, but was diplomatic enough not to voice it.

The radio tower was below us, thus giving me a course for home.

'How far?' She asked.

'About ten miles, and eight minutes.' I replied, feeling almost confident.

'Now, do a check for engine performance, radio volume and fuel gauges.'

I glanced at the panel: RPM fine, radio was clear.

Fuel gauges--my stomach jumped, they both registered empty! I looked at Humphrey but she was happily chewing gum and looking out the rear window.

'ER.... I began, the fuel gauges.' She turned and tapped them.

'Well, now what?' and she wore her Julie Andrews expression.

'I'll turn away from built up areas, check the gauges again and switch tanks if applicable.' I quoted from the manual.

I banked to start the turn, saying, "I thought you checked the fuel."

'You're the Captain, that is your job,' she answered looking straight at me.

I was thinking what beautiful blue eyes she had, but felt, this was not the time to voice that observation, and continued the turn.

She was nodding her head: 'First thing you've done right today.'

She held her clenched fist up, opened it to reveal two silver fuses in her palm, which she then deliberately and slowly replaced in the fuse box. Eyeing me with raised eyebrows as she did so. The gauges sprang back to nearly full again.

'Never trust anyone to check your aircraft, that is your job and responsibility. Plus the life and well being of any passengers, who maybe desperate enough to want to fly with you.'

The landing was fairly smooth, but I did have to brake a little hard to turn onto the first taxi way. Which incurred the rebuke: 'I can see you're not paying for your own brake linings.'

We reached the Flying Club, she jumped out, saying as she did so: 'Your instructor will let you know any suggestions I make for your improvement, thank you,' and she walked briskly back across taxi the strip to the office, her pony tail swinging in rhythm to the click of her cowboy boots.

I needed a consolation coffee, and was sitting nursing it, feeling quite deflated when Jack walked in and sat down.

'Well.... how did it go?'

'Don't ask,' was my unhappy reply. He let me wallow in self pity for awhile, then he said, 'She is quite the instructor.'

The more I thought about it the more I agreed, I had learnt a lot in that hour and a half. I started to cheer up, my humour returning, and recounted a few events of my ego busting check ride.

I told Jack how she had put her cigar packet on the dash board, then must have caught it while recovering from a spin.

Jack shook his head and adapted an expression of disbelief, "Amazing!" he said.

As we left the cafe, he beckoned to me. He whispered: 'She has two packets, one always in her shirt pocket!'

I must have looked dumb founded, and Jack was laughing so hard he had to hold onto the gate...but she did have beautiful blue eyes!

MRS REMBISH

After thirty-two hours of dual instruction and eighteen hours solo, Jack felt I was ready to take my license. However I was to be subject to a pre- flight test by an impartial instructor. This was as much to examine Jack's method of instruction, as my ability to learn.

Jack and I walked into the office to arrange the day and time, the Chief Flying Instructor checked on the roster. Pointed at an empty square and said, 'Rembish is available that morning,' and proceeded to write my name and the words Pre-flight in larger letters.

While the CFI was engaged in his clerical duties, I noticed the secretary and Jack had exchanged a look that personified the word--collusion.

What was I missing? Once out the office I asked Jack if this was another blue eyed, ego busting, tail spinning juggler. He laughed, 'no Mrs Rembish is quite different, but it's not done to discuss the senior instructors.' He continued, 'you'll be fine, just relax and take your time with everything.'

It was the 9th of August 1970, I was thankful it was a clear day, not a cloud in the sky.

The office smelled of coffee and cigar smoke, the secretary looked in the appointment book. 'Oh, you're with Mrs Rembish, you will be using her Cessna, a yellow one, she has just gone to move it out the hangar.'

I had seen this aircraft before and it was quite unique, as was the pilot. The aircraft was bright yellow, not easy to miss.

Mrs Rembish was kneeling by the propeller in a position of prayer, talking softly. Not a sight to inspire confidence in a would-be-pilot, about to be tested.

I hesitated at the door but she sensed my presence and looked up. 'Please join me in a word of prayer Mr. Scott.'

I was not sure what to pray for at this point, so played it safe (or rather prayed it safe) by thanking God for a sunny day and asking him to keep me cool, calm and collected during my forthcoming test.

'I am sure he will,' Mrs. Rembish added, as if she had a direct link to the almighty. 'You will also gain inspiration from these.' She pointed at the yellow fuselage, which was covered in Biblical Quotations printed in black gothic letters.

During my moments of prayer, I had been distracted by the mini-skirted secretary mounting a ladder to clean the office windows.

The first quotation stated:

'Set your affection on things above, not on things on the earth.'

As I watched the ascending young lady, I felt this was rather appropriate.

I passed to the next quotation.

'Faith is the substance of things hoped for, the evidence of things not seen.' This seemed almost beyond coincidence.

My fantasies were terminated by Mrs Rembish, 'Just push on the right wing and we'll clear the door.'

We were now out the hanger, her polished yellow Cessna shimmering in the morning sun, the black quotations standing out as a reminder of man's fallibility. Not to mention my own.

'Climb in,' she said. The quotation on the door read:

'The love of money, is the root of all evil.' I would bring this to the attention of the office next time they sent me a bill.

During my flight with her, she was the epitome of tranquillity, only one instruction given in a calm gentle voice.

'Head to Drayton Valley, do a touch and go and return.'

Once airborne I turned to a heading of 230 degrees and climbed to 4000ft.

'Good, but don't forget the wind from 320 at 12mph,' I nodded and I added a few degrees to my heading.

Navigation for this trip was quite simple, cross the twisting North Saskatchewan River four times. The forth time Drayton Valley is, or should be straight ahead.

The airstrip was deserted, but the radio is still used, other aircraft listened for, eyes scan in all directions. She instructed me to land once with no flaps, again with full flaps and make this approach as slow as possible.

The first landing was uneventful, the second I tried a little too hard, slowed too quickly, the stall warning blowing shrilly in our ears. I expected her to take over at that point, but she sat very calmly, watching as I added full power, thus avoiding too heavy a landing.

Climbing for my return she said, 'I've changed my mind, return via Wabamun Lake.' This was part of the test, of course.

I looked at the map and using a pencil as a guide, figured my new heading to be 010 degrees and the distance about 25 miles.

In about 15 minutes Lake Wabamun was ahead to our right. I turned to 060 degrees and maintained 5000ft. Fifty miles ahead lay Edmonton and home.

During our flight she told me of her flying life, starting on a farm near Regina, in her father's home built aircraft, doing crop spraying and ferrying friends and family when required.

She was twenty-two in 1940, she moved to San Francisco to obtain a commercial license. Here she learnt of Jacqueline Cochran, and in March of 1942 was one of the twenty five women pilots taken to England to fly for the British Air Transport Auxiliary.

These women were used to ferry every type of aircraft from the factory to active stations, for the Royal Air Force all over England. Thus, freeing the male pilots for active duty.

Later she changed to the US equivalent and became a member of the Women's Air Force Service Pilots. She then ferried bombers made in the USA across the Atlantic to England.

As she was telling me this I began to feel my fifty miles to Edmonton was rather insignificant, and I said this to her, she said, 'it doesn't matter whether it is fifty miles or five hundred you still have to know your position.' This made me feel a little better, and I nodded in the direction Lake Wabamun with a new confidence.

History neglected these women pilots for many years and it was not until November 1977 President Carter passed a bill recognising the work of the WASPs.as they were then known. Plus it was March 1979 before any of the women were given a certificate, granting them an honourable discharge from the US Air Force.

I'll never know if it was my reluctant prayer before the flight, or her presence in the cockpit, but I did feel cool, calm and collected all through the test.

I offered to buy her lunch, but she said she had to hurry home to prepare her husbands lunch.

'What would Jacqueline Cochrane say?' I laughed.

She gave me a grin, that transformed her into that plucky, gutsy bush pilot of 1942.

'Jacqueline Cochrane would have said two words about my husband, and it wouldn't have been ....bless him.'

THE MARS BAR.

During the next week I passed my three exams, which gave me a Private Pilots license. 'A license to continue learning,' as the Chief Flying Instructor put it.

Now I could fly off on my own, take friends up and practice for the next level.

Three mornings a week, would find me heading out to one of the practice areas around Edmonton. Here I would try to perfect all the techniques passed on by Jack, the assertive Miss Hansen and the cool calm Mrs Rembish.

I felt I had become quite proficient in all areas, but should have recalled Jack's words, when he said: 'Never take anything for granted in the air.'

I was so relaxed with stalls then spinning three times before levelling out, that on this occasion I was holding the yoke in my left hand and a Mars bar in my right, while pulling the wrapper off with my teeth.

I pulled back the throttle until the engine was just ticking over, pulled the nose up, the stall warning sounding irritatingly loud in my ears, the nose dropped, I applied full left rudder and started the three rotations. Cooking Lake was glistening in the morning sun, three thousand feet below.

I rotated twice, I've got lots of height, I thought, I'll do another stall.

I levelled out and pulled the nose up, but the aircraft was still rotating.

I'll add power to stop the rotation, but I rotated even faster. I pushed the yoke forward to drop the nose but nothing happened. I just kept rotating. I now knew I was in a flat spin and Cooking Lake was moving up at an alarming rate.

Jack's words clicked in my mind: If all else fails take your hands off the controls and these aircraft will correct themselves.

Slowly the rotation stopped, the nose dropped and I added power, knowing I had control again. I was only a few hundred feet above the lake and could see a fisherman sitting in his red aluminium boat looking up in alarm at my unintentional aerobatics.

Once my pulse settled, my attention focused on my Mars Bar. Where was it? Not on the seat or on the shelf in front of me, in fact, no where to be seen.

Well, I'll find it when I land, I thought.

I searched everywhere, but no sign. I guess Mars Bars, and the wrappers, are digestible, given the right circumstances.

YOU NEVER KNOW.

Having given up on finding my Mars Bar, I went to look for Jack and found him in the cafe waiting for his next pupil.

When I told him my saga he groaned,'didn't I tell you not to take anything for granted in the air? Another few seconds and a few hundred feet and it would have ruined my whole evening. We would be fishing around in Cooking Lake for you. If you want to be a helicopter pilot take lessons.'

I was thoroughly chastised, and I guess I looked it, because he added, 'at least you didn't panic.'

I was relieved when the secretary put her head round the door, saw Jack and walked up to him. 'Jack your next pupil has had a car accident and can't make it,' she said.

'Well at least I didn't teach him to drive,' Jack didn't sound too happy.

'Come on I'll give you a ride home,' I said.

'No Mars Bars,' he almost shouted at me. The secretary backed away at his out-burst, and raised her eyebrows at me. I shrugged and we pushed our way through the wire gate to the car park.

'How would you like to see my world,' I asked as he got in my car. I think mainly, because I wanted him to know I was accomplished at something.

We headed down Whyte Avenue to The Drum Shop, and being a Sunday, the area was quiet and almost deserted. I unlocked the front door and I led Jack up the stairs.

He enjoyed looking at the different types of drums, many from the States some from England, India, Mexico and the new arrivals from Japan.

In one of the studios I had him sit behind a full drum set, he looked so out of place and confused by all the drums, cymbals and pedals. I tried not to laugh.

'What do you do with all these?' he asked, waving a drum stick in the air.

'You just bang them at appropriate times.'

'How long does it take before you know what is appropriate?' Again waving a stick in the air.

'Well..... that is a hard question, because you need to spend two or three years learning to read music, and practice at least two hours a day. Then you have to decide if you want to be in jazz, rock or symphony. Learn timpani, xylophone and vibraphone etc. After about five years you should know where your percussionistic talent lies.'

He looked surprised and replied, 'I didn't know they had music for drums and five years. That's longer than taking a commercial license.'

I put an Eagles tape on and told him to just tap along with it.

It was strange to see him out of his environment, no longer the experienced flying instructor, but looking like any nervous pupil on their first lesson.

Later I showed him my four new copper timpani from England and explained their use in an orchestra. I was showing him a Mozart overture when he asked, 'What is the number 182 for?'

'That is the number of bars rest,' and I went on to explain how they were counted. 'It's a bit like flying, hours of boredom interspersed with moments of sheer terror and hoping you've counted your bars rest correctly.'

As I drove Jack home, he told me he had just passed the entrance exam for an Air Traffic Controller and would be moving to Ottawa for his training. Plus he was to be married soon and confessed his future wife was pregnant... but only a little bit.

We were laughing as we drove past the hospital on Whyte Avenue, the usual line of wheel chairs and occupants lined up on the pavement to enjoy the afternoon sun.

Jack looked back at me. 'We're so lucky, all we have to worry about is were our next sex is coming from.' (Or words to that effect), 'and those poor people are stuck in that hospital probably for the rest of their lives.'

The irony of that statement reoccurred to me every time I drove past that hospital.

Jack's 'rest of life,' was to be only six days.

It was a week later when listening to the CBC morning news, I heard the

announcer talking about a plane crash near North Battleford the previous night.

The pilot, Jack Topa, his fiancee and a friend were killed.

Weeks later, when I felt I could visit the Flying Club again, I asked about the accident.

I was told he was flying overnight to Edmonton so he could clear up his affairs and move to Ottawa the next day. He had flown into heavy icing conditions, the aircraft ahead of him had turned back, but Jack decided to press on.

Why? when this is one of the situations you are always advised against.

I can only think, that the necessity of having to be in Ottawa the next day, had goaded him to take that fatal risk.

GEORGE.

Night flying has always fascinated me, because so many books written by the worlds best pilots, had given such glowing reports about this area of flight.

I decided to take my night endorsement at the Aero Academy, situated on the other side of the field to the Flying Club.

Part of the building had been the original control tower, going back to the days of Wop May and many other historical figures in the early days of bush flying and exploration in the north.

There was an informal atmosphere, everyone on a first name basis, lots of leg pulling and the deciding factor, low wing Piper Cherokee trainers.

The instructors taught in their own aircraft which were maintained and polished to perfection.

I had been told to ask for George, and when I met him was pleased to see he was older than myself, maybe ten years or more.

'Come up to the office,' he said, and led me up the wooden stairs of the old control tower to a small square room at the top. From here you could see the air field in all directions.

He sat behind a battered wooden desk and from the drawer pulled out a stack of pilots' log books dating back to 1940.

'Just so you'll know something about me,' George said.

I thumbed through a few, the notations indicated George had flown everything from Harvards to Hurricanes to Typhoons.

The areas were just as varied, Biggin Hill, Topcliffe, Le Touqet, and all stations to Germany. I was impressed and spent the next hour listening to some of his war time experiences.

I could see George liked to talk, but then I liked to listen.

He was explaining how complicated today's aircraft are, and added, 'never take anything for granted in the air.' He leaned forward, expecting me to ask for clarification on this statement, but I already knew.

'Tomorrow at eight and I'll check you out on the Cherokee 140, you'll love it after the Cessnas.'

As we bounced down the runway building speed for the take off, I did like the low wing and the clear view I had above me.

George was chatting on the radio as we lifted off. He broke off his conversation to tap the airspeed indicator, '85mph to 5000ft' he said, and carried on his conversation.

When we reached the practice area he had me go through my basics, interjecting a series of helpful hints as I did so. 'I'm a great believer in Murphy's law, we have to keep outwitting him,' he concluded.

I had just started the turn towards Edmonton and George was recounting how they flew low level attacks in France to disrupt the transportation system, by blowing up trains.

We were about 2000ft above Spruce Grove, below us was the railway line stretching as far west as the eye could see. Several miles away and moving toward us was the tell tale smoke of a locomotive.

'Tighten your belt and hold onto your hat, nothing like a demonstration.'

Down went the nose and I watched the airspeed move from the yellow towards the red overspeed line at 170mph, the wind whistling past the fuselage. Nervously I pointed to the overspeed line.

George quickly glanced at me: 'Don't worry, this is my own aircraft,' and down we went to about 100ft. The locomotive was straight ahead and growing in size until it filled the windscreen; 'Now!' George yelled and shouted, "boom !boom ! boom.!" Then he climbed to what seemed a few feet above the train and flew the length of it booming away.

Laughing he shouted above the noise of our engine, 'we have to keep going otherwise someone may get our registration number, it's time to head back anyway.'

Though I did find him a little unnerving, he had many years of experience from which I hoped to benefit.

'Link trainer tomorrow,' he said as I climbed down to the safety of the ground.

The Link trainer with little stubby wings and just enough room for the pilot, looks like a cartoon drawing of an aircraft. When you sit in it, there are the controls and instrument panel, plus a hood that can be lowered to put you in complete darkness to simulate night flying. The good thing is, it never leaves the ground and if all else fails you can always have a cup of tea, and try again later.

You sit in this claustrophobic situation until you can hold a course, turn, climb and descend. Plus, obey instructions voiced into your headset, by an instructor intent on your theoretical destruction, while he sits, feet on desk, sipping a coffee and chatting to the secretary.

After about five hours of the Link, all you have learnt is transposed to a real aircraft.

With the instructor by your side, you wearing what looks like a baseball cap with a large tubular peak. This cuts out all outside vision, except for the instrument panel directly in front of you.

The instructor gives verbal commands, you concentrate on the instruments, and give no credibility to your instincts, but rely entirely on the dials on the panel.

This requires great concentration, even after two weeks practice, but the first time, after an hours flight, that you remove your cap, and there is the runway 200ft below and straight ahead, gives you a feeling of great accomplishment.

George was still introducing me to Murphy's Law and I realised he was a master at setting up hypothetical, and some times, all to real scary situations.

During a lesson he would produce four rubber discs, these he could stick over any of the instrument dials, thus simulating failure of that instrument.

Every so often, plonk would go a rubber disc. George would lean back saying, 'you have lost your airspeed indicator, now what?' then it would be the artificial horizon, and so on until he had used up all the available permutations.

It kept me on my toes and only once did it back fire on the Murphy conquering George.

We were taking off and had reached about 100ft, when George turned off the engine and plonked a disc on the airspeed indicator. 'Now what?' he asked with a mischievous grin.

The manual flashed before my eyes, 'you lower the nose, keep up the airspeed and land straight ahead.'

'Good, that's the idea,' and he turned the ignition key--nothing happened. George looked at me as if it was my fault and tried again, still not a peep from the Lycoming failure proof engine.

By this time we were just a few feet above the runway and I did a gentle landing and turned off onto the grass.

The tower called and asked if I had a problem. 'No,' I panted, 'the instructor switched the engine off.'

'Hold your position and we will send a tow, then please report to the tower.'

'You shouldn't have said that,' George said, 'now I'm in trouble.'

'That's Murphy's law,' I laughed.

George knew the controller but they still had quite an argument.

He explained that we were doing a simulated engine failure, that turned into a real engine failure.

The controller told him it was against regulations to practice engine failure on an active runway and that all emergencies should be practised away from the airport. George said an accident doesn't pick a safe location or it wouldn't be an accident, and so on. I was just a silent witness to this confrontation.

NIGHT FLIGHT.

My cross country night flight was from Edmonton to the VOR beacon at Rocky Mountain House, and on the return, do a touch and go at the Edmonton International.

It seemed strange to be doing my pre-flight check with a flash light, the office closed, and George giving me instructions where to park his Piper on my return.

He drove off and I climbed into cockpit. Had I felt alone on my first solo, now I felt positively deserted.

I had phoned in my flight plan indicating a 9 p.m. take off, this left me a few minutes to check all the dials especially the VOR for Rocky Mountain. I knew this would not register immediately, maybe not until I reached 5000ft. But I set it anyway along with the ADF to my favourite country station. Thus giving myself two points of reference once in the air.

I followed the blue lights of the taxi ways, feeling rather conspicuous, on what seemed a deserted airport.

'BLC clear for take off,' came the voice of the controller, 'and have a nice evening.' I noticed that the mood of the controller varied with the activity on the airport. Tonight I was it.

With the cool night air I was climbing smoothly, and very rapidly reached 5000 ft., which I intended to hold to the beacon.

I was relieved when the needles swung to their correct positions. I checked my ADF and heard a current hit song.

Anytime I wanted music I just had to turn up the volume. But for now I was enjoying the feeling of solitude, probably the furthest I had been from mankind, since I was born.

I had about ninety miles to cover and noted how beautifully the engine purred at night. I looked down at the city lights, thousands of homes each with their own built in set of problems.

On my left I could see the twisting river glinting in the moonlight, and knew that if my heading was correct, I would be crossing it after about thirty miles.

Ahead habitation was very scarce and I would cross only one highway with a rail line alongside, before my destination. So I watched my VOR very carefully correcting for any drift of the needle.

Ahead I could see the outline of the Rocky Mountains, looking like a backdrop to a Wagnerian opera and as I neared my turn around point, I knew the ground would be rising beneath me, and that at Rocky Mountain I would be about 1500ft above ground level.

On the dial the needle wiggled; the little flag moved to the from position indicating I had passed over the VOR station. Below several groups of lights twinkled, looking like inverted constellations.

I turned climbingto 6000ft for my return, and adjusted my VOR to the Edmonton International. When the lights of Edmonton glimmered in the distance, I called the tower at the International Airport, and asked for permission to do a touch and go .

'Clear for touch and go on runway 01. Straight in approved, call on final,' came the quick response from the tower.

Runway 01 is 11,000ft long but I only needed about 700ft. It was quite visible in the moonlight, but to my surprise, when I was lined up with the runway and called I was on final, the whole runway lit up. It stretched into infinity until the lights met at a point on the horizon. I was just about fifty feet above touch down point, when they all went off, and the other runway, number 29 on my right was lit up Going from a lit runway to total darkness, was quite a shock because suddenly the ground was no longer visible and I had to look at my artificial horizon, add power and climb away carefully. The voice of the controller cut in.

'Sorry about that BLC but we have a 747 for runway 29.'

'Never take anything for granted in the air,' clicked in my mind as I climbed to 4000ft, looked behind me and saw the landing lights of the 747 to my right and below.

I followed the highway for the rest of the flight, enjoying the tranquillity of my cockpit and the pop music from CFRN.

I called the tower, was given clearance for runway 34 and was asked if I required runway lights. 'No thank you,' and I switched on my landing lights, it really did give me a feeling of great independence.

After I had tied down BLC for the night, I sat at a little table enjoying a coke and the peacefulness of the evening, trying to imagine all the great flyers who had been guided from that tower: From the first world war flyers, to the bush pilots of the thirty's and all the pilots who learnt their craft for the second world war.

I reasoned, they probably all felt the same trepidation as myself, before their first cross country night flight. And, I hoped, the same feeling of accomplishment when it was over.

I am ashamed to admit that I always wondered about George and his wartime adventures. Ashamed I should be, because now, 30 years later courtesy of the Internet and todays sources of information, I found out more about the Murphy beating George.

He was F/O George Grant Wharry of No 245 Squadron. He had 35 missions, leading his squadron deep into Germany. He was a member of the first wing to be established on the beachhead in Normandy. On being awarded the Croix de Guerre it was noted: that at all times he showed courage and enthusiasm of the highest order.

Whilst I, was complaining about the drudgery of attending school, George was taking off in his Typhoon from a temporary runway constucted between two opposing armies and flying at the battles of Mortain and Falaise. Then on to help in the fall of Paris.

If I had known all that, I would have felt very humble in the presence of the instructor--who introduced me to Muphy.

THE FLY IN

A pleasant way for a novice pilot to spend a summer Sunday, was to attend a Fly In. These were held at many small airports in Alberta and people arrived in everything from home built aircraft constructed in a barn, to a bright yellow Harvard Trainer. The main ingredient of these get-togethers, was pride of ownership.

A bright sunny day in July 1972, a day I had been looking forward to for weeks. It was to be the, Edson Fly In.

I thought I would ask a young lady, who, (without her knowledge I'm sure) had placed me in the temporary condition of insanity, politely called love.

She was a violinist in the orchestra, and though possessing an aristocratic beauty, always looked sad, and when spoken to, reminded me of a startled deer.

After a few enquires, I was told she was the daughter of the owner of a large store on Jasper Avenue. Even so she still aroused my protective instincts and I hoped a Fly In to Edson would be a different, and intriguing way to give wings to a potential relationship.

I approached her during our rehearsal break, her startled look registered rejection in my mind, but she told me she had never been in a small plane before and would look forward to it.

Trying to hide my delight at her acceptance, I said, 'Seven o'clock Sunday morning, I'll pick you up.'

She gave the address, which was in a plush part of town and added: 'Don't tell Daddy when you meet him.'

As I rang the bell I made a mental note not to be intimidated by Daddy, but when Daddy answered the door, I could see why she had that startled deer look. I was ready to hide behind the nearest bush.

He was well over six feet, and had a look of permanent outrage on his face. This face I had seen at many of our symphony concerts.

I noticed he came to the Sunday afternoon concert, always sitting on the front row, accompanied by an elegant lady, who frequently jabbed him with her elbow if he showed signs of nodding off during a slow movement. Then goading him to his feet for a standing ovation to the soloist of the concert.

Plus, like most concert goers he would be just settled in his seat, when I did the drum roll for the National Anthem, then have to stagger back to his feet again, while glaring at me, as if I was responsible for the inconvenience.

I had the feeling that these Sunday afternoon concerts, were not the happiest occasions of his life.

'Oh, it's you,' he said. 'The drummer.'

'Timpanist.' I replied.

'What ever,' and he directed me into an elegantly furnished sitting room.

Joan arrived a few minutes later, 'lets go before Mummy appears,' she whispered.

Too late, Mummy strode in, blond hair tantalisingly moist from a recent shower, wearing a white bath robe, and shoeless.

'Good morning, Mr. Scott, nice to meet you in person, I have only seen you buried behind all those drums.'

'Timpani,' was my reflex reply.

'Sorry, of course timpani,' and she gave a little curtsy, that revealed more than her personality, and asked, 'would you like coffee?'

My instinct was to say, 'yes, breakfast lunch and dinner!' But Joan was already opening the door and I reluctantly replied, 'no thank you, and sorry for disturbing your Sunday morning.'

With a beguiling smile she held the door open for us. 'Have a wonderful day, Henry and I can now head back to bed, for a morning of unrestrained passion.' I was about to say, 'he looks like he needs it,' but felt it was not a good idea to push my luck, on what I hoped, would be the first of many visits.

As we left, I heard her father say, 'where are they off this early in the morning?'

'Edson, dear.'

'Who the hell would want to go to Edson on a Sunday morning; or at any other time,' was his disgruntled reply.

'I like your Mum,' I said, to cover the uncomfortable silence.

'Most men do, she always has to dominate, one way or another.'

I thought I would try another tack. 'You look great.' I was going to add, as well but managed to restrain from that catastrophic addition. One foot in was enough.

Joan wore a black pant suit with a white scarf, her blond hair parted in the middle and held in place by a black ribbon.

She glanced at me, 'really--if I wanted to impress you, I'd have worn a bath robe.' I felt I better just drive to the airport.

The Cessna was parked outside the hanger and I helped Joan into the right seat, making sure her seat belt was fastened and her handbag tucked in the pocket behind us. Then I stowed our top coats, and two one pound bags of flour.

'What are these for?' she asked.

'You'll see later.' I hoped maybe a mystery would restore her humour.

It was a cool, clear morning with vivid blue Alberta skies and the Cessna purred up to 5000 ft. with no other aircraft in sight.

Joan pointed to her house, below us and by the river. 'How do you know which way?' she asked. 'I follow the railway lines all the way to Edson.' I passed her the map, which displayed the rail lines in heavy black. Then I explained the other methods of navigation, and she settled into a more receptive mood.

Wabamun Lake passed on our left, then Entwistle, where the rail lines and the highway met beneath us. Chip Lake was on our right, then Carrot Creek and lastly Wolf Creek.

Here I reached for the mike, and radioed we where ten miles east of Edson.

Unlike the Air Traffic Controllers at a major airport, we were greeted with :

'Good morning to you, the pancakes are on, descend to four thousand and stay to the right of the rail tracks, two aircraft ahead of you, call when you have visual.'

Joan looked surprised, 'they sure sound friendly,' she said.

'They'll treat you like a princess, tell me when you see the airstrip.'

She leaned forward, and I had a moment to admire her fine features and the contrast of her blond hair against the black ribbon, these features highlighted by the morning sunlight through the canopy.

She pointed like my daughter when she saw her first dog, 'there,' she said, 'lots of planes.'

'That's it' I said and radioed, 'VGX about three miles east of the field, with two ahead of me.'

'VGX you are number three for 27 and straight in approved. Remember if you make the white line, breakfast is on us and you win a prize.'

Joan eyed me quizzically, and I explained that meant, if I could land with my wheels on the white line, which was painted just beyond the threshold of the runway, we would win a two week, all expenses paid trip to Bali.

I exaggerated a little, the prize was really a plastic money box in the shape of a logging truck.

However, I tried my best, put the flaps down for a slow approach, bounced about twenty feet before, and twenty feet beyond the white line, landing on my third bounce.

Joan gave me her startled deer look; I tried to look, as if that was usual procedure.

'There goes Bali.' I said, trying to sound relaxed and humorous.

'There would have gone my breakfast if I'd had one.' Joan said, but she was actually laughing.

I braced myself for the leg pulling which I knew would follow. We taxied off the gravel runway onto the grass following the directions of a flag bearing official.

He approached, and laughing shouted above the surrounding noise, 'Captain Kangaroo and Princess Wallaby, park here please, then you can hop over for some breakfast.' (Much laughter at my expense).

Joan was not used to the openness of a small community, where the first impression you give, is the one you're stuck with.

She found it hard to believe that I had never met any of these people before, but she was soon laughing, when a lady said, 'you two been bouncing around together very long?'

The lady led us to the breakfast area, gave us a coffee, raised her own cup saying, 'well nice of you to drop in --all three times.'

When I told her this was our first date, she whispered to Joan, 'there is a bus back to Edmonton at 4.30.'

The event I was looking forward to, was the bombing run, hence the two bags of flour. I thought I better explain to Joan, what this entailed, as she too would be involved in this exercise. I pointed to a large bulls eye drawn in the centre of the field and explained that each aircraft had two chances to hit this target with a flour bag, which looked like a smoke bomb when it burst open.

Two hundred feet was the lowest you could fly, and the sequence was monitored by radio.

Joan and I sat in our aircraft and I began to explain her part: 'You hold the bag on your lap, and as we get close you move it to the open window. I try to put us right over the target, then, when I shout, NOW! you push it out.'

'How do I open the window?' she asked.

'Release this little catch, then it opens upwards and outwards.' I enjoyed leaning across her to demonstrate. She nodded and wiggled the catch several times. Then turned and asked, 'can I put your coat on my lap, one of these bags is leaking and I don't want to get flour on my pant suit?'

'Sure,' and I reached over and spread my coat over her knees.

We taxied to the take off point, several other aircraft ahead of us. 'Make sure your seat belt is tight.' I cautioned.

We bounced along the gravel and into the air, flew to the holding area and circled behind the two aircraft ahead, waiting for permission to start our bombing run.

'VGX clear to go, and remember 200ft minimum.' The instructions came through loud and clear.

I looked at Joan who was holding the flour bag against the window. She wore a look of concentration I had only seen previously when she was playing away in the symphony orchestra.

I turned towards her, 'open the window,' and I felt a gust of wind as she struggled to hold the window with her left hand and the bag with the right.

'NOW! ' I yelled and down went the flour bag. I banked to the right and saw the bag explode about twenty feet beyond the circle.

'We'll do better next time,' I shouted above the sound of the wind blustering around the cockpit, and turned for our next attempt.

'This time I'll dive a little, to give more speed and make the target easier to see.'

Joan had the bag at the ready, window open and a look of even greater concentration. I put the nose down, built up speed, the target was right under our nose. 'NOW,' I yelled, and I'm sure it would have been a bulls eye, except for one mishap.

Joan in her excitement forgot about the catch on the window which ripped the bag from end to end, the wind took over and blew the contents into the cockpit. Suddenly, visibility was down to a few inches and we both started sneezing, not a situation to be in when you are nose down at 100mph and 200ft.

'VGX, do you have a cockpit fire.' The voice of the controller was loud and clear. 'No, our flour backfired,' I shouted between sneezes.

'You're cleared to land and taxi off the runway.'

As we touched down the little red fire truck followed us. We rolled to a halt and a fireman ran and opened our doors, a large extinguisher at the ready.

His look of concern turned to laughter as he surveyed us. He looked at Joan and said, 'I think you've been a bit heavy on the talcum.'

Her once black suit was now a dusty grey, her face and hair covered in white flour. He reached up and helped a very dazed Joan to the ground.

'Stay there, I know how to clean you up. Close your eyes,' and he lifted a snow blower from the back of the truck, plugged it in and directed the nozzle at the immobile Joan.

She looked almost angelic as the white cloud rose above her, her blond hair streamed out behind, her black pant suit clinging to her body like a second skin.

Next it was my turn, then the aircraft. The coffee lady wandered over, saying to Joan, 'That bus still goes at four-thirty.'

All was not lost however, Captain Kangaroo and Princess Wallaby won a prize, for the most unusual flight of the day.

It was a plastic bear with a Mounties hat that could be used as a money box. I presented it to Joan, who said, 'I really wanted a logging truck.'

'Next year,' I replied hopefully.

At the Sunday concert, her parents were in their usual seats. Her father looking as if he wanted to be anywhere but here, her mother waved and projected a devastating smile that almost made me forget the drum roll for the anthem.

At the end of the concert she waved again and I was drawn towards her.

'What did you do with my daughter last Sunday, she's still trying to get the flour out of her underwear? I think you are a very kinky drummer.'

'Timpanist,' I said indignantly.

'Sorry, kinky timpanist,' and she performed her delightful curtsy for me.

Allan F Scott

The End.

Kenya 1970

NIGHT RIDE TO MOMBASA

Kenya and East Africa, is a part of the world that has always fascinated me since my teen years when I read the novels of Ernest Hemingway and Robert Ruark. The tales of the Mau Mau and Jomo Kenyatta intrigued me and names like Nairobi, Tree Tops, Norfolk and Stanley Hotels, had a magic sound.

I had tried to join the Kenya Police when I was seventeen, but failed my medical, because I was not tall or heavy enough and we still had several years of food rationing, before I could hope to expand to the required size of a Kenya Policeman.

It was to be 1973 and 25 years later before I would set foot in Kenya, not as a member of the police force, but as a tourist. During my stay I had a series of wonderful safaris, so wonderful, I would pinch myself to make sure I wasn't dreaming. The wildlife, the scenery, the visits to places I had fantasised about in my teens, all outshone my imagination.

The previous weeks had passed exactly as my itinerary had predicted, always the right place at the right time. However the next entry read: 'Drop off at cross roads near Sultan Hamud.' From here I was to be taken to Mombasa.

It was early morning when we arrived at the cross roads, and I waved a cheery good-bye to my guide and companion of the last five weeks. He was known as Evans, a Kikuyu, educated, always immaculately dressed. He boasted three wives, with the three sets of problems that created.

Most of the time he was very calm and easy going, except when he came across members of another tribe. Then his whole personality changed and he became what us westerners would call––Crazy.

If we were driving on a lonely gravel road, and Evans saw anyone walking, women, children, old people, whom he identified as Samburo he would swerve our Volkswagen bus at them and try to knock them into the ditch. He even did this to a group waiting in the pouring rain at a bus stop.

We had many discussions about his serial killer tendencies, but he could not understand why I was even concerned. 'But they are only Samburo,' he would laugh.

I drew his attention to an item at the bottom of the Nairobi newspaper that stated: 'One hundred and fifty thousand Hutus killed by Tutsies in Rwanda last week.'

'Oh, they usually exaggerate,' he said, 'anyway they're only Hutus.'

I was glad I was member of a tribe that met his approval.

My itinerary was correct as usual, it was a cross roads, a gravel cross road, covered in red dust common to that area. The pick up point was a gas station, with one pump, one table with umbrella, a telephone with crank handle and a coke machine. All supervised by a Maasai boy of about ten years old.

He waved me to the table with the grace of a Savoy maitre d' and suggested tea, which he poured with a flourish, from a pot boiled over an elephant dung fire.

I piled my three cases against the table and surveyed my surroundings. Flat is the best description, and in all directions. I could see 360 degrees of horizon.

I looked at my watch, 10:15 a.m., pick up time 11 a.m. Noticing the red dust had started to move with the breeze, I decided to change out of my new safari suit into jeans and a T-shirt.

I did ask a silly question, 'Anywhere I can change?' I asked my companion when next he approached, tea pot in hand. He shrugged which I gathered, meant it didn't matter. It didn't of course, because privacy is relative to ones surroundings.

As I stood in my underpants, I had a mental picture of an English Bobby riding up on his bike and arresting me for indecent exposure. I think the sun was already getting to me.

At noon I asked if I could phone Nairobi to see what had happened to my pick up. When eventually a voice answered, I was told there was a two hour waiting time for phone calls to Nairobi, but my message would be relayed, then in two hours they would phone back a reply.

Tea and Coca Cola was plentiful but food was none existent. My miniature maitre d' explained that he had never had anyone spend all day at his gas pump, and he offered me what I had seen him snacking on. However, he was Maasai and I knew their choice of a snack was a mixture of: ox blood, donkey urine and wood ash. I politely declined.

At four o'clock the phone rang, and I was told the taxi was on it's way but had to pick up a few people first. It was just nice to know someone knew I was here.

I sat and watched the sun move to the west and the cumulus clouds build up from the south. Then just after six p.m. I noticed a moving red cloud of dust on the horizon, as it got closer it materialised into a red Vega. Which slid to a stop at my oasis.

The driver, a six foot Maasai with flopping ear lobs, jumped out and ordered the other passengers out. He placed three in the rear seat, a tall Samburo woman in the luggage space behind the rear seat, then piled my luggage on top of her.

By her gestures I could see she was not amused, and I offered to change places with her. But our lofty chauffeur explained, 'She is a woman and must do as she's told.'

I was placed in the front passenger seat, given a package wrapped in plastic and told, 'Look after this.' Then off we set on the road to Mombasa.

I have been in a bus filled with intoxicated Liverpudlian mill workers enjoying a pub crawl on Saturday night , but the volume of passenger noise could not compare with what was happening in the little red Vega on this trip into the African sunset.

The driver sang what sounded like Maasai war songs, the three Arabs behind me yelled at each other and punched the roof of the car to add weight to what ever point they were trying to put across. The Samburo lady kept up a barrage of verbal abuse directed at the driver, which he ignored and not one word of all this did I understand. Which probably was just as well.

Our driver had his own style, gas pedal to the floor and hand on the horn. We headed into Tsavo National Park, famous for it's elephant population.

Darkness fell, the rain poured in torrents. We slid from one side of the road to the other as our Kamikaze chauffeur, who I had now nicknamed Stirling drove as if he were the only item on the road.

I pointed out a sign indicating an elephant crossing, hoping we would slow down a little. But our driver just nodded and said, 'Elephants, sometimes.... they try to cross.'

As we sped through the villages, Stirling never let up, full speed, horn blasting. People leaping out of the way of our speeding machine.

We turned a corner to find the street full of people, enjoying a festival of some sort, we roared through the throng, some jumped to one side but, two people not agile enough were hit, one bounced off the hood the other went over the roof. Stirling slid to a halt, the angry crowd gathering round the car.

He was yelling, the Arabs were yelling, I was looking for my Canadian passport.

The crowd started to rock the car, and I felt it would not be long before it was up side down. Then the Arab behind Stirling grabbed him round the neck yelling and trying to choke him. Stirling shifted into gear and away we went leaving the confused and angry crowd behind us.

For once we had momentary silence. 'What was all that about ?' I asked Stirling. He was rubbing his neck and laughing.

'Those three behind us are Arabs, and the people here, hate Arabs, the crowd would have lynched them.'

'Why them?' I asked.

'Because the Arabs sold the African into slavery, and they always remember that.'

'What about you, you were driving?'

'I am Maasai, and they saw it was an accident.'

He laughed when he saw I still had my passport in hand.

'That wouldn't do you any good, nobody can read around here.'

We dropped the Samburu lady off, several Arabs met her and proceeded to cry, wail and hug each other.

'What's all that about?' I asked Stirling.

'They always do that when they come back off a trip.'

'How long has she been away,' I said.

'Three days,' Stirling replied. 'They are very emotional.'

'I would never have guessed,' and I laughed for the first time in many hours.

The rain continued and the wind howled as we arrived at the outskirts of Mombasa. Stirling pulled into the courtyard of a large house and told me to stay in the car. 'White are people are not welcome in this area, have you got my parcel?'

I had forgotten all about the mysterious parcel, but located it under the seat. I was sure it contained heroin or something illegal.

He left the car and stretched to his lean six foot four, for the first time in many hours, strode across the yard opened a large double door and slid through.

I waited, but my curiosity was aroused and after a minute I followed Stirling's steps to the large doors. One of the doors was open enough for me to see inside the house.

It was like a scene from the Arabian nights. A large room with a circular fire place in the centre, the stone walls of the room hung with colourful tapestries.

Divans and cushions were arranged round the fireplace and soft music filtered into the night. The occupants were all women as for a I could see, black beautiful and wearing long white diaphanous dresses.

Stirling was talking to a lady and I saw him hand her the mysterious package, then turn in the direction of the door. I retreated back to the car and tried to look bored when he returned.

'What was in that package,' I asked as casually as possible.

'Just beef for my supper, it will be ready for me after I leave you at your hotel.'

'Lucky you,' I said, not necessarily referring to his forth coming supper.

My hotel was called the Whispering Palms which would probably be applicable during most of the year, but now it was The Howling Palms.

The wind was so fierce it bent the trees until the tops almost touched the ground and the rain stung like hail. This I observed as I carried my cases into the lobby. To my relief the desk clerk called me by name and I started to relax. 'You have a cabin on the beach,' he continued. 'Henry will help you, then you can have dinner.'

Henry to my relief was about five feet tall, and thankfully not a Maasai. I didn't need any more displays of tribal courage tonight.

He put one case on his head and one in each hand and we headed into the monsoon. It was pointless to worry about getting wet and I almost enjoyed the soaking as I followed Henry to my abode for the next three days.

Henry singing to himself, led me to a brightly lit cabin about five hundred yards along the beach. 'Your place,' he shouted above the howl of the wind.

It was raised about four feet off the sand, with a small open porch at the front. A removable ladder leant against the rail of the porch.

I was about to climb the ladder when Henry said, 'You better wait until I clear the dogs off.' I thought he was joking, because I couldn't see any dogs.

He picked up several stones off the beach and threw them onto the porch.

This was followed by yelps and growls and several large evil looking dogs leapt down onto the beach. Henry shouted and swung at them with my cases until they slunk away.

'Never trust those wild dogs, sometimes they go crazy,' he panted as he reached up and placed my cases on the porch.

'Dinner is on for twenty minutes,' were his parting words as he retreated into the wind and rain.

I climbed the ladder and dragged my cases in the front room, shutting the door behind me. Ahead was the bedroom complete with mosquito net and to the right a bathroom, which I hoped to use before dinner. However, there were several hundred reasons not to.

Every inch of the walls, mosquito net, bath and shower were covered with every type of flying insect imaginable. I was about to sit and ponder this, when I saw even the chairs had their share of nocturnal visitors, all drawn to the bright lights of my cabin.

'How about if I turn off the inside lights, then just leave the outside on? They should then fly out to that source,' was my brain wave.

Looking at myself in the mirror, I hardly looked fit for a dining room, but by now I was too tired and hungry to care.

The screen door seemed stuck when I tried to open it, then I saw movement through the mesh, the dogs had returned and one was slumped against the door.

What I needed was a large stick, this I obtained by screwing a leg off a kitchen chair. I banged on the door, shouted and waved my weapon, the dogs retreated enough for me to make my exit.

I jogged along the beach towards the lights of the hotel, found the washroom, washed, dried off and hid my chair leg behind the toilet bowl.

The dining room was immaculate, which only emphasised my grubby state, the equally immaculate maitre d' asked me if I had a choice of tables.

I had lots of choice because I was the only diner, the only other occupants of the room were four waiters, who stood in each corner of the room like statues. They too, were in immaculate white uniforms with gold buttons and wearing a red fez.

The food was wonderful and as I finished each course one of the statues would spring to life and remove my plate. With the good food and wine I was beginning to relax, when I felt something brush against my leg. I looked under the table and there was an ugly one eyed cat staring up at me. I began to think I was in a Hitchcock Movie.

My fantasy was interrupted by the waiter telling me coffee and dessert would be served in the bar.

The bar was facing the ocean, had a white marble floor and was enclosed on three sides. The front was open to the ocean which gave me a sheltered view of the raging storm. I was enjoying my coffee, enthralled with the view, the moon, the sand and the huge breaking waves.

Then I heard a strange tapping sound which seemed to come from all directions.

I looked down and saw the noise was created by hundreds of crabs of all sizes scurrying across the marble floor, attracted by the lights and piling up against the bar.

I lifted my feet onto a chair and told the barman we were being invaded.

He yelled for Henry, who arrived with a large wide broom, and swept them down the steps back onto the sand. It was then I saw the whole beach was a mass of moving crabs.

Henry grinned over at me. 'High tide and bright lights.' I nodded trying to look cool in this eerie situation.

I was just thinking, 'No one would believe this,' and wishing I had someone to tell, when I heard several female voices, one with an unmistakable London accent.

The voices materialised into two air line hostesses and a honeymoon couple. Val, petite and slender with glowing red hair and Denise, large, buxom with black hair and a loud voice from years of instructing how to don a life vest and grab an oxygen mask. Fred and Betty just married in Halifax in the UK, both tired, wet and wishing they'd gone to Blackpool.

They had arrived too late for dinner, but were to have sandwiches in the bar.

'Do you like crab?' I asked. 'Lovely,' Denise replied.

'Well here they come!' and I pointed at the long line of crabs just advancing up the top step. Denise let out a scream and jumped onto the table, quite the feat for one so rubenesque. The others looked alarmed but kept their composure.

Henry leapt into action, keeping the swarm at bay with his super wide broom.

Val and Denise had a cabin next to mine, but, I thought after Denise's reaction, I better not mention the forth coming hazards.

Several drinks later, it was time to head for the cabins via the crab infested shoreline. I offered to give Denise a piggy back not realising she had two suit cases.

I remembered to retrieve my chair leg from the wash room, and was eyed with suspicion by the desk clerk as I returned to the bar.

Val didn't seem to care and was enjoying Denise's terror, even adding to it by saying things like, 'Don't drop her, or they'll gobble her up in a second.'

'What's that for?' Val asked, eyeing my club.

'That's to fight off the wild dogs.' I replied trying to sound casual.

'Yes, and this is to put on the elephants' tails.' Val laughed, grabbing a salt shaker. She thought I was joking.

We noticed the crabs retreated into their holes as we approached and reappeared when we passed, giving the beach a sense of perpetual scurrying movement.

I struggled along the beach, a suitcase in each hand and my club under my arm. Denise hanging on my back was almost hysterical. The rain poured and the wind howled.

Val ever the witty cockney, said, 'To think we actually pay for this.'

I was already having a struggle to keep Denise on my back, and Val making me laugh was too much. My knees buckled and I lay gasping in the sand. Denise seeking safety from the crabs by standing on my stomach.

I looked up at them both, rain running down their straggled hair, sand to their knees and their uniforms sticking to them like a second skin.

'I only have three days of this to look forward to.' I choked.

Val looked at me and said, 'Lucky you. Next year, how about a wild weekend in Siberia?'

With much huffing and puffing, they climbed the ladder to what was called in the brochure, A cabin on a sun soaked beach.

They had no lights on, so no insects, but our voices did attract the dogs.

Up to this point Val insisted these were a figment of my imagination.

When she looked down and saw the pack of rain soaked black creatures, their bright eyes focused on us, she was the first in the door. We locked the doors and windows, and it was time to relax with several miniature bottles of brandy, courtesy of British Airways.

Next morning the sun was shining, the ocean blue and a wonderful breakfast taken on the patio. During breakfast we decided to take a trip of fifteen miles into Mombasa, taxis were expensive, but.... earlier I had met a young man, Albert, who was resident here, studying of all things--crabs!

I suggested to Val that she chat him up and see if he would offer to take us to Mombasa. I set the plot by introducing them and walking away.

A few minutes later I observed Val in earnest conversation, she was using the intensity that a pretty woman can create, to make us gullible males believe we are the only man on earth. Her eyes never left his, but her thumbs up sign behind her back informed me that she had achieved her objective.

Val, Denise, Fred, Betty and myself were to be taken to the Rio Club in Mombasa that evening. Albert our chauffeur and crab expert, informed us that long dresses for the ladies, suit and tie for men, were mandatory.

The first sight of our transportation was disappointing, an ancient Austin seven stuttered to the front entrance and choked to a halt.

Albert leapt out, umbrella in hand, the weather of the previous night had returned. Albert supervised our seating or rather squeezing arrangements. Three on the back seat and Val on my knee (at my suggestion) in the front seat.

The guards at the front gate warned us not to stop for anyone, and to watch for snakes. A snake warning had been issued due to the heavy rain.

I should have been sceptical when Albert told us, it may take an hour and a half to drive the fifteen miles. I looked back to see the security gate close behind us, and the bright lights of the hotel fade into the mist and rain. Before us, a red mud track that climbed into the oblivion created by the beams of our headlights. Either side the trees rocked by the wind discharged large rain drops and broken branches around us.

I felt warm and secure with a perfumed Val nestled on my lap, listening to the adventures of our honeymoon couple from the rear seat and the comforting chug of the Austin engine in front.

We slipped and slid on the red mud path, but made progress. Denise ever the pessimist noted how the tree branches on the road looked like snakes and every dark tree a terrorist waiting to pounce.

I was just thinking, as I nuzzled the back of Val's neck, enjoying the softness and scent of her hair and the warmth of her body, that the journey could go on for ever as far as I was concerned.

Then our chugging motor ceased to chug. I looked at Albert , he looked at me. 'Maybe water on the distributor cap,' I suggested.

'May...be,' was the limp reply. Obviously, I was the one to get out and check.

I reluctantly unravelled my self from the soft nuzziness of Val and moved out into the world of wind and rain. By the time I had the bonnet open I was soaked, I checked what I thought was the problem, without success.

'Pump the pedal,' I shouted.

'Squeek-squeek,' the sound of the connections to the carburettor.

'No smell of petrol,' I shouted.

'How is the petrol gauge?'

'It doesn't work,' Albert shouted back.

I found a stone and knelt in the mud to bang it on the petrol tank. It emitted a hollow, empty echo.

'Think you're out of petrol,' I sounded more relaxed than I felt.

'Could be, I lent it to someone this morning,' Albert answered, as if this was a daily event, and continued, 'we'll just have to roll back down the hill and see if we can get some. Just push Allan, and I'll turn around.'

I pushed, but the soft mud and narrowness of the road made it impossible.

Albert voiced an unwelcome suggestion, 'If everyone gets out and pushes we should be able to turn.' Out they climbed into the mud and rain, shoes caked in two steps and clothes soaked in two seconds.

Denise saw a snake in every broken branch on the road, which kept us is a perpetual state of panic. But we still were unable to rotate the Austin.

'No luck,' Albert said, from the dry comfort of the drivers seat. 'I'll just reverse down if someone will lead the way.'

'How about you,' Fred shouted.

Albert shook his head, 'No I'm responsible for you all, and this maybe tricky.' I realised that our crab expert was smarter than I thought.

Fred echoed my sentiments when he muttered, 'I'd like to drag him out and jump on him.' Val laughed and said, 'Remember he is doing us a favour.'

I looked at Val, who was illuminated by the headlights, and I thought I'd never seen a woman so beautiful. Her now translucent dress clung to the soft curves of her body, her wet hair shone with rain droplets and her eyes sparkled with merriment.

I was shaken out of my reverie by shouts of, 'Push!' from our bedraggled group. Slowly Albert backed down the hill, Val leading and walking backwards, using her shoes to gesture and point.

It took us over half an hour to reach the gate, where the guard, trying to be pleasant, asked if we had enjoyed ourselves.

'It was wonderful!' Val replied, 'I've always wondered what a lady mud wrestler felt like. Now all we have to do, is battle the crabs, fight off the dogs, kill about three thousand flying ants and another day in paradise is complete.'

We staggered into the bar still laughing at Val's repartee, looked at ourselves and laughed even more. We were all saturated and covered in red mud to the waist, we had to abandon our shoes at the door. Betty had fallen while pushing and didn't look too bad from the rear but her front was covered in red mud from toes to neck.

'Into the pool,' Betty yelled and ran out the bar, Fred and us not far behind. Here, tragedy was narrowly averted when Fred grabbed her as she was about to jump into an empty pool.

We all jumped into the other pool fully clothed, Henry arrived with our drinks which we placed on the floaters. In a few minutes Albert arrived at the edge of the pool, dry, groomed and apologetic.

Val shouted, 'Here's a toast to Albert,' she swam up to him, raised her glass, and grabbed him round an ankle with her free hand.

'Thanks for fuck all Albert. In the pool with him!', she pulled.

His pleas of––'I can't swim,' fell on deaf ears.

'Who ever heard of a crab expert that couldn't swim?'

Allan F Scott

The End.

Edmonton, Alberta 1965

THE SYMPHONY WITH BRIAN PRIESTMAN

It was 1965, and I was timpanist with the Edmonton Symphony Orchestra. We were just coming to the end of the Saturday morning rehearsal for the two weekend concerts.

Our conductor was not a happy man, and only two minutes were left in rehearsal time, so he decided to cut to the last few bars of the movement.

I was still trying to find where he had cut to, when he started waving at me and throwing one of his tantrums. "How can you be so stupid to miss that entry, it costs hundreds of dollars an hour to rehearse this orchestra, and you're too lazy to count a few bars " Etc, etc.

So he raved on, until my little six year old daughter, who had been waiting in the wings with her mother for her Saturday lunch pizza treat, leapt into action.

She ran onto the stage, hands on hips she glared up at the Maestro, and yelled: "Don't you shout at my Dad."

That ended the rehearsal, even our frustrated Maestro collapsed into fits of laughter.

My daughter--, was voted the union rep. of the month.

Allan F Scott

The End.

Grand Prairie. Alberta

BRIAN PRIESTMAN CONDUCTOR

The new policy for the orchestra was to travel throughout Alberta, spread culture and hopefully arouse interest in symphonic music. Our new conductor, fresh from London, had no idea of the distances involved, or the lack of interest and lack of enthusiasm we could expect from the hardworking locals.

We arrived in Grande Prairie at lunch time after about five hours on the road. The schedule was to play a children's concert in the afternoon and one for the adults in the evening, both in the school gymnasium. However, no one in the school office admitted knowing anything about either of these events.

Our conductor was quite upset, but eventually a truck with a loudspeaker on top drove the streets announcing that: 'A band from Edmonton would perform two concerts.' Our Maestro was even more upset.

The afternoon concert was the usual light affair, mainly demonstrating the instruments and playing short excerpts. The kids enjoyed themselves and asked lots of questions.

But, the evening performance was not blessed with a display of youthful curiosity and interest, but rather a noisy group of males fresh from the bar, who wandered in an out during the overture, sipping on their beer bottles.

The end of the overture was greeted with a smattering of applause and boisterous requests for rock'n roll. Our conductor put down his baton, turned to the audience and said: "I refuse to play for a bunch of backward Ukrainian Peasants!" then stomped off.

The concert master rose to his feet, shrugged and told us to pull out our 'Pops' folders, and out came such gems as 'Leroy Anderson's Sleigh Ride,' 'Perpetual Mobile,' 'The Turkish March' and the 'Blue Tango.' He stood up, nodded to the audience, then played, joked and held their interest for over two hours. The highlight was when a neatly dressed and happy little girl from the afternoon concert was invited to conduct. We had the 'Thunder and Lightning Polka' on our stands.

Our concert master told us to follow her movements exactly.

The expression on that little girls face was worth the price of admission as she gave her first downbeat, and Whump, went our orchestra. She stopped, we stopped. The concert master whispered to her and away we went again, slowly at first, then picking up speed as the concert master nodded his encouragement. She was laughing, we were laughing and then she stopped to turn and wave to her parents. We stopped. "Sorry!" she shouted to us. Her next downbeat had a little more authority, and away we went to a rip-roaring jumbo presto finish. I'm not sure which was loudest, the laughter, or the applause.

The finale of the concert was the 'Colonel Bogie' march conducted with great enthusiasm by the Mayor of Grande Prairie.

Our concert master said it all when he voiced: "If orchestras would remember that they are here to entertain, and not educate. It would be a lot easier for all of us."

Allan F Scott

The End

Edmonton Alberta

THE CHRISTMAS CONCERT WITH BRIAN PRIESTMAN

The Christmas concert was regarded with even less enthusiasm than a Pop concert by our Maestro. "One rehearsal--will be more than enough," he grouched.

He had programmed the usual pop stuff, then the British members of the committee insisted on a grand transformation scene. "Just like a pantomime back home." They voiced. Then at this point, the presents could be distributed to the children.

This highlight of the concert was to be accomplished by using our new hydraulic lift at the front of the stage, which, when in the down position became a pit for an orchestra. On this occasion, it would be in the down position for the first half of the concert. Here it would be loaded with: Santa, the deer and a large sleigh containing gifts and imitation snow that would be blown out over the audience by several electric fans. Santa's eight elves were to toss the snow-like confetti in the air and the fans would do the rest.

The hydraulic lift could only be raised or lowered by a union man, who sat in a steel cage in the wings and pressed a large red button, housed in a small red box.

How will he know when to press it was the problem?

I solved that problem by saying. "There are no chimes in the program, so I'll play a church-like peal on the chimes and this will be his clue to press his red button.

The pit will rise, Santa, the sleigh and the sumptuous elves will appear at stage level, the snow will be blown out, and the elves will prance into the audience distributing the presents and good will to all."

Everyone nodded, including the union red-button-presser who placed aside the paper- back he was engrossed in, to agree to perform this act of infrequent union agreement.

The button presser introduced himself as Walt and asked what chimes were. I showed him, then gave him the mallet and let him have a few heavy swipes at them.

"So," I said, "as soon as you see me walk over to these and you hear the first chime you press your button." "Right, no problem." he said.

I set up my percussion gear, walked to the front of the stage and peered down into the pit as the sleigh was moved into position and the rain deer, (courtesy of Canadian Tire) placed in a neat row. Santa was surreptitiously placing a case of Molsons under his seat, where he was joined by a delicate elf. The other elves were removing hiking boots, thick sweaters and backpacks ready for their magical appearance about an hour from now.

I climbed onto my riser at the rear of the orchestra and to prevent any wobble or worse checked that all wheels on the chimes had their brakes applied. I looked between the chimes and could see Walt, the button-presser settled in his cage, paper-back in hand and the little door guarding the red button wide open.

The auditorium was full as expected, the children restless and already looking forward to yet another appearance (by kind permission of Canadian Tire) of yet another Santa.

Our conductor was showing more enthusiasm than expected, but, then I had noticed the champagne in the Green Room. Orchestral Committee Members Only was the sign on the door, of what was normally, the musicians' lounge.

Our first two short pieces were greeted with much applause. Then I noticed the librarian moving amongst the orchestra and placing a sheet of music on our stands.

"Extra encore, on next," he whispered to me.

The conductor was having a reparteé with the children and parents. Then he turned to us and said, 'Leroy Anderson's Christmas Medley.' Down came the baton and away we went. I followed my percussion music moving from timps, to snare drum, to glockenspiel and lastly chimes.

As I hit the first chime, I felt an apprehensive twitch, (surely Walt will know this isn't the promised church-like peal of bells we had discussed) I glanced in the direction of the button presser. He had dropped his paper-back, and was moving towards the little red box, and giving me the thumbs-up. I replied with a frantic shake of the head and a desperate wave, but, by now he had his back to me and was pressing the button.

I felt the whirr of the hydraulic lift and slowly the rain deer's antlers rose into view, Santa and the elves were not prepared for such an early arrival and lay comfortably, partially dressed and each clutching a dark bottle of Molsons, whilst reclining on the sleigh.

Santa was the first to shake himself into activity. He jumped up, braces dangling, shirt askew and bottle in hand to voice to our Maestro: 'What the f***'* happening.' Much to the delight of the audience.

This Christmas spectacle was hardly the expected grand transformation scene, when everyone had to watch Santa dress himself, fix his beard and then help the elves into their green spandex skin tight outfits.

The elves threw the snow, the fans blew, and the kids ran around enjoying the excitement and confusion plus the early arrival of their presents.

The conductor was gesturing to me and pointing in the direction of the button presser, I shrugged. Walt gave the thumbs up, I grinned weakly at him and realised that sign language fell far short of any clarification in this situation.

However, it was the shortest Christmas concert in the history of the orchestra.

Allan F Scott

The End

Hay River. Northwest Territories.

LAWRENCE LEONARD CONDUCTOR

Hay River is about 500 miles north of Edmonton on the banks of the Great Slave Lake, and was to be one of the stops on our winter tour of northern Alberta and beyond. I was hoping the conductor, just fresh out from London, would pick a program that required a minimum of percussion, as there was only one of me, and flying was to be our method of transportation. However, he insisted that, "The Young Persons Guide to the Orchestra," was to be on the program and could I manage it on my own?

He also scheduled a piano concerto to be performed by Katrina, his lady friend. This would justify her travelling with us. It took several of us to persuade him that the chance of finding a grand piano in Hay River was very slim and maybe he should forget that item.

So he compromised, and settled for the 'The Ritual Fire Dance.' This he pointed out was quite showy for piano, but not as demanding as a concerto. Our manager nodded his approval, and Lawrence was happy, Katrina was happy and I was happy. However, she insisted on taking her piano stool. This was to be weighed in with the percussion gear and hopefully, an upright piano could be borrowed in Hay River.

The hotel we lodged in had a pub downstairs. I changed into my tuxedo and with several other musicians headed down to the bar for a sandwich and coffee. A tanned and grizzled man in a cowboy hat sat next to me, and asked me why everyone was dressed up.

'We're playing a concert in the High School gym later, will you be coming?'

'What kind of music?' he asked.

'It's a symphony orchestra, very nice and relaxing.' I replied.

' No, I don't think so, I heard one once.'

'It's a different program each time.' I laughed.

He shook his head, "No, anyway, I play spoons with the band here tonight, do you ever use spoons in the orchestra?" He was looking very seriously at me. Then he pointed to a piano on the little stage. 'We're lending that to you this evening.'

'Are you sure?' I asked and looked closer at a war torn upright that appeared to have been used for target practice by the hockey team.

'Sure, as soon as Harry gets his fork lift we'll bring it over. My name's Wilf.' I hesitated, then shook a knarled hand, thinking I really didn't want to be on a first name basis with the spoon playing piano mover. Knowing familiarity could bring responsibility.

The first row of the audience were smartly dressed men and women of professional status in the community. From here it passed to blue jeans, work boots and T-shirts at the rear.

We were set up on the floor, my percussion gear forming the rear rank. I set Katrina's piano stool on my left. 'The Marriage of Figaro,' overture was well applauded. Next was listed two movements from a symphony. Lastly, before the break was to be 'The Ritual Fire Dance.'

We had just finished the first movement of the symphony and the conductor, eye's closed and head bowed was waiting for the applause to cease.... so he could start the last movement. With a rattle and clatter the side doors swung open and in blew the cold wind, snowflakes and the piano balanced on a forklift. Wilf, looking very important, his cowboy boots clacking on the polished floor strode over to our Maestro.

'Where would you like it chief?' Our conductor looked pleadingly over at me.

'Just here, Wilf." I suggested.

'Over here, Harry!' Wilf, shouted.

Katrina sat on her stool, music in hand, as the piano was gently plonked down in front of her.

'There you go sweetheart, bang away.' Wilf grinned at her.

Harry carefully retracted the forklift, swung around and out the door, followed by a waving Wilf. Their short appearance aroused the most applause of the evening so far.

We opened the front of the piano, removed several beer cans and a charm bracelet.

The last movement of the symphony forgotten, Katrina nodded at the Maestro and attacked the piano with great ferocity, and 'The Fire Dance' never had so much fire.

After the concert, back in the hotel our manager thanked the hotel owner and I thanked Wilf and Harry for their efforts.

Wilf impressed us all with a spoon solo in an arrangement of 'Orange Blossom Special' that left the cutlery in the establishment rattling. His finale was to rhythmically work his vibrating spoons over the well endowed barmaid, who was known as, 'Miss Twin Peaks.'

'How about having them perform at our next 'Pops Concert?' I suggested to our manager.

'That spoon player isn't even in the union,' he replied, rather sullenly I thought.

'Yes... but I am,' I said hopefully.

Allan F Scott

The End

Jubilee Auditorium Edmonton 1972

I WENT TO A CONCERT AND A HOCKEY GAME BROKE OUT

If I had been the music critic attending this concert, that would have been quite the eye catching headline to my revue. But, I was playing in the orchestra, so had a first hand view of all that transpired on that cold Sunday afternoon in the Jubilee Auditorium.

This event requires some background to set the scene. The aggressor, whom, I'll call George, was an oboe player from Winnipeg, who had played several seasons with us, but, was replaced (without his knowledge) by an oboe player from Toronto.

I met a very frustrated George in the shopping centre the night before our first rehearsal and he told me he had arrived from Winnipeg ready for the symphony season in Edmonton. At the sympnony office he was told by the manager that the conductor (Lawrence Leonard) no longer required his services. So he approached the conductor, to ask why. The conductor told him, the manager had chosen an oboe player from Toronto, so there was nothing he could do about it now.

This left George a long way from Winnipeg with no job, no money and getting the run-around from the manager and the conductor.

Anger must have eaten away at George, so that by Sunday he was a coiled spring of frustration. He decided that words were not enough and took himself to the auditorium and lurked in the wings, waiting to enact his revenge.

At the end of the concert the orchestra stood to acknowledge the standing ovation. Lawrence Leonard bowed, and baton suspended between thumb and forefinger, eyes half-closed and head thrown back, marched into the wings. A second later, he staggered back on-stage. Some of the audience laughed and applauded again. This little bit of spontaneous choreography was repeated and I felt it was hardly appropriate after the rendition of a Beethoven Symphony. But then Lawrence... did tend to clown about sometimes.

The applause ceased, and I was placing the covers on my timpani, when I noticed George running along the brass risers behind and above me. Just at this moment the manager arrived on stage and started to chat to me. George yelled, then jumped from the top riser onto the back of the manager knocking him to the ground, and with fists and legs flaying threw himself on top of our unfortunate manager, knocking over music stands, cymbals and most of the percussion gear.

Quite a commotion erupted, the retreating audience turned to see what was happening and were greeted with the vision of two of bodies battling amongst the debris on the percussion riser.

I must admit, for a moment I just stood in a state of bewilderment. The manager was yelling, George was kicking and cursing, someone yelled, “Bring down the curtain!”

Being closest to the action and not having a $10,000 violin in my hands I grabbed one of George's legs and pulled, others members of the orchestra also grabbed arms and legs and pulled. But no one was quite sure who the antagonist was, so some pulled on George and some on the manager. No penalty was called, but eventually they were separated and to ensure an end to hostilities, sat on by members of the brass section.

I turned and saw two stage hands supporting the dazed and bleeding Maestro from the wings and across the front of the stage. His last contribution to the arts for this concert, was to aim a kick at the now restrained, panting and prostrate unemployed oboist.

As the confusion subsided I rubbed a bruised knee and picked up my many pairs of timpani sticks that had scattered across the stage during this fiasco. I glanced over at one of the largest members of our orchestra--who happened to be the player's union rep-- and asked why, he offered no help during this fiasco.

'Well... I thought I'd let George have a few minutes with the manager first,' he grinned.

Allan F Scott

The End

Whitehorse 1972

DRUMS ALONG THE YUKON

One morning in May 1972, I was happily shaving and listening to CBC Radio, the guest was Alan Fry and he was promoting his new book, Come a Long Journey.

It was about a trip on the Yukon River, from Whitehorse to Dawson City, just himself and Dave, a native Indian. As they paddled, Dave related the history of the area they passed through. I was fascinated, and as the interview concluded, the announcer asked Alan Fry if this was a difficult journey.

'If you like camping, boating and the weather co-operates, it can be a wonderful trip. About five hundred miles in all.'

Sounds great to me, I thought from the comfort of my Edmonton home, plus, we were due in Whitehorse with the Symphony Orchestra the next week, I made a mental note to ask more about this trip.

Our concerts in Whitehorse were enjoyed by all and we in turn enjoyed their hospitality. Everywhere we went the welcome mat was out. At one of the receptions I met Ken, the manager of the music store. He knew I did percussion workshops, and he asked of I would like to do one in Whitehorse. The fee offered was quite good, and we agreed on the weekend of June 17th.

As the wine and conversation flowed, I told him of my interest in kayaking.

'Why don't you kayak the Yukon, middle of June, the ice should be gone, you could go right after the percussion clinic.'

Next day back in Edmonton, I wondered if I would ever hear from him again, maybe it was just the wine talking. However a few days later, a package form Whitehorse arrived containing: the book Come a Long Journey, a contract for the percussion workshop, and a copy of the Whitehorse Star.

The newspaper had an advertisement for the workshop, but the headline read: 'Drums will come before kayak trip.' Later the phone rang, it was Ken telling me they had twelve people for the workshop, and the sport store had offered to lend me a kayak.

'Fine,' I replied, 'but I do have my own folding kayak that I can bring with me.'

Next morning found me in the government map office to purchase maps for the intended trip. 'What are these little squiggles on the river,' I asked the man behind the counter. 'They are rapids and gravel beds,' his voice adopted a fatherly quality and I expected him to pat me on the head.

'This is the most dangerous, Five Finger rapids, one hundred and eighty people drowned there during the gold rush. But they had no experience.' At this point he gave me a quizzical look.

'Fancy that,' I said retreating out the door.

The airline to Whitehorse was very co-operative and I was welcomed along with my five drum cases, camping gear and my kayak folded into two canvas bags. Fourteen items in all. 'Quite the expedition,' the hostess said. 'Maybe you should just get a one way ticket.' 'Everyone's a comedian,' I thought.

The hotel room was cosy and warm and I started sorting out my percussion gear for tomorrow. Ken picked me up early and we drove to the school where I set up my drum stuff for the weekend. A good time was had by all, and we swapped stories, mine from London, theirs from all areas in the Yukon. Here they thought nothing of a fifty mile sled trip in twenty below, then playing from after dinner until breakfast time.

'Sometimes it's too dangerous to stop,' one of my pupils said. 'What do you mean,' I asked. 'Well, they shot a guitar player who wanted to quit at midnight.'

'That would motivate you to keep going,' I replied.

'Glad the Mecca dance halls never heard about that,' I thought.

Everyone wished me, 'Good Luck on your trip.'

'Thank you,' I replied with more conviction than I felt.

Ken reminded me I was to be at the CBC studio next morning for an interview, this was regarding a recording I played on performed by the Edmonton Symphony Orchestra, and a rock group called Procol Harum from England.

Apparently it was having tremendous success on the pop charts and had sparked a lot of interest. The interview went well and I related some of the problems and humorous aspects of recording an orchestra, a choir and a rock group.

Just as I thought I had escaped, he looked at his clip board and said, 'Now, about this river trip to Dawson.' I tried to be evasive, but he insisted on knowing my departure date, place and time. Here I found myself quoting from the book, 'I will launch by the old paddle wheelers on the river bank.' Then I went on to explain that I wanted to try and follow the book, and if possible, camp in the same places as Alan Fry and Dave, this would enable me to absorb some of the history from Dave's stories.

'Well we hope to be there to take a few pictures and wave you off.'

Any chance I had of testing the waters and changing my mind was gone, all of Whitehorse knew about my trip. 'How did I get into this?' I thought Next morning, as required by anyone making a river trip, I reported to the RCMP. I was instructed to report as soon as I arrived in Dawson, or after two weeks they would start looking for me.

Then it was on to Allan Innis Taylor, who was the last of the paddle wheel river boat captains , a wonderful and interesting man. He pulled out a map for me, and traced the course I should follow in red pencil.

'Use binoculars to look well ahead for log jams, stay in the right channel of Five Finger Rapids and don't get turned sideways.'

Talking to him was an inspiration, his last words of advice were to have my knife and axe sharpened.

'They are your best friends.' were his parting words.

That evening Ken and his wife took me out to dinner, during the meal a tall distinguished man came over and said, 'stand up please.'

I obeyed and he took out a tape measure, then measured me head to toe.

Stepped back, looked me up and down, said, 'one hundred and sixty pounds, I think.' Turned and walked out the dining room.

'Who was that?' I asked my friends.

'The undertaker.' Another Yukon comedian.

Next morning Ken drove me and all my gear to the river bank, where I started to set up my Klepper kayak.

A small group of well wishes followed me into Taylor and Drury, where I was going to buy my supplies for the trip.

Luckily I had made a list, so I ignored all the suggestions offered, otherwise there wouldn't have been room for me in my kayak.

By the time we arrived back at the launching site, CBC had arrived, and I had more questions to answer, plus pose for a few shots. I had to load very carefully, declining help from all directions and leave enough room for me to slide in.

Then at last I was on my way, with shouts of farewell interspersed with:

'Watch our for the moose.'

'Watch out for the grizzlies.'

'Watch out for the wolves.'

The river was moving at about ten knots, so it was not long before the waving group and the paddle-wheelers faded into the distance.

Once I had rounded the first bend I rested my paddle and relaxed. I wanted to camp early, check my gear and wax the rubber hull of my kayak. I had hoped to do this in Whitehorse, but it would have created another frenzy of questions.

About three hours later I saw a nice flat spot on the bank, hopped out and unloaded my tent and cooking gear. This is really the wilderness I thought as I sat by my tent, a pot of water boiling on the fire. Out came the tinned stew, my next quest was for the can opener.

'Nobody would be stupid enough to have a kayak loaded with tinned food and not have an a can opener,' I moaned to myself.

Well, here was my first mistake, it was all those people milling about when I was trying to organise everything. I had to blame someone.

The newly sharpened axe would do, just split the tin in two and pour the contents into a pan. I placed the can on a tree stump, and carefully aimed my stroke at the centre. The stroke was accurate and it neatly bent the can in the middle. I had the axe raised for a second attempt when I heard the sound of a car engine.

'What! I'm at least thirty miles from a road.'

The unmistakable shape of a Volkswagen appeared moving through the bush in my direction, I hastily hid the battered tin behind the stump.

A young couple scrambled out complete with camera and tripod.

'We're with the Yukon Tourist Bureau, we would like to ask you a few questions and take a few pictures. Plus we have a questionnaire you can fill out at your leisure.'

'How did you get here?' I asked.

'We just drove through the bush when we saw your smoke, would you stand by the fire holding your pan for this picture... That looks great.'

She was asking me information about myself, and when I told her my occupation, she asked if I was on the recording with the Edmonton Symphony and the Procol Harum.

'Yes, I was.'

'Wow, that's neat.'

'Bye have a good trip, you can drop off the questionnaire in Dawson.'

So much for wilderness!

I retrieved my tin from behind the tree, and changed my tactics. I used the knife like a tin opener, and it worked like a charm. Thank you Mr. Jones!

Day two found me at the end of Lake Leberge, I was lucky and had, had the wind behind me for the thirty mile trip.

I had a morning break on the skeletal remains of the Caska, her ribs rising out of the gravel. This had been used as a landing stage for Lower Leberge and had lasted since 1911, and still made a fine view point for tea drinkers like me.

I camped at Lower Leberge at what had been a road house for the paddle-wheelers. Now all that was left were a few forlorn looking cabins. I explored and found in one, a little white table and chair. These I moved to a spit of land where I had set up my tent. I stayed two nights, and enjoyed having dinner at my table, with a thirty mile view of the lake, the sun lowering to the horizon, but never setting.

Later that year Pierre Berton did the same trip with his family, and wrote in his book Drifting Home, that his daughter had imagined a 'Fellini-like sequence' on seeing the table and chair set up on the spit of land.

The next stretch of the river is called Thirty Mile and is joined by the Teslin River, plus logs, tree stumps and debris freed from the ice. From here the river narrowed and picked up speed, the cliffs on either side crumbling and sliding into the river like miniature avalanches, this was caused by the sun warming the freezing soil. Here I kept to the centre of the river.

In the distance I saw a paddle wheeler and was beginning to think I was hallucinating, then another appeared. This was Hootalinqua and at one time had been the repair depot for paddle-wheelers. As I stopped paddling I heard an eerie hissing sound as if I was rubbing on a sand bar, I checked this out and realised it was the thick silt in the river flowing past the boat. I worked my way into the inlet where the Paddle-Wheeler was and saw the name Evelyn, on her wheelhouse.

'Tea time,' seemed like a good idea.

As I sat on the deck it was easy to imagine the ghosts of the past, people laughing, eating, dancing and enjoying the view, as the elegant ship chugged along the river. It must have been quite the romantic adventure.

Big Salmon, was to be my next camping spot, here again another river joined the Yukon, adding more debris to the now cluttered river.

This was my fifth day, I had begun to think I was the only traveller, when ahead of me I saw a large heavyly loaded aluminium canoe with two paddlers.

I silently paddled until I was right behind them, and said, 'Good afternoon.'

They nearly fell overboard with fright, and like myself had not seen anyone for a week.

My fellow boaters were John and Randy, both fresh from military service in Vietnam. John was small, efficient and very talkative. Randy, heavy, slow moving and rather quiet. Quite the contrast I thought.

John advised me to camp with them at Little Salmon. I hesitated to accept, and John continued, 'you may need us, we have five finger rapids ahead.'

As we unloaded at Little Salmon, I was amazed at the equipment they had.

Cameras with extra lenses, bags of rice, two rifles, two hand guns and a first aid kit, that was an emergency ward in itself. Two tents, waders, fishing gear and several hats.

It was beginning to rain so we stored our gear in one of the buildings. It had Little Salmon Mission painted above the door.

John pulled a manual from his first aid kit, 'Have you had your appendix out? he asked.

'Yes,' I lied, not wanting to be wanting to be part of his, do it with a friend medical training."

The population of Little Salmon had been decimated by the flu epidemic after the first World War, and like many of the other villages on the river had been abandoned.

Next morning I was up early and as it was Randy's birthday, I decided to take him a cup of tea in bed.

I found my primus in the hut, poured fuel into it, struck a match. What I hadn't noticed, some of the fuel had spilt onto the floor. This also ignited and then I saw the grass under the hut was burning.

Panic Time! everything we had was stored in that hut. I grabbed a pan rushed to the river, ran back and poured the water down the cracks in the floor. This I did five or six times, until no flames were visible under the hut. I sat for a few minutes trying not to think what the consequence of my carelessness could have been.

I took the tea to their tent and John remarked, 'you look wide awake.'

He would never know just how awake I was!

For Randy's birthday, John offered to make a special stew, I offered a bottle of rum (my medical kit) then John asked if I would read some Robert Service as my accent would make it more realistic.

Later we explored the trails around the village and came to the burial ground. It was like a miniature village, little houses about four feet tall with windows and pitched roofs. About thirty in all. When I looked through the windows I could see what had been the possessions of the deceased. A tin cup, leather suitcase, sewing awl and sadly in the window of the last grave-house a toy truck and a toy pistol.

The last of the inhabitants of Little Salmon were buried here, even John stopped talking as we read the names on the tomb stones. It was a solemn trio that headed back to 0camp. John broke the silence, 'I have to get dinner,' and he left us, a twenty-two gauge rifle slung over his shoulder.

I spent the afternoon re-waxing my kayak as the silt had done a great polish job on the rubber hull.

I heard sporadic rifle shots in the distance and eventually John returned with a bulging canvas bag and a triumphant expression. Their tents had now a plastic cover over them with the Stars and Stripes fluttering in the breeze. All I could find was a large maple leaf that I tied to the top of my tent.

As I prepared my birthday treat, peanut butter on digestive biscuits, the aroma from the American camp drifted my way. And very good it smelt. Later the three of us sat under the mosquito netting between the tents, the smoke from the camp fire blowing over us, we had quite the feast.

Wild green onion soup, ground squirrel stew, biscuits and rum and coke.

We drank a toast to Randy, I read The Cremation of Sam McGee, right on the bank of the Yukon. I think Robert Service would have been pleased to join us by the camp fire, it was quite a memorable evening.

I left before my friends were up, and we had agreed to rendezvous later in the day. I just had to make a smoky camp fire when I camped. The river still moved at great speed and as I came to the junction with the Little Salmon River floating trees would be sucked under and then bob up twenty or thirty feet down river. That area was to be avoided.

Later in the day I saw a weather worn battered sign hanging from a tree, Britannia Creek, how could I resist? I pulled in, lit a fire and made lunch. I was just enjoying a siesta when the unmistakable sounds of Randy and John arguing reached my ears. I half hoped they would continue on, but in they came.

'Where else would an Englishman camp?' John yelled as they fought the current to shore. Tea was enjoyed, then John said, 'If you lend me your shotgun, we'll have duck for dinner.' I told John about the kick from this grouse gun as it was called, I explained it had nearly knocked me over the first time I fired it. This was no Lee Enfield.

John laughed, 'I grew up with shot guns,' Randy gave a silent shrug.

As they climbed into their canoe, I passed the gun to John who was sitting in the bow, then four shells. Randy paddle in hand was pushing off from the bank.

John had asked me to walk ahead of them up the creek and throw stones into the reeds to chase the ducks from cover.

I trotted along the river bank until I was about fifty feet ahead, then I tossed a few stones into the reeds, sure enough a group of ducks paddled quickly into mid stream.

Randy was paddling hard, John kneeling in the bow shotgun at the ready.

From upstream I waved and pointed at the ducks. John brought the gun to his shoulder, but as he did so the ducks took flight and climbed steeply away from us.

As the ducks rose so did John, a look of grim determination on his face, he was now standing--he fired--and went over the side of the canoe faster than the shot left the barrel.

When he surfaced he was yelling at Randy for not turning the canoe fast enough. I was laughing so hard I had to sit down. Even though I thought I'd seen the last of my shotgun.

Randy had more luck with fishing, and I was careful not to mention lack of duck on the menu. However the fish was delicious.

Next day we hoped to reach Five Finger Rapids, and I showed them my map with the route carefully drawn. 'Just follow us,' John said, 'and you'll have no problem.' I could hear the roar of rapids long before I saw them, the river moved faster and faster, took control of the kayak, all of my efforts went into keeping the bow pointing downstream.

John and Randy were about fifty feet ahead of me, they disappeared into a wall of water, I followed and felt the cold water rush up the sleeves of my jacket, then a drop as I went over the shelf. I paddled hard to avoid a pinnacle of rock, then through the frothing channel and into smooth fast water.

I looked around for my compatriots, two heads appeared, then shoulders and arms still paddling. As I drew level with them I could see their canoe was swamped. I tried to push them towards the bank. The current did most of the work but we landed puffing and gasping on a sand bar.

They started to empty everything out, so the canoe could be bailed, arguing as usual. I left them to sort out their differences and belongings.

The next time we met was two days later at Fort Selkirk.

I could see the buildings of the Fort from quite a distance, and made a landing below the once thriving settlement. I pulled the kayak on the bank and climbed up carrying my tent. This I wanted to set up as soon as possible to avoid the mosquitoes, which during the last few days had started to be very active.

I knew the settlement had a warden and I saw smoke coming from a building on the far side. I just finished setting up my tent when Warden Danny Roberts arrived guest book in hand.

'How did you get here?' he asked.

I pointed at the kayak. 'You know you are the first person the dogs haven't smelt coming down the river.'

'That's probably because I smell like a dog.' I laughed.

Danny took me around the settlement and introduced me to his teenage daughter who was sitting next to a charcoal fire, the smoke blowing over her. She was reading a comic and seemed unimpressed at my arrival.

He had about ten large dogs that he used for his sleigh in the winter, and as a deterrent for bears in the summer. I had just finished eating and was dozing in my tent when the dogs started howling, then the sound of John and Randy still arguing. They joined me in my tent to eat. Then went off to explore, cameras drawn and at the ready.

Next morning I left while my friends still slept, I paddled and drifted most of the day, enjoying the perpetually changing panorama of the river.

On the side of a hill I spotted two grizzly bears chasing ground squirrels. They ran after the squirrel, then dug like mad as it ran down into its burrow. It was something to see the speed with which these huge bears moved.

I read somewhere that bears have difficulty running up hill, these two must have neglected to read this. I made sure I would camp a long way from these two large and athletic bears.

A few hours later I saw the roof of a cabin in the woods and pulled onto the bank, I prepared to move on, if it was occupied. But it was empty, and in wonderful condition.

I set my tent up in the garden and explored the house. It was a log, two story house, all it needed was glass in the windows.

I was fascinated by the wall paper in all the rooms. They were covered in newspapers from 1915 and 1916. From floor to ceiling, newspapers.

I spent the rest of the daylight hours reading the walls.

I found out later that this house had been built by a wealthy family from Paris, even a grand piano had been installed. Several years later, as their daughters matured they had moved back to Paris, leaving history on their walls.

I pressed on the next morning and I was never to see John and Randy again. Though they did write several times and stayed at my house in Edmonton on their return trip, unfortunately I was away at the time. They had decided on a slower pace, as they were going all the way to the Bering Sea. This would take them about another three months. My last night was spent on an island, the only evidence of previous occupation was a water logged sign that read, Ogilvie.

The mosquitoes were really out in force, and I put on my full mosquito gear, even then they stung at the bend in my elbows. I gave up on a fire and cooked in the tent. Next day I figured I was about twenty miles from Dawson City.

So today was clean up day. I had a very cold bath in the river, a shave, put on clean clothes and boots and left the remainder of my tinned food in the hut for another traveller.

I reckoned on two paddling hours to Dawson and I was right. Dawson appeared as I rounded a bend in the river. I paddled to where the main street met the river. There was a log landing stage, with a little hut on it, sitting outside was an Indian lady knitting.

She never looked up as I approached just kept her eyes on the needles as they clicked rhythmically. I was thinking, 'Tonight I stay in a hotel, have a hot bath and eat a steak without having to extract it from a can with a hunting knife.'

Carefully I paddled the kayak parallel to the logs, took the line in my mouth and climbed out onto the logs. I had one foot on each log when I noticed they started to move apart. I froze until my legs would part no further, then gracefully, I slid down between them, putting an arm round each log as I did so.

At this point I was up to my chest suspended in very cold muddy water, but I still had my kayak line in my mouth.

The lady glanced up from her knitting and without breaking her rhythm said, 'They're not tied together you know.'

'I noticed,' I mumbled, as I slowly worked my way between the logs until my feet touched bottom. I pulled the kayak onto the shore, took out my duffel bag and shotgun then headed up the main street in search of a hotel.

In most cities of the world a soaking wet man carrying a shotgun down the main street would cause comment. But no one gave me a second look as I headed into the hotel. Though I could see the two ladies who had just polished the lobby floor were not amused by my muddy footsteps, or the puddle I left at the reception desk.

I kept my eyes on the registration form, and for method of arrival put down...boat.

The clerk looked at me and said, 'Oh..I thought you swam!'

Allan F Scott

The End

Victoria 1975

THE TRANSITION

Edmonton in 1975 was a very sociable city, especially for people involved in the arts. As the timpanist with the Edmonton Symphony I was invited to a cocktail party, the theme being, Meet your orchestra.

We were encouraged to chat to the financial supporters of the orchestra, consisting of the richer members of the Edmonton community and yearly subscription holders, who braved blizzards and sub-zero temperatures to hear us perform.

I was explaining to a doctor how temperature can effect the tuning of an orchestra, when I noticed he was getting that glazed look, people attain when they find something.... almost interesting.

He turned to me, 'Do you do anything besides bang things?'

I was trying think of an appropriate answer, when he continued, 'it's rather a juvenile way of earning a living.'

'It's very good therapy,' I joked.

His eyes narrowed and he leaned towards me. 'You have problems then?' This was posed as a question. I thought I better excuse myself, in case I admitted anything I might regret. However, it did sow the seeds of doubt in my mind. Here I was at forty-five years-old, and all I had done over the last thirty years was bang things.

The outcome of this short conversation found me attending a summer course at the University entitled, Choose your Career.

The finale of the course was to take Dr. Strong's Vocational Interest Test.

This involved answering a book of questions, and we were instructed to: 'Not think, just tick what ever answer comes instantly to mind.'

The next week we were presented with the computer generated results of our efforts. Here we received one hundred and thirty-seven vocations, marked accordingly with our ability to perform same.These results were transcribed to a graph and then to a tower graph.The darker the colour the more this was you.

I was surprised when I followed the lines and number one read, Priest!

I expressed my amazement to the professor, who took it, looked at it and said, 'You have it upside down.' To my relief, number one now read.

'Musician Performer.'

I absorbed this information and realised it had taken me six weeks and two hundred dollars, to confirm I was best suited at doing what I was doing.

As we moved into the Edmonton winter it seemed half my life was spent shovelling snow. If it wasn't the driveway to be cleared, the car was stuck in the back lane or your overshoes stuck in a snow bank.

The day that was the turning point for myself, began with a miserable opera rehearsal with our new, devoid of humour conductor.

I returned home to shovel my way into the house, then shovel a space for my car.

'May as well live on the moon,' I thought as I stowed the snow shovel and broom by the back door, removed my overshoes and tossed the soggy newspaper onto the kitchen table. It fell open at Brithish Columbia Business Opportunities, my eyes followed the print as I rotated the sausages in the frying pan..

'Picture Framing Shop for sale, offers on $25,000.' I read it again, I always did like burnt sausages.

A phone call, and I had arranged to visit Victoria the next week.

I left Edmonton in a blizzard and was welcomed to Victoria by sun and flowers. The male menopause swung into action, and at forty-five I wanted a change.

Any doubts I had were dismissed when I arrived back in Edmonton, and saw my car was the third dome of snow in the parking lot, I couldn't wait to return to Victoria.

I sold my house, most of my instruments and my shovel. This gave me enough to make the move.

The Picture Framing store was downtown on busy Fort Street, and having had a month to find an apartment and settle in, this was to be my first day. The owner or rather ex-owner had agreed to stay on for six months to teach me the intricacies of the art world.

Mrs. Hale, was an efficient, no nonsense type of woman. When I told her my only knowledge of art, was a paint by numbers picture I did twenty years ago, she said, 'Well at least I don't have to eradicate any preconceived ideas about art.'

I admitted she had a mental vacuum to work with. She showed me how to cut glass in squares, ovals and circles and mats in every shape and size possible. How to cut moulding without loosing my fingers, and if everything was done correctly, the finished product fitted into the frame.

To accomplish all this I had to practice at night, Sundays, and early mornings, rather like learning an instrument.

The customers, of course didn't know I was a novice and if they succumbed to my suggestions, would often say, 'Well, you're the professional.'

Mrs. Hale would smile and say, 'must be a relief when you find someone who knows less than you do about art.' I was never sure if this was a compliment.

Customers came in all types and sizes, one of my first was a fussy rotund man who brought in, what looked to me, like four grubby pictures of old army officers.

'I'd like these framed,' he said.

I looked at them and replied, 'are you sure?'

The nudge from Mrs. Hale indicated this was the wrong thing to say. I changed tactics and began placing moulding samples on the corner of the pictures.

Mrs. Hale and I now had a secret system, when I eventually placed a suitable moulding, she would tap my leg with her foot. After two or three tries, I felt the tap and could be assertive as to my choice for the customer.

The satisfied customer left, and I was told these were, Spector Prints and quite expensive. They still looked like old grubby army officers to me.

As the days went by I learnt to be more tactful, and when a lady came in with ten small dog pictures. I told her we had small pre-made frames, that would be perfect.

I placed the frames on them and she was delighted.

Next week she was back and sought my advice again, she reached into her bag and pulled out two books containing dog pictures, which she opened flat on the counter. I placed the box of frames next to her and she began picking them out and placing them over the pictures.

'How does that look?' she asked.

'Fine,' I said, then I noticed a stamp in the books.

It read, Greater Victoria Public Library!

'Do you cut your dog pictures out of library books?' I asked in surprise.

'Oh yes, and the cat ones too, but just the ones I like, no one else reads them anyway.'

Only in Victoria, I thought.

Sea life photographs were popular and a very attractive lady came in with a colored photo of a creature, I had not seen or heard of before. She told me it was a sea anemone.

I spent more time than usual with this young lady, until I could no longer ignore the tapping on my leg. 'Yes, I will have it ready tomorrow for you, I'll do it myself.'

Mrs. Hale rolled her eyes and said, 'You would have thought it was the Mona Lisa.'

Next morning I had it ready and approved by Mrs Hale. The young lady arrived and I laughingly greeted her, 'You look like a lady that's come for an enema.' I heard muffled laughter from the workshop, and noted a cool indifference from my customer.

When she left Mrs. Hale explained my faux pas.

'I better phone her and explain,' I said.

'What if her husband answers, and you have to tell him his wife doesn't really need an enema.'

'I guess so,' I answered dejectedly.

Later that month, I attended a three day workshop in Seattle covering all areas of picture framing. I came away with a mountain of new found knowledge and a plaque that stated: I was now a member of the Professional Picture Framers Association.

It was too big to wear round my neck, so I proudly stood it on the counter, thus proclaiming myself an instant authority on all things relating to art.

A nervous but pleasant looking man entered carrying three framed pencil sketches, laid them on the counter and asked if I would be interested in taking them on consignment, as he was moving away.

I saw they were three nude drawings, of a rather overweight, but attractive lady. Nicely done I thought and voiced, 'Yes, I am sure they will sell.' He then gave me a minimum price of seventy dollars each. He left and I hung them on the rear wall, because last time I hung a nude in the window, I had several complaints. This was Victoria after all.

Saturday morning was busy as usual. An attractive lady wearing fashionable sunglasses was exploring the gallery. Mrs.

Hale realised I gave top priority to attractive ladies and didn't compete for her attention.

She had stopped by the three nudes, I wished her 'Good Morning.'

'How much are you asking for those?' She asked softly.

'I think the owner would be happy with two hundred and fifty. They are a consignment from a disillusioned lover.' I said, trying to pique her interest, and added,

'I really like them, but she is a bit tubby.'

She turned to face me, lowered her sun glasses and said firmly, 'That is me, drawn by my soon- to-be ex-husband.'

My mind raced to amend yet another faux pas, but Mrs. Hale saved the day.

'I think it's lunch time Allan.'

A few hours later the soon-to-be ex-husband appeared and nervously asked if he could retrieve the drawings. 'Of course,' I replied with relief. Mrs. Hale, a mischievous glint in her eyes, said, 'Oh what a pity, Allan nearly sold them this morning.' It was my turn to kick her under the counter.

Oil paintings were my favourite, because no glass or matt was required.

I had just taken in an oil, it was a farm scene with blue skies and puffy white clouds. I placed it behind the counter, leaning it against the wall, until I had time to move it to the workshop.

Later, as I was serving a customer, I stepped back and felt my heel scrape the oil painting. I had removed about an inch of the blue sky. 'Help, Mrs. Hale,' I whined. She rebuffed me for putting the painting on the floor, but went on to explain how a repair could be made.

She said it would be impossible to replace the blue as it wouldn't blend, but she could paint in another puffy white cloud over the scratch. The white cloud was added and I fitted the oil painting into frame. I pondered how to explain the deteriorating weather conditions to the customer. I thought to myself, another scratch and she could have had a thunder storm.

I was a little apprehensive when the customer arrived and relieved when she said how delighted she was with my work, then added, 'It's amazing how much fuller a painting looks when it's framed.' I ignored the stifled laughter from the workshop.

It was nearly closing time on a Friday evening, when a lady brought in a new challenge for me. It was a 3ft x 2 ft. piece of hardboard on which were glued sea shells of every size and colour. The result resembled a colourful Spanish Galleon under full sail.

I advised her that a box frame about an inch deep and glass would protect the delicate shells and give an appearance of movement. She left and I placed it carefully on the work bench and covered it with brown paper.

On Fridays, the owner of the fish store next door, often brought me cooked shrimp and sauce as an end of the week delicacy. I heard his knock, and let him in anticipating the gourmet delight to come. I poured him a beer and offered him the desk chair. I put my hands behind me and levered myself onto the work bench.

I was poised with my rear end six inches above the bench when I realised my mistake, but too late, the forthcoming crunch, confirmed my mental prediction.

The Spanish Galleon looked as if it had scuttled itself. As I emptied the broken shells into the garbage, my appetite for anything in shells considerable diminished.

It was time to phone damage control.

Mrs. Hale commiserated with me, but calmly told me the customer probably gathered the shells locally, and as I now had two days off, I could try and replace them. 'Gather as many as you can and we'll see what can be done.'

Tuesday morning I arrived early after a cold and wet couple of days on the windswept beach. I had a cardboard box under my arm, containing shells of every size and colour.

We matched and glued until the resemblance of a Spanish Galleon began to take shape. But we had no way of knowing what the original looked like. I just hoped the customer hadn't taken a photograph of it.

I framed our creation and phoned the customer to say her masterpiece was ready.

'How does it look?' she asked.

'Well the frame does influence the content.' I replied. (I read that in a book somewhere). 'I'll be in later today,' she said, and I made a mental note to take a very long lunch. However, I met her as I was returning and she said, 'I just can't wait to see my galleon.'

'I hope you'll be pleasantly surprised,' was all I could venture.

I placed the framed nautical nightmare on the counter with a feeling of trepidation, removed the dust cover and stood back.

There was a seconds silence while she studied her work of art. She looked up. 'That is the most beautiful one I have ever done, and you are right the frame does change the content.'

I interrupted her, 'not change, influence.' I said.

'Yes, influence,' she replied.

From the corner of my eye I could see Mrs. Hale convulsed over the workbench.

As Mrs. Hale left for the day, she said, 'I'll be sorry when the six months are over, every evening my husband says, tell me what happened at the store today. Before you came he never asked.'

Allan F Scott

The End

Victoria 1980

TAKING A CHANCE.

Answering an advertisement in the personal column, does require courage and a little soul searching. Will this change my life? In my case, could this be my dream woman?

The advertisement that caught my eye was written by a lady who claimed to be blond, a non-smoker, witty, under fifty and possessing a beautiful pre-teen age daughter.

She then continued to list twenty-seven qualities required in her choice of male companion. I ticked each one off to see how I would measure up, honesty prevailed and three ticks was all I could muster.

I was fifty, single for many years and rationalised that I had nothing to loose.

A recent photograph was requested in the reply. I sent one of me relaxing in my recliner, smoking a cigar. (That would leave two ticks)

I added a few details but wrote that I only had three of the twenty-seven qualities she required. However, I would inform her which three, if she replied.

Two weeks later on answering the phone, I was greeted with, 'This is Lil from the paper.' I waited for further clarification, and the voice added, 'You know from the advertisement.'

'Oh... what a surprise,' was my nervous reply.

'I've had three hundred replies,' she continued. 'My friend and I have spent two weeks sorting them, and you are about number seventeen.'

'How does your process of elimination work,' I inquired.

'Well, I have been out with three already, and they didn't match up at all, in fact all they seemed interested in was sex. You're not like that are you?'

'Of course not,' I lied. Thinking, that leaves me with one tick.

We kept talking, and I felt she was beginning to warm to me. She said that she enjoyed my letter and could see I had a sense of humour.

'Was I over six feet tall?' was her next question. Here goes my last tick I thought as I replied, 'No, afraid not.'

This didn't faze her, and she continued, 'Well we must meet, I'll give you my address and you can visit.'

To me this didn't sound like a good idea, and I told her so. 'You shouldn't give your address to strangers, I could be anyone, why don't we just meet for coffee first,' I suggested.

'OK. I'll meet you at the White Knight Restaurant, seven on Saturday,' and she hung up.

Saturday evening I was washed and polished, just ready to leave, when the phone rang.

'Lil from the paper, sorry I'm not ready, could you pick me up from my apartment?' I agreed with some trepidation.

It could be a set up, I thought, and took the precaution of removing my wallet and putting the money in my shoe.

Her address was in a non remarkable apartment block, and next to her door was a child's bicycle. I assumed it belonged to the pre-teen age daughter, and I began to relax.

I pressed the buzzer and a voice from inside said, 'Come in, door's open.'

The hall was quite dark, the first room I passed was the bathroom, the door was open and I saw a silhouette in the bathroom mirror, it was a small female with curlers protruding from her hair.

'Go into the living room, and have a seat, the blue chair is great,' the voice said. I did as instructed and sat on the blue chair, I was greeted with a very embarrassing sound, it had a whoopee cushion installed. The obvious happened and was greeted with much laughter from the bathroom.

I sat in uncomfortable silence observing the plastic butterflies interlaced with the curtains and eyeing a large collection of country and western LP's with apprehension, afraid to move in case it provoked another blast from beneath.

After a few minutes a small elderly lady with hair parted like spaniel ears, and balanced precariously on platform shoes entered, put out her hand and said, 'Hi I'm Lil.' I started to shake her hand and felt the shock of a metal palm tickler. Instinctively I pulled back, again to much laughter.

'I tried four different outfits on,' she said.

'What made you decide on that one?' I asked.

'You don't like it, well I'm not going to change.' She growled.

I started to get that married feeling and only ten minutes into the relationship.

She turned and I followed her down the hall, she pointed at a small cabinet door. 'Would you get my gloves please?' I reached and opened the door. I jumped back when a small boxing glove on a spring hit me between the eyes. This cabinet had it's own built in laughter, which was joined by another outburst from Lil. 'I collect jokes,' she laughed. I felt I was being added to her collection.

She wobbled down the steps and I helped her over the grass to my car.

'I made a reservation at the James Bay Inn, it's seafood night.'

Her only reply was an unhappy grunt. I hoped I was being down graded on her list of potential suitors.

The pretty and statuesque hostess , greeted me by name and showed us to a corner table.

Lil frowned and asked, 'How come she knows your name?'

'Well I come here quite often,' I replied.

'Why did you reply to my advertisement if you know lots of people?'

I shrugged and said, 'I was just curious, that's all.' I was relieved when the waiter appeared and told us salmon was number one tonight.

'Great, that's for me,' and I expected Lil would join me. But she put the menu down and said, 'I'll have a coke float.' The waiter hesitated, expecting an addition to that request then she added, 'Can't stand that seafood crap.'

He retreated obviously taken aback, and I saw him relate the strange request to the hostess on his way to the kitchen. She smiled looked over and raised her eyebrows in a quizzical gesture. I resisted the urge to raise my arms in a non-committal Italian manner.

There didn't seem much point in asking Lil if she wanted desert, but as I ordered apple pie, she asked the waiter for a martini.

'You said you didn't drink.'

'Not true,' she replied. 'I said, I wanted a man that didn't drink.'

My gut reaction was to order a vodka! But I ordered coffee and Lil had another martini.

I began to feel a descending cloud of depression as I received the bill from the hostess. (Who I felt, was feeling some empathy for me) and we exchanged conspiratorial smiles.

I helped Lil to her feet and as we approached the cash register, I was feeling for my wallet--then realised I didn't have a wallet. My money was in my shoe.

The hostess took the check and extended her hand for payment. She looked perplexed when I hesitated, and surprised when I took my shoe off and pulled out several crumpled twenty dollar bills.

She hesitated, took them and held them with the tips of her fingers, dropped them in the cash register with the same motion as a doctor discarding his rubber gloves.

Lil, one elbow on the counter observed my loss of savoir faire with annoying amusement. 'I found him in the paper,' she stage whispered to the hostess, extending a limp wrist in my direction.

I glanced over my shoulder as we left and saw the hostess and the waiter engaged in a ritual head shaking.

Lil seemed friskier now, 'Which is your favourite dance place?' She asked.

'You said in your letter you liked dancing.' This I reluctantly admitted.

The Forge was a large, noisy dance hall but it always had a live band, all of whom I knew, having worked with them over the years.

As we descended the stairs I kept a firm hold on Lil as she had developed quite a wobble.

The band was on a break, and several of them sat grouped at the bar, I waved and a couple came to chat.

'More people you know.' Lil said accusingly. I ignored her and did the introductions.

'I found him in the newspaper,' she announced. This was greeted with much laugher and witty remarks, such as:

'What year?'

'In the lost and found?'

'The obituaries?' I was relieved when they had to return to the stand.

A martini later she decided it was dance time, removed her shoes and disappeared into the gyrating mass on the dance floor.

I found her moving with no sense of rhythm, her back against a pillar in the centre of the floor. Thankfully the set ended and I supported her back to the bar.

'I enjoyed that,' she said and continued, 'Can I ask you something?'

'Go ahead,' I ventured.

'Why don't you and I buy a condominium together?'

'Don't you think we should wait until our second date?' I replied.

The band was about to play again and I felt it an opportune time to leave and eased her towards the exit.

She was intent on me listening to some of her good old country records, but I explained I had to be up very early for stock taking.

A week later she phoned to say I had risen to number three on her list, and when could we meet again.

I told her I was going on holiday, which was true, but I did extend the time a little.

I went on vacation, sent her a change of address card and didn't move.

Allan F Scott

The End

Victoria 1996

I KNEW I WAS RIGHT

It was a bright summer evening in June 1941, I was living in the fantasy world that contains I am sure, many eleven-year olds. I was in our back yard, a Liverpool back yard. This is a stone floored enclosure surrounded by twelve foot walls that divides the row housing and provides access to the narrow back alley.

Wearing a toy version of a steel helmet, I was lying on my back, my Woolworth's binoculars focused on the white puffy clouds moving slowly overhead. My space odyssey was interrupted by the sound of aircraft. The engine sounds were enough to bring me to my feet. Not the smooth purr of our RAF aircraft but the pulsating wum-wum-wum of the German synchronized twin engines. This sound was as familiar, but not as welcome as an ice cream bell to me.

Having left the shelter of the clouds, the two aircraft dove to the level of the silver elephantine barrage balloons glowing pink in the evening sunshine. Black puffs of smoke appeared around them as they continued to lose altitude hoping to confuse the anti-aircraft guns, drop what ever they had and escape. All this activity, and no air raid siren.

What motivated me next were three black cylinders tumbling end over end from beneath the first plane, which I recognized as a Heinkel 111. As I leapt up the back steps into the house I heard the whistle of the three bombs as they accelerated towards the ground. I ran into our large kitchen, frantically pulled open the first wall cupboard door and jumped into darkness, one shattering explosion and then another. From above, all sorts of debris fell and slid on top of me. I crouched awaiting the third explosion, but nothing.

As I sat on the floor of thc cupboard, my imagination kicked in. What if the gas main bursts? What about the hot water tank? That was next to, and above me. I reached up and felt the warm smooth copper surface. Maybe the house was on fire?

I could be trapped here for hours? The door had clicked shut behind me, it was designed to be opened from the outside.

As my father used to say, *If all else fails... panic.* This I did, braced my back against the wall and pushed the door with both feet, it burst opened, I scrambled out pushing the junk aside. The debris covering me was from the top shelf that I dislodged as I jumped in. It consisted of dishes, old toys, papers and many years of discarded items.

There was momentary silence; then distant cries for help that prompted my father to run up the stairs from the basement. He pointed out the kitchen window at what had been the house across the alley, now a sloping pile of rubble. I followed as he ran out the door.

The voices came from what was left of their outdoor shelter. Three walls had collapsed and the two-feet thick concrete roof was resting at a precarious angle on the fourth. Here in this cramped triangle the people were trapped, buried up their necks in bricks and debris.

My father and several neighbors scrambled over the rubble and started to carefully remove the bricks from around the trapped victims. As the dust settled I could see a man, and a woman, who was holding a cat in her arms. She was gently stroking the cat and smiling up at her rescuers. I heard someone tell them it might take awhile and to try to keep still.

'We'll get you some tea while you hang on,' one of the rescuers said to her.

'No sugar please,' she replied still stroking her cat. Even at my tender years it seemed laughable that a person with a huge concrete slab resting precariously about ten inches above her head, would worry about sugar in her tea.

'Tea,' my father admonished pointing in the direction of our kitchen. As I returned with two full mugs my hands were shaking so much I was spilling most of it.

'Here mate, hold them tight against your chest,' one of the burly rescuers whispered, 'you wont spill so much.' He winked at me, and I remember the gratitude I felt at not being ridiculed for my display of nerves, plus he called me mate. I hugged the mugs as I scrambled up the pile of loose bricks, feeling some of the contents splashing hot and wet against my chest.

The mugs of tea were carefully edged through a gap in the rubble. Out the same gap, a dust covered black and white cat was gently lifted out, shook itself and settled onto the cement roof where it sat licking its paw and washing behind its ears. Probably thinking, *I still have eight lives left.*

When I returned to the kitchen my aunt was standing hands on hips and surveying the jumble that reached from my cupboard retreat across most of the floor.

She looked puzzled. 'Strange what these bombs do, not one ornament broken but all this stuff blown out the cupboard.' What could I do but agree?

Over dinner that evening, during which the adults discussed events of the day and children may be seen but not heard. I bravely interrupted when I heard my aunt say two bombs had fallen. 'No it was three.' 'Shush!' Was the only interest shown in my addition to the conversation.

Moving out of slapping range, I continued. 'I saw three falling end over end.'

'Sit at the table and finish your spam and chips or I'll eat them,' my aunt replied.

My father added, 'bombs fall nose first and head straight down, otherwise how would they aim them?' 'Well they missed this time,' was my indignant reply.

My father raised his hand. 'Look, the bomb aimer looked down his sight, saw you, panicked and missed. Now eat your dinner... because I won't miss.' Their laughter put me into my pre-teenage sulking mode.

Seven years later I was enjoying a few days leave, sitting in the kitchen catching up on the local gossip, on which my aunt was an authority.

'Never guess what Mrs. Bradshaw found in her coal shed when she cleaned it out.' I shook my head to confirm I would never guess.

'A 250 lb. bomb wedged between the side of the shed and the house. The UXB people moved us all out, just like the old days, did their stuff with the fuse and then let us all have a look the bomb. It was very rusty and they said it must have been there for about seven years.'

Indignantly I replied. 'I told you there were three that day, one in the front, one at the back and one that didn't go off.' 'Yes, but you were just a kid and we didn't take much notice.'

'Well I was right... and that was nice, for once.'

It was many years to July 17, 1996, and I was now happily living on Vancouver Island. I read a poster placed by the *Sidney Air Museum* advertising a fly-in visit by two aircraft from the *Confederate Air Force.* This is a group of aviation specialists from the USA whose passion is restoring aircraft from the two World War eras. One was to be a *Flying Fortress* the other a *Heinkel 111.*

The *Heinkel* was not hard to spot parked on the grass by the museum. The black Swastikas and the crosses on the fuselage still made my stomach tighten, how forbidding it looked, even after fifty-five years.

I approached camera in hand and was greeted by the gentleman standing under the nose, visually a text book pilot. Leather jacket, dark glasses, crows feet creases at the corners of his eyes from years of squinting along primitive air strips.

'Can I look inside?' I asked.

'Sure you're the first today, it's a rebuilt Heinkel. Jack is my name, spent many hours helping renovate this one. Any questions, just ask.'

I nodded, 'I lived through the war years in Liverpool, so I saw a few at an unsafe distance.'

As I climbed into the fuselage I was surprised how small and compact it was. I sat in the pilot's seat, just to see how it felt and looked at the controls and instruments. Jack joined me explaining the new additions to the instrument panel needed to update it for today's flying. I told him about my first flying lessons in a *Tiger Moth* with an irate Australian instructor. I was all of fourteen.

He was still laughing as I moved to the front gunner/bomb aimer position and looked down the bombsight. I was flat on my stomach surrounded by clear perspex, it was like being suspended in a goldfish bowl. *I wondered if he did see me in my tin hat?*

Halfway back down the fuselage I saw the bombs in their racks, three on each side, inverted resting on their tail fins. Black, sleek and menacing.

'Did they carry the bombs like that?' I asked Jack.

'Sure, they dropped tail first from here then tumbled,' he demonstrated with his hands, 'until they were stabilized by the fins and down they went.'

'You said tumbled.' He noticed my elation and paused.

'I have a story to tell you,' I said.

We dropped onto the grass and sat under the wing as I took him back to 1941 in Liverpool and the scene at the kitchen table with my doubting family.

'Twenty minutes and two good stories,' he laughed. 'You Brits never lack a good story. You should write that down.'

'I may one day, but you know...I was right!'

Allan F Scott

The End

ABOUT THE AUTHOR

1930 was not a good year to be born, the depression was in full swing, World War ll was on it's way and Liverpool was not a very happy place to arrive in. However, here I was and there was nothing I could do about it.

The first photos of me show a rather worried baby, an unhappy Mother and a bewildered Father.

I was farmed out for a time to the Gittens family. My benefactors being Mrs. Gittens, her daughter Ronnie and their small Pekinese. My first memories of daily treats was to have a small dog biscuit with Woo. I liked the black ones. I'm sure the daily snack had no adverse effect on my health, but, I've been told I bark at people sometimes plus, I admit, I find a lamp post irresistible.

The first time I remember seeing my mother she was sitting at a desk in the front room. I noted how tidy and shiny her hair was. She offered me half of a cream puff, this was one up on a dog biscuit and I didn't have to wrestle her for it. I felt life was about to improve.

At eighteen I was happy to start my national service. Plus lucky enough to be placed in the RAF Music Service. Ten years later I left the RAF for the RCAF Music Service. We travelled a lot in the UK but, nothing compared to the distances we covered in Canada.

Edmonton Alberta was my home base, here I left the RCAF for the Edmonton Symphony Orchestra. Percussion in any form was my main interest, This enabled me to keep up with the Jazz and Pop world.

Having visited Victoria several times, the temperate climate and relaxed atmosphere won me over and in 1975. I shelved my musical ambitions, bought a picture framing store and over two years learnt how to stick a picture in a frame without it falling out. Well...not very often.

I have a daughter, Lorna, in Cape Town whom I had only seen a few times. She was now sixteen. My paternal instinct twitched, I sold the business and took off to spend time with my daughter before she developed an independent life of her own.

Lorna and I were the first Canadians to visit the Transkie. My ex-wife had lent me her ex-car. It was quite the trip and much to my surprise the car and us survived.

After Africa I spent time in Rio de Janeiro, where drumming is a religion and never stops. But having maxed my credit cards it was time to return Victoria and start paying them off.

Here I worked for two music stores until retirement. Retirement I can recommend. So it is kayak one day, skate the next, write a little, take photographs and just put my feet up when fatigue wins out.

Allan Francis Scott.